From Eden to Egypt

Exploring the Genesis themes

Peter Williams

Day One

© Day One Publications 2001
First printed 2001

British Library Cataloguing in Publication Data available
ISBN 1 903087 07 4

Published by Day One Publications
3 Epsom Business Park, Kiln Lane, Epsom, Surrey KT17 1JF.
01372 728 300 **FAX** 01372 722 400
email—sales@dayone.co.uk
www.dayone.co.uk

Designed by Steve Devane and printed by Creative Print and Design

To my grandsons
Ben, Jack and Harry

From the time I was a young Christian I have always loved the book of Genesis with its great narratives of the patriarchs, and the vivid and exciting story of Joseph and his brothers. But that was not the only reason I was attracted to this book. As I considered the great themes of Creation, the Fall, the Flood and the Tower of Babel I found it satisfied me both spiritually and intellectually. It also answered my questions about the origins of life and the universe, the meaning of our human existence, God's purpose for mankind, and where human history is leading. I must, of course, make it perfectly clear that this is not a technical commentary that attempts to answer the many critical questions associated with Genesis. My concern has been with the spiritual purpose of the book, and to draw out those profound truths, which still apply to God's people today.

During my ministry I have often preached from Genesis, but I never thought I would ever attempt to write a commentary on the whole book. But I have enjoyed doing so and have profited from the exercise, and I can only hope and pray that it will give equal satisfaction and help to those who read it.

As always I must express my heart-felt thanks to my dear friends Ruth and Brian Kerry for their labour of love in preparing the manuscript for publication.

Peter Williams
Bournemouth 2001

Contents

The work of creation

There is a very real sense in which the book of Genesis is the most important book in the whole Bible. Not because it comes first in the biblical canon, but because it is foundational for the understanding of the other books of the Bible. The title 'Genesis' in both its Hebrew and Greek forms means 'beginnings' or 'origins' and comes from the Hebrew phrase 'bereshith' (In the beginning) with which the book opens. In the chapters that follow we learn about the beginnings of the universe, of mankind, of evil, of marriage and family life, of culture, language and nationhood, and in particular of the beginnings of the chosen people of God.

Both the Jewish and Christian traditions have long held the belief that Genesis was written by Moses along with Exodus, Leviticus, Numbers and Deuteronomy. With its fifty chapters it is the longest of these five books which grouped together are known as the Pentateuch or the Torah (Law). There are scores of references and allusions to Genesis in the New Testament, and nowhere do we find even the slightest suggestion that we should treat it as anything but inspired scripture and therefore totally reliable and historical. In studying it we are not moving in the realm of allegory or Babylonian myth or legend as liberal scholars would have us believe. Furthermore, the Mosaic authorship of this unique and remarkable book was clearly recognised by our Lord (Matthew 19:7; Mark 12:19–26; Luke 16:31; and John 5:46–47), and for Him its contents were true, authoritative and divinely inspired.

The primacy of God

"In the beginning God created the heavens and the earth. Now the earth was formless and empty, darkness was over the surface of the deep, and the Spirit of God was hovering over the waters" (Genesis 1:1–2 NIV). What a haunting phrase this is with which the Bible opens: "In the beginning God".

It says it all! For if we accept, in faith, the truth of this statement then we shall have no difficulty whatever in believing the rest of the Bible's message. On the other hand, if we reject the truth of this opening statement then we shall not only find it impossible to believe much of what the Bible teaches, but we put our souls in grave peril. Many Bible scholars describe the name of God (Elohim) as a 'uni-plural' noun, meaning that God is to be understood as being both ONE (unity) and more than One (Plurality) at the same time, thus foreshadowing the doctrine of the Trinity in the New Testament. The opening verses also anticipate the unity of the Godhead in another way. The statement "In the beginning God created the heavens and the earth" asserts that God is the source and origin of creation. The statement, "and the Spirit of God was hovering over the waters" asserts that the Spirit was the divine energy through which creation was brought into being. And the expression (Genesis 1:3) "And God said" describes the Word of God as the divine agent of the creative process. This reference to the creative Word of God is exactly what John says in the opening verse of his gospel: "In the beginning was the Word, and the Word was with God, and the Word was God. He was with God in the beginning. Through Him all things were made; without Him nothing was made that has been made" (John 1:1–3). In the very opening verses of the Bible therefore we have this early indication of the reality and unity of the Godhead. Later, in verse 26, when God makes man we have the expression 'Let us', which is another anticipation of the Trinity.

When, as a young Christian, I began reading the Bible seriously, one of the first things that impressed me was the fact that nowhere do the writers of God's book attempt to prove His existence. Throughout history many learned and philosophical arguments have been formulated to try and prove God's being, and yet God Himself, and the writers through whom He speaks, make no such attempt whatever but simply assert God's reality. The Psalmist says that this reality is so obvious that only a fool would seek to deny it: "The fool says in his heart, 'There is no God'" (Psalm 14:1). Such a denial is said to be foolish because there is so much evidence to the contrary. There are the immensities of the universe and the variety and complexity of earth's numberless life-forms, including man himself, all of which demand an explanation intellectually more satisfying than simply to be told that it all 'just happened with a big bang'. Such an explanation is too incredible for words! If I see a building which has sprung up overnight on a spot where there was no building before I am not content with being told 'it just happened'. I am likely to go further and ask, 'Who put it there? How was it built and for what purpose?' Similarly these are the kind of questions Genesis addresses itself to in relation to man and his world when it opens with the words: "In the beginning God created the heavens and the earth".

It must also be said that a further evidence for the reality and being of God lies within ourselves. There is in the human heart a primal need for the existence of a God whom we can worship and adore. It is, if you like, a kind of natural instinct man has that a Supreme Being who is the source of life and the controller of all things does exist. Unlike the rest of creation, man is a creature who asks questions about his own existence and the meaning of what goes on around him, and the attempt to find answers to these questions leads him to persist in reaching out beyond himself and to express his inquisitive desires in worship. This instinct or intuition, call it what you will, lies within all men from the primitive tribesman who worships the spirits in rocks and trees, to the sophisticated businessman who believes his destiny lies in the astrological significance of the stars and planets, right through to the evangelical Christian who worships God at his local church on a Sunday morning. Where does this inward urge and desire come from? The only sensible answer is that God the Creator put it in man's heart when He "created man in his own image" (Genesis 1:27). As the writer of Ecclesiastes puts it: "He has also set eternity in the hearts of men; yet they cannot fathom what God has done from beginning to end" (Ecclesiastes 3:11).

Creation out of nothing

Whenever we use the word 'beginning' in ordinary speech we have in mind the idea that it is the beginning of something. In these opening verses it means the beginning of creation in an absolute sense. That is to say the very materials out of which the universe was created were themselves willed into existence by God. Theologians call this 'creation ex nihilo' (creation out of nothing). When we read, "Now the earth was formless and empty, darkness was over the face of the deep", we are being given a description of the original unformed state of these materials when God brought them into being and before He began to impose order and system to transform them into the wonderful universe we now know. Speaking of God's creative work the writer to the Hebrews says: "… what is seen was not made out of what was visible" (Hebrews 11:3). If the materials were not visible then clearly they did not exist originally.

But not everyone, it would seem, agrees with that as is evident from certain versions of the Bible. For example, the Revised Standard Version has the alternative reading: "When God began to create the heavens and the earth the earth was without form and void". The Living Bible has: "When God began creating the heaven and the earth the earth was at first a shapeless, chaotic mass". Both those versions are saying that the raw materials were already in existence when God began His work of bringing the organised universe into being. But that is not absolute or primary creation but 'secondary' creation, and is more like the kind of thing we ourselves are able to do when we 'make' or 'build' or 'construct' something out of materials already to hand. The fact is we tend to use the word 'create' very loosely in everyday speech as for instance when we describe a great painting as a 'creative work of art' or even a beautiful evening gown as the dress designer's latest 'creation'. But the fact is the word create (bara) is unique, and can never be truly used of anything we ourselves are able to do. We are builders, makers, designers, constructors, but we are not creators. God alone is a creator simply because He is God – the absolute and ultimate reality.

Creation by fiat

As we continue reading chapter one from verse 3 to its conclusion we come repeatedly upon the phrase, "And God said". Like a refrain this phrase comes at the opening of each of the six days' work of creation beginning with the introduction of light to dispel the darkness on the first day. "And God said, 'Let there be light,' and there was light" (Genesis 1:3). "And God said, 'Let there be an expanse between the waters to separate water from water'" (Genesis 1:6). "And God said, 'Let the water under the sky be gathered to one place, and let dry ground appear'. And it was so" (Genesis 1:9). "And God said, 'Let the land produce vegetation'. … And it was so.

(Genesis 1:11). "And God said, 'Let there be lights in the sky to separate the day from the night'. ... And it was so" (Genesis 1:14). "And God said, 'Let the water teem with living creatures, and let birds fly above the earth across the expanse of the sky'" (Genesis 1:20). "And God said, 'Let the land produce living creatures according to their kinds'" (Genesis 1:24).

This is sometimes called fiat creation, meaning that God simply speaks or commands and things immediately spring into existence. Referring to this creative Word the Psalmist says: "By the word of the Lord were the heavens made, ... For he spoke, and it came to be" (Psalm 33:6 and 9). And the writer to the Hebrews says: "By faith we understand that the universe was formed at God's command" (Hebrews 11:3). From the expression 'And God said' we learn that God's Word is power – power to bring light to dispel the darkness and power to bring life into being in the form of vegetation, birds, reptiles, mammals and finally man. And not only was the world created by the power of God's Word, but its continued existence is totally dependent upon that same Word. Speaking of Christ the Divine Word, Paul says: "... all things were created by him and for him. He is before all things, and in him all things hold together" (Colossians 1:16–17). And in Hebrews we read: "The Son is the radiance of God's glory and the exact representation of His being, sustaining all things by His powerful word" (Hebrews 1:3).

Ecologists speak of eco-systems which govern the earth and which are constantly adapting to sustain the various life forms in plants, animals and insects. Everything has its own specialised function and particular part to play in giving coherence and order to the whole. But we are bound to ask: "Who keeps all this together so that the world doesn't fall apart? Who, or what, is performing this incredible 'juggling act' whereby everything is so finely tuned and so sensitively balanced?" The same ecologists answer by referring to the 'laws of nature' and the 'evolutionary process'. But we must go further and ask: 'Who made these laws and set these processes in motion and keeps them going?' And the Bible answers, 'The power of God's Word'.

Furthermore, the power of God's Word to bring light and life extends beyond the physical world and into the spiritual realm, thus anticipating in a wonderful way the redemptive work of the Lord Jesus Christ. Paul echoes Genesis 1 when he says: "For God, Who said, 'Let light shine out of darkness', made His light shine in our hearts to give us the light of the knowledge of the glory of God in the face of Christ" (2 Corinthians 4:6). The power of the divine Word that dispelled the primeval darkness at the dawn of the physical creation is the same power that dispels the darkness of sin in our hearts through the light of Christ at our spiritual creation. In both instances light and life come through the power of God's Word.

Evening and morning

It was made clear in the Introduction that this is not a technical commentary which seeks to answer the critical questions generally asked of the events in the early chapters of Genesis. But now that we are in day six, which deals mainly with the creation of man, something needs to be said about the controversy surrounding the length of the days mentioned in the creation account. For some Christians this issue is very troubling. Each of the creative six days is followed by the formula: "And there was evening and there was morning". This seems to indicate a specific time period, which we normally associate with the twenty-four hour day. But the problem for some Christians, not to mention unbelievers, is that modern scientific theory teaches that the earth was formed over vast periods of time, called geological time, involving millions of years, and during which the rock strata of the earth was laid down.

In an attempt to square the Genesis account of creation in terms of days, with the geological interpretation involving millions of years, one measure has been to formulate the Day-age theory which says that each of the six days of Genesis represents or symbolises the vast periods of time involved in the geological formation of the earth.

But there isn't the slightest reason for believing that theory on the basis of what we are told in God's Word. Why use the formula "and there was evening and there was morning" after each period if we are not meant to accept them as six literal or natural days? Furthermore, back in verse 5 we are told that God specifically associates light and darkness with day and night: "God called the light 'day' and the darkness he called 'night'. Those who favour the Day-age theory sometimes quote the words of Peter in support of the argument that the word 'day' can mean a vast period of time. "With the Lord a day is like a thousand years" (2 Peter 3:8). But Peter doesn't say that a day is a thousand years but like a thousand years. Furthermore, you have to look at the second part of the verse: "and a thousand years are like a day". In other words Peter is simply saying that time is meaningless where God is concerned. What takes man a thousand years to do, God can do in a twenty-four hour day. Similarly what man can do in a twenty-four hour day, God, should He choose to do so, can take a thousand years to do. It follows therefore that God can do what He likes with 'time', including compressing the millions of years of geological evolution into a twenty-four hour day.

If we find it difficult to accept the six natural days of creation then it seems to me that it becomes equally difficult to accept the miracles of the Lord Jesus. For example in Mark 3 we read of Jesus healing a man's shrivelled hand instantaneously. That hand may have been shrivelled from birth, perhaps twenty or thirty years or more, yet in an instant it was exactly like the other hand which had taken all those years to grow! The truth is we find it all difficult to understand because we are earthbound creatures and prisoners of time, but God is the God of eternity.

The creation of man

"Then God said, 'Let us make man in our image, in our likeness, and let them rule over the fish of the sea and the birds of the air, over the livestock, over all the earth, and over all the creatures that move along the ground. So God created man in his own image, in the image of God he created him; male and female he created them" (Genesis 1:26–27). We are now in the sixth day of creation and the world has been furnished with everything needed to make it a beautiful and habitable place. But as yet it has no inhabitant. At this point we are told that a council takes place among the persons of the Godhead and a divine deliberation taken to create man to inhabit the earth; hence the expression 'Let us' instead of the former 'And God said'. This collective deliberation in itself tells us that man is unique among the creatures of the earth and is the crown of God's creation. Everything that had gone before was a preparation for man's place in the divine plan for the universe and for his dominion over the rest of creation. The Psalmist confirms this: "The highest heavens belong to the Lord, but the earth he has given to man" (Psalm 115:16).

This account of man's creation is a direct contradiction of modern evolutionary teaching. We cannot accept both that man arrived at his present position as the result of a long process of animal evolution, and that he was directly created in the image and likeness of God, thus making him special and unique from all the other creatures. It must be one or the other, and for my part the Biblical account is infinitely more convincing and satisfying. Not only is man's body structure more complex than that of the lower animals, but unlike them, he has a spiritual side to his nature. He has a moral awareness, he is able to think abstractly and logically, he has a sense of the aesthetic and is able to appreciate his environment and what goes on in the world around him. But above all, because he is made in the image and likeness of God he has an affinity with God and is able to communicate with Him in worship and in prayer.

For the Christian there are other considerations that follow from the belief that man was directly created by God in His own image and likeness. If Adam was not a real person then it becomes difficult to accept other parts of the Bible as speaking the truth. For example Romans 5:12 tells us that sin and death entered the world through Adam. "Therefore, just as sin entered the world through one man, and death through sin, and in this way death came to all men, because all sinned". It follows that if Adam did not exist then sin does not exist either, and if sin does not exist, then Christ's death on the Cross was meaningless. Paul's whole argument for the redemption of sinners rests on the truthfulness of the Genesis account that man was directly created by God in His own image and likeness.

But there is more here. Man's understanding of his own unique place in creation must inevitably affect his attitude towards himself and towards others. If he believes that he was created in the image and likeness of God it will give him a reverence and respect for humanity he would not otherwise have. In today's world human life is cheap and is treated with contempt as we see all too clearly in the hatred and bestiality of war, in the increasing murders and violence taking place in society, and in the thousands of needless abortions that take place every year. In all these ways human personality is devalued and robbed of its dignity. But what else can we expect if we continue to teach our children that man is not a unique spiritual being but is simply the product of impersonal and mechanical evolutionary processes and therefore not essentially different from the lower animals? Proverbs in its description of a man says it all: "For as he thinketh in his heart so is he" (Proverbs 23:7 AV). If a man thinks of himself as an animal, however sophisticated, he is likely to act like an animal, and that is precisely what we see happening all too often in today's world.

Man's dominion

"God blessed them and said to them, 'Be fruitful and increase in number; fill the earth and subdue it. Rule over the fish of the sea and the birds of the air and over every living creature that moves on the ground'" (Genesis 1:28). This is sometimes called God's 'cultural mandate' to man giving him the right to govern and control the earth with all its intricate processes and complex systems. He is to be the steward of the earth's resources on God's behalf and to use them for the good of all mankind. This is man's authority to study his environment, to investigate its mysteries, and in general to increase his knowledge and understanding of the universe through his science and technology. The Bible therefore is in no way anti-culture or anti-knowledge but, on the contrary, man is given the divine benediction to use these gifts to subdue and rule the earth for his own benefit. "God blessed them and said to them, 'Be fruitful and increase in number; fill the earth and subdue it'" (Genesis 1:28).

The great tragedy is that man in his arrogance and sin has forgotten that his ability and authority to govern and control the earth has come from God, and that as the steward of creation he is answerable to God. He thinks he can do as he likes with this planet of ours and the result is he abuses his environment by wasting its natural resources, polluting its lakes and rivers and oceans, poisoning the very air we breathe, denuding its forests, exterminating the wild life, forming vast dust bowls where nothing will grow, and in general reducing the quality of life on this earth which God intended all should enjoy.

It was clearly God's original intention through His providential goodness that man and the animals should live in mutual harmony and that both should enjoy the benefits of creation. Man's dominion was not intended to be a brutal dominion over the other creatures, killing them either for food or pleasure or even because he feared them. Both man and animals were to live on a vegetarian diet. "Then God said, 'I give you every seed-bearing plant on the face of the whole earth and every tree that has fruit with seed in it. They will be yours for food. And to all the beasts of the earth and all the birds of the air and all the creatures that move on the ground – everything that has the breath of life in it – I give every green plant for food.' And it was so. God saw all that he had made, and it was very good. And there was evening and there was morning – the sixth day" (Genesis 1:29–31).

It is only after the Fall when sin came into the world that we find man eating the flesh of animals, and nature itself became 'red in tooth and claw'. That idyllic world of the primeval creation of which we read: "God saw all that he had made, and it was very good", was shattered and henceforth disharmony and isolation characterises the earth, and the relationship between man and the animals becomes one of fear and hostility. But looking down the corridor of time we see in the great promise of the Gospel a day dawning when there will be a redeemed creation (Romans 8:20–21), a new heaven and new earth in which harmony will be restored and "The wolf will live with the lamb, the leopard will lie down with the goat, the calf and the lion and the yearling together; and a little child will lead them ... for the earth will be full of the knowledge of the Lord as the waters cover the sea" (Isaiah 11:6–9).

The completed creation

READ GENESIS CHAPTER 2

The theological college I attended in my student days was liberal in its theology and we were taught as students that in Genesis 2 we have a second account of creation totally different from that given in Chapter 1, because it comes from a different source. We were taught that Genesis was made up of a series of independent documents known as 'P' for priestly, 'J' for Jehovah, 'E' for Elohim, and 'JE' for a combination of Jehovah Elohim. Furthermore, we were taught that someone, at a later date, edited and brought these documents together to make a single account of creation and this is why we have differences and contradictions between chapters 1 and 2.

Even as a young student I didn't find this documentary theory very convincing, but as I got older and began studying the Bible in greater depth I became increasingly dissatisfied with it and eventually rejected it altogether. E. J. Young in his wonderful little book 'In the Beginning' says that Genesis is a remarkable piece of writing and whoever the so-called editor was who put the documents together in their present form must have been a true genius. But then he goes on to make the important point: "If he was such a genius, would he not have realised that it was not very sensible to put two conflicting accounts of creation together?" And the answer must be "of course he would". The truth is that until the higher critics came on the scene no one ever considered for one moment that Genesis 1 and 2 are different accounts of creation. It seems to me that once we have grasped the purpose of each chapter, we shall have no difficulty at all in accepting them as a single account of creation with chapter two as a natural sequel to chapter one.

In the first chapter we have an account of creation from the original materials that God first brought into being. In the second chapter what we have is not another account of the earth's creation, but a particular and more detailed account of what took place on the earth after it had come into existence; including the formation of man and woman and the planting of the Garden of Eden. But first, we have the institution of the Sabbath.

The Sabbath Day

"By the seventh day God had finished the work he had been doing; so on the seventh day he rested from all his work. And God blessed the seventh day and made it holy, because on it he rested from all the work of creating that he had done" (Genesis 2:2–3). When we are told that God rested on the seventh day it doesn't mean that He was no longer interested or concerned with the world He had brought into being, but that He had completed His creative work. And that is where the significance of the Sabbath lies. God was setting a meaningful pattern for man's cycle of work and rest when He "blessed the seventh day and made it holy". The essential meaning of the word 'holy' is 'set apart' or 'different from'. The Sabbath was to be different from other days because it was set apart for the special purpose of rest from daily work and for the worship of God. By the time of the Exodus the Sabbath had become a covenant obligation and was enshrined in the fourth commandment. "Remember the Sabbath day by keeping it holy … For in six days the Lord made the heavens and the earth, the sea and all that is in them but he rested on the seventh day" (Exodus 20:8–11).

By New Testament times the celebration of the Sabbath had changed from the seventh day to the first day of the week, or what we now call the Christian Sunday. "On the first day of the week we came together to break bread" (Acts 20:7). Also 1 Corinthians 16:2 "On the first day of every week, each one of you should set aside a sum of money in keeping with his income, …". The first day of the week when the early church gathered for worship was also called 'the Lord's Day' (Revelation 1:10). The first day was celebrated as the Christian Sabbath because this was the day of Christ's resurrection and the day when the Holy Spirit was poured out on God's people at Pentecost and the Church came into being (Acts 2). But although the day was changed the principle underlying the institution of the Sabbath at creation as a day set apart for the worship of God was still observed. The Sabbath was a creation ordinance instituted before the Mosaic law and therefore it has a permanent validity and obligation.

It is a sad fact that for many today what God intended to be a day of rest for man's body and soul has become a day of restlessness; a day of hectic activity. Ours is a neurotic age in which people are living on their nerves and they do themselves no great service by passing up this God-given opportunity to pause and bring a little quiet into the turmoil of their noise-rocked lives. But for the Christian believer the Lord's Day has a much more positive aspect. It is a day when we celebrate the triumph of the Lord Jesus Christ over sin, darkness and the grave. It is a day to be 'enjoyed' in the true sense of that word because of our freedom in Christ. That will mean that our worship and prayers, our fellowship with fellow believers and our listening to God's Word will all be a joy and pleasure more than a duty and obligation.

The formation of man

"When the Lord God made the earth and the heavens, no shrub of the field had yet appeared on the earth and no plant of the field had yet sprung up; the Lord God had not sent rain on the earth and there was no man to work the ground, but streams came up from the earth and watered the whole surface of the ground. And the Lord God formed man from the dust of the ground and breathed into his nostrils the breath of life, and man became a living being" (Genesis 2:4–7). We are not told **how** God formed man's body from the dust of the ground, simply that He did so. But that is the important thing the Bible wants us to know about our body in the first instance, that it was formed directly by the hand of God the Creator and did not evolve from any lower form of life. Second, being formed from the dust of the ground is a reminder to us of our mortality and prepares us for that humbling statement which comes later after man's fall: "for dust you are and to dust you will return" (Genesis 3:19). We need that reminder today because ours is the age of the cult of the body, when it is treated as though it will last for ever. A whole industry these days in centered on pampering the body, both male and female, to an excessive degree with cosmetics, lotions, beauty treatments and cosmetic surgery. And all this is done by people who frequently give little or no time to the needs of their soul. As someone once said: "Man is made from the dust, and from the care some people give to it you would think it was gold dust!"

Of course there is a proper and more balanced view which, as believers, we should take of our bodies. The fact that man's body was formed directly by the hand of the Creator indicates that it is special in God's sight and not to be abused or treated contemptuously as happens all too often today when the body is wasted and debased through drugs, heavy smoking, excessive drinking and sexual abuse. The Apostle Paul takes a very strong line on the Christian's attitude towards the body. "Do you not know that your body is a temple of the Holy Spirit, who is in you, whom you have received from God? You are not your own; you were bought at a price. Therefore honour God with your body" (1 Corinthians 6:19–20).

But man is more than a body, much more, he has received a divine in-breathing. "The Lord God formed man from the dust of the ground and breathed into his nostrils the breath of life, and man became a living being" (Genesis 2:7). Animals too have the life principle in them and come from the dust of the ground (Genesis 2:19) but that is where the similarity ends. In animals the life principle was given by divine fiat or command in common with the rest of creation, whereas God breathed into man directly and imparted to him His own Spirit thus making him a living soul created in His own image and likeness.

The Garden of Eden

"Now the Lord God planted a garden in the east, in Eden; and there he put the man he had formed. And the Lord God made all kinds of trees grow out of the ground – trees that were pleasing to the eye and good for food. In the middle of the garden were the tree of life and the tree of the knowledge of good and evil" (Genesis 2:8–9). This is the point at which the history of man on the earth begins, and a wonderful beginning it is, for God puts him into a beautiful garden which has been specially prepared for him. Here was the perfect environment, being both beautiful – "trees that were pleasing to the eye" – and practical – "good for food". Now there are two important truths that follow from this. First, it tells us that man, as the crown of God's creation, is treated differently from the other creatures and is the special object of God's love and providential care. Everything he needs for his happiness and well being is provided in the garden. In the Bible the doctrine of God's providence develops in two ways. There is on the one hand what we might call God's General Providence, by which we mean His government of creation for the preservation of His creatures and the supply of their needs. Our Lord put it like this: "He causes his sun to rise on the evil and the good, and sends rain on the righteous and the unrighteous" (Matthew 5:45). All are the recipients of the gifts that come daily from God's providence, whether they believe in Him or not. But there is also what we might call the Special Providence of God, or the special love and care he has for those who have a personal relationship with Him in the Lord Jesus Christ, just like the close intimate relationship Adam had with God. This special or particular providential care is expressed in many different ways in the New Testament but nowhere better than in the words of our Lord: "My sheep listen to my voice; I know them, and they follow me. I give them eternal life, and they shall never perish; no one can snatch them out of my hand. My Father, who has given them to me, is greater than all, no-one can snatch them out of my Father's hand. I and the Father are one" (John 10:27–30).

Second, the provision of the perfect environment in the form of this beautiful garden in Eden teaches us that, where man is concerned, environment is not everything. For many years now the humanists and the environmentalists have been telling us that the answer to the evils of society lies in the provision of a better environment. Even the churches took up this theme at one time and the emphasis was laid on preaching the 'social' gospel. The thinking was, and still is with many, that with better education, better living standards and full employment we would produce better people, and crime, violence and greed in our society would gradually diminish and life would become happier for all. But that has not been borne out in practice. A good and pleasing environment is certainly desirable and plays an important part in the proper development of our children as they grow up and take their place in society. But with all the progress we have made in education and the betterment of social conditions, we still have today enormous problems relating to crime, violence, drug addiction, alcohol, divorce, the break-up of the family and so on. And that is because the greatest problem of all is man himself; the Garden of Eden experience is meant to teach us that. The first man, Adam, had the perfect environment but he still gave way to sin and disobedience, as we shall see shortly.

The name Eden means 'pleasure' or 'delight' and there has been a lot of discussion among Bible scholars as to its actual location, but no firm conclusions have been arrived at. The only clue is mention of the river with its headwaters flowing out of the garden. "A river watering the garden flowed from Eden, from there it divided; it had four headstreams. The name of the first is the Pishon; it winds through the entire land of Havilah, where there is gold. (The gold of that land is good; aromatic resin and onyx are also there.) The name of the second river is the Gihon; it winds through the entire land of Cush. The name of the third river is the Tigris; it runs along the east side of Asshur. And the fourth river is the Euphrates" (Genesis 2:10–14). Pishon and Gihon can no longer be identified, but the second two rivers the Tigris and Euphrates, suggest the possibility that Eden may have been situated in the area of ancient Mesopotamia or today's Persian Gulf. But there is no certainty about this, and also there is the additional complication that colossal changes would have taken place in the geography of that part of the earth following the catastrophe of the Flood, thus making identification virtually impossible.

Man in the Garden

"The Lord God took the man and put him in the Garden of Eden to work it and take care of it. And the Lord God commanded the man, 'You are free to eat from any tree in the garden; but you must not eat from the tree of the knowledge of good and evil, for when you eat of it you will surely die" (Genesis 2:15–17). From the very first the concept of work or service was intended by God to be one of the basic principles of human existence. Man was put into the garden "to work it and take care of it". What that work entailed exactly is difficult to say for there were no noxious weeds since sin had not yet entered into the creation to spoil it. It is only after man's fall from grace that God cursed the ground and said to man: "It will produce thorns and thistles for you" (Genesis 3:18). Nevertheless the lesson is clear. Man's life on the earth was not intended by God to be one of idleness but characterised by activity and useful service. Work is a necessary part of being human. We notice however that there is a difference between the work man did before the Fall and his work after the Fall. In the garden his work and service were a pleasure and delight but after the Fall they became hardship and toil. "By the sweat of your brow you will eat your food"

(Genesis 3:19). We all know something of the difference between work and service that is a pleasure, and work that is a burden. A man may work all day in the office or the factory and find it hard and boring, but then he comes home and spends his evening working in the garden or playing in the local band and he expends just as much energy, but finds it all a joy and delight. Even in the perfect environment, like the garden of Eden, work and service had their place, but were a source of pleasure. Between Adam and ourselves the difference is: he lived to work, but we work to live.

The time Adam spent in the garden is sometimes described as man's 'probation'. Today, when a young offender commits a crime, particularly a first offence, the courts will sometimes put him on probation but with certain conditions attached. This is intended to be a period of trial to see how he behaves and if he doesn't keep the conditions, such as reporting to his local police station every day, or he fails to keep out of further trouble then his probation immediately ends and he is punished. This is not an exact illustration of Adam's position since he had committed no wrongdoing, but it comes close to it. God put conditions on his probation: "And the Lord God commanded the man, 'You are free to eat from any tree in the garden; but you must not eat from the tree of the knowledge of good and evil, for when you eat of it you will surely die'" (Genesis 2:16–17). Another tree is also given special mention, the tree of life (Genesis 2:9), but the significance of that will be seen later.

Man is given total freedom to enjoy all the delights of the garden and God puts only one minor restraint or condition on his freedom – he is not to eat of the tree of the knowledge of good and evil. This was intended to be a test or trial of his love for the Creator Who had given him so much, and of his obedience to God's command. But he was to fail on both counts. After all, the basis of any truly loving relationship must be absolute trust. That is why the break-up of a marriage because of the adultery by either of the partners can be so hurtful and leave such a deep wound. Nor should we forget that as believers we can, by our infidelities and disobedience, wound God's heart. "And do not grieve the Holy Spirit of God, with whom you were sealed for the day of redemption" (Ephesians 4:30). There is much more to be said about this matter of trust and obedience, about the tree of life and the tree of the knowledge of good and evil. But what is said so far is only a preparation for a much deeper understanding of these things in chapter 3.

The formation of woman

"The Lord God said, 'It is not good for the man to be alone. I will make a helper suitable for him.' Now the Lord God had formed out of the ground all the beasts of the field and all the birds of the air. He brought them to the man to see what he would name them; and whatever the man called each living creature, that was its name. So the man gave names to all the livestock, the birds of the air and all the beasts of the field. But for Adam no suitable helper was found" (Genesis 2:18–20). What we are told in these verses clearly cannot be reconciled with the modern theory of man's animal evolution. The loneliness of man is mentioned, thus emphasising the distinct difference between himself and the animals and that they could not provide a helper with whom he could correspond and have fellowship on equal terms. Man could name the animals but the animals could not name him! How this naming process was carried out we are not told but its purpose would have been for Adam to familiarise himself with their individual characteristics and their potential for serving him. Furthermore, we do not necessarily have to imagine some kind of animal parade passing in front of Adam as he named them: it could have taken place during the course of his lifetime. But however it happened the important thing to remember is that it was man who named the animals because he was different from them and of a superior intelligence.

"So the Lord God caused the man to fall into a deep sleep; and while he was sleeping, he took one of the man's ribs and closed up the place with flesh. Then the Lord made a woman from the rib he had taken out of the man, and he brought her to the man. The man said, 'This is now bone of my bones and flesh of my flesh; she shall be called 'woman', for she was taken out of man," (Genesis 2:21–23). The Hebrew word for 'rib' can also be translated 'side', but it is of no great significance since the important thing the passage teaches is that the woman was made in equality with the man, her life came out of his life. Adam doesn't say that the woman acquired her soul and spirit from him but only her body. "This is now bone of my bones and flesh of my flesh". We are told earlier in Genesis 1:27 that both man and woman were created in the image and likeness of God. But why did God put the man into a 'deep sleep'? It couldn't have been the purpose of avoiding pain since pain, and suffering had not yet come into the world. One reason might have been that God was stressing his sovereignty by making man an inactive participant in the making of woman. A similar truth is taught in the doctrine of the Virgin birth. Joseph was a by-stander whilst God alone brought about the miraculous act of conception in Mary so that later the angel could say: "So the holy one to be born will be called the Son of God" (Luke 1:35), and not the 'Son of Joseph'. Salvation is God's work alone through Christ, and man has no part in it. Similarly, the making of woman was God's work alone, and man would never be able to say that he had an active part in it.

That grand old commentator Matthew Henry, when speaking of Eve being made out of Adam's side, says: "… not made out of his head, to rule over him; nor out of his feet, to be trampled on by him; but out of his side, to be equal with him; under his arm, to be protected; and near his heart, to be beloved". This is a quaint, but nevertheless, almost perfect description of the kind of relationship God intended between man and woman. She was meant to be a 'help' to man and this clearly implies headship and authority in keeping with New Testament teaching. "For man did not come from woman, but woman from man; neither was man created for woman, but woman for man" (1 Corinthians 11:8–9). This relationship was then given expression in the institution of marriage. "For this reason a man will leave his father and mother and be united to his wife, and they will become one flesh" (Genesis 2:24). As with all other ordinances of God, marriage too has become distorted and marred by human sin and perversion, but this in no way minimises the importance of marriage and family life as God's intended ideal for the welfare of society. Our Lord Himself when speaking of the sanctity and insolubility of marriage referred to this very passage, thus showing that we are not dealing with allegory or myth but with the authentic Word of God. "'Haven't you read,' he replied, 'that at the beginning the Creator made them male and female,' and said, 'For this reason a man will leave his father and mother and be united to his wife, and the two will become one flesh'? So they are no longer two, but one. Therefore what God has joined together, let man not separate'" (Matthew 19:4–6).

Our failure today to accept the Bible's teaching on the sanctity of marriage and the headship or leadership of the man in God's scheme of things, has brought with it disastrous consequences for society. Broken marriages and broken homes on today's scale have meant more crime among children and young people, growing problems with drink and drugs, more vandalism, and children on the streets, greater hardship for single mothers, a greater number of homeless young people in our towns and cities and an ever increasing demand for housing by separated families. From the Christian perspective the failure to accept fully the doctrine of the headship of the man has also had its effect upon marriage and family. In this regard men have been influenced by today's unisex philosophy rather than by the clear teaching of the Word of God. Many pastors will relate how wives have complained to them that their husbands are not giving the lead in the home, and that responsibility for disciplining the children and taking family devotions is left to them or else it will not be done at all. The same is true in many church fellowships where women are engaged in leading, guiding, teaching and in general giving direction and counsel, not because they particularly aspire to these roles, but because the men are either not available or else, if they are, they opt out of leadership responsibility.

Primal innocence
"The man and his wife were both naked, and they felt no shame" (Genesis 2:25). Sin distorts everything, but perhaps more than everything else connected with the human condition, our attitude towards sex has been so warped and twisted by sin that instead of being something beautiful and fulfilling, as God intended, it has become a source of guilt and shame for many, for others an obsession that leads to misery and even destruction, and for society at large a problem we simply cannot cope with. Adam and Eve had no sense of shame with regard to their nakedness and sexuality, because they had no sense of sin and guilt. The moment they fell from the state of grace through disobedience to God's command they were enveloped with guilty shame before God and in the presence of each other (Genesis 3:7).

Sin enters the world

READ GENESIS CHAPTER 3

We said at the outset that Genesis is a book of 'beginnings' and in this chapter we have the account of the beginning of sin in the world. And although this is the only satisfactory explanation of the origin of evil in the universe, those who approach the Bible from the perspective of critical analysis interpret this story of the fall of man very differently. Here is one such critical approach to Genesis: "Obviously, the book begins in the misty region of tradition and transmitted myth in which imagination precede knowledge. Few will suppose that Adam and Eve and the Garden of Eden belong to factual history" (*Interpreters Bible* Volume 1 page 460). What intellectual arrogance! The great Apostle Paul accepts the account of the entry of sin into the would through Adam as factually historical, and makes it the cornerstone of his doctrine of the Cross. "For if, by the trespass of the one man, death reigned through that one man, how much more will those who receive God's abundant provision of grace and of the gift of righteousness reign in life through the one man Jesus Christ" (Romans 5:17). That tells us clearly that if this account of Adam's fall into sin is mythical then Christ's atonement for sin is also mythical.

The serpent

"Now the serpent was more crafty than any of the wild animals the Lord God had made. He said to the woman, "Did God really say, 'You must not eat from any tree in the garden?" (Genesis 3:1). A talking snake! – that is the first thing the critics seize upon and immediately conclude that we are dealing with a fable in which animals have the power of speech. But that is a literary device, which in the context of a fable, is used for the purpose of teaching a moral lesson. But what we have here is no artificial literary device to teach a moral lesson, but a historical event that determined the eternal destiny of mankind. The serpent is real, the speech is real, and the craftiness is real, because behind it all there is that malignant personality

Satan whose definite strategy was the undermining of God's good work in creation.

In the book of Revelation Satan is actually described as: "... that ancient serpent called the devil or Satan, who leads the whole world astray" (Revelation 12:9). As to his craftiness and subtlety the Apostle Paul urges the Ephesian believers to "take your stand against the devil's schemes" (Ephesians 6:11). Also his ability to possess the serpent's body has its parallel in the incident of the healing of a demon-possessed man where Jesus allowed the demons to enter into the bodies of a herd of pigs (Luke 8:32). Moreover, Paul tells us that Satan "masquerades as an angel of light" (2 Corinthians 11:14), so there is no reason for not believing that he could also masquerade as a serpent. But behind all this the really important thing to keep in mind is that Satan himself is a reality. When confronted with evil in the world we are not dealing with an abstract principle, but with a malignant personal intelligence whose deliberate objective is to hinder and, if possible, to destroy the work of God's kingdom by every means at his disposal. His cunning may be chiefly seen in the fact that he has succeeded in convincing a good many people of his own non-existence. But the New Testament teaches otherwise. In his parable of the Sower our Lord says: "The seed is the word of God. Those along the path are the ones who hear, and then the devil comes and takes away the word from their hearts so that they cannot believe and be saved" (Luke 8:11–12). Or this: "Then he will say to those on his left, 'Depart from me, you who are cursed, into the eternal fire prepared for the devil and his angels'" (Matthew 25:41). In such passages there is no suggestion that evil is an abstract principle, rather our Lord is speaking of a definite personality who directs and organises the evil powers of this world.

The serpent and the woman
The craftiness of the serpent quickly becomes evident in his approach to the woman. "He said to the woman, 'Did God really say, 'You must not eat from any tree in the garden?'" The woman said to the serpent, 'We may eat from the trees in the garden, but God did say, 'You must not eat fruit from the tree that is in the middle of the garden, and you must not touch it, or you will die" (Genesis 3:1–3). The Devil's strategy is clear, it was to plant doubt

in Eve's mind first by distorting God's Word – "Did God really say", implying that God is being mean and small-minded and not at all as good and gracious as Eve thinks He is. Second, he denies God's Word altogether: "'You will not surely die' the serpent said to the woman. 'For God knows that when you eat of it your eyes will be opened, and you will be like God, knowing good and evil'" (Genesis 3:4–5). This same strategy he employs today, and very successfully it would seem, from the way the Word of God is being distorted in many pulpits and its truth ultimately denied altogether. Paul was acutely aware of this strategy when he warns us in his letter to the Corinthians to guard the veracity of God's Word. "Therefore, since through God's mercy we have this ministry, we do not lose heart. Rather, we have renounced secret and shameful ways; we do not use deception, nor do we distort the word of God" (2 Corinthians 4:1–2). The Authorised Version reads: "nor handling the word of God deceitfully", and J.B. Phillips states: "we use no dishonest manipulation of the Word of God".

From the moment Eve entertained the distortion of God's Word by the Devil, the seed of doubt concerning its veracity and authority was planted in her mind and she was headed for disaster. And the same is happening today when liberals manipulate and distort the scriptures to make them say what they want them to say. They adapt the Word of God to fit in with so-called modern progressive thinking. References to the supernatural such as miracles, the virgin birth, the bodily resurrection and the return of Christ in glory and power are either explained in a rationalistic manner or else denied entirely. But such distortion is disastrous since it destroys the power and vitality of God's Word and no longer accomplishes the very end for which God gave it – the salvation of people's souls. Instead they remain dead in their sins (Ephesians 2:1). For when God warned Adam and Eve against eating the fruit of the tree lest they die, it was both physical and spiritual death He was talking about.

The fall
"When the woman saw that the fruit of the tree was good for food and pleasing to the eye, and also desirable for gaining wisdom, she took some and ate it. She also gave some to her husband, who was with her, and he ate it. Then the eyes of both of them were opened, and they realised that they

were naked; so they sewed fig leaves together and made coverings for them-selves" (Genesis 3:6–7). Underlying all temptation to sin is the desire for self-assertion as opposed to subordination to God's rule and God's law. That is what made the big lie of the serpent so attractive: "… your eyes will be opened and you will be like God, knowing good and evil" (Genesis 3:5). Their eyes were indeed opened but not to the delights of being like God, but opened to the awareness of their own guilt and shame which they vainly tried to cover up by covering their nakedness. And Satan has been busy perpetuating that big lie ever since, leading people to believe they can be their own god, going their own way independently of their Creator but bringing upon themselves the same misery and guilt that is always a conse-quence of sin and disobedience.

When we analyse the temptation of Eve we see that it has three basic characteristics. It was physically satisfying – "the fruit of the tree was good for food". It was aesthetically appealing – "pleasing to the eye". It was intel-lectually attractive – "desirable for gaining wisdom". According to John these are always the essential features the world holds out to the believer to seduce him from his love for Christ. "If anyone loves the world, the love of the Father is not in him. For everything in the world – the cravings of sinful man, the lust of his eyes and the boasting of what he has and does – comes not from the Father but from the world" (1 John 2:15–16).

"The cravings of sinful man" – what does he mean by that? He means all the things that pander to our indulgences and physical appetites in the way Eve craved the fruit of the tree because it was physically satisfying. It will include gluttony in food, selfishness in the use of personal possessions and extravagance in the gratification of our personal desires. In short it is a soft, flabby approach to life which thinks only of its own pleasures and comforts. We see a lot of that today and the believer needs to be on guard against it.

"The lust of his eyes". Eve found the fruit of the tree 'pleasing to the eye'. It appealed to her senses. She liked what she saw and she wanted it. So it is still. A feature of worldly society is a spirit of discontent with what we already have, and a covetous desire to possess more of the things we see around us. It is an attitude of life and a spirit that is always impressed by the outward appearance of things – 'the lust of his eyes' – and is captivated by outward show and ostentation in the mistaken belief that happiness and contentment is to be found in the accumulation of the things money can buy. The believer on the other hand is in touch with 'reality' and looks beneath the surface appearances of the world because he knows that "the world and its desires pass away" (1 John 2:17).

"The boasting of what he has and does". If there is anything that characterises the spirit of the world it is man's pride in his own achievements independently of God. Eve found the fruit of the tree intellectually attractive because it held out the possibility of 'gaining wisdom' and being 'like God'. Modern man, in the boasting of his own intellectual achievements and his pride in the advances of science, has long since eaten of that fruit and deified his own interests. He no longer sees a need of prayer, of the Bible, of salvation or of God, he sees himself as his own god. But we have only to take a long hard look at our modern world to see the brilliant mess our boastful progressive humanity has got itself into as a result.

Hiding from God

"Then the man and his wife heard the sound of the Lord God as he was walking in the garden in the cool of the day, and they hid from the Lord God among the trees of the garden. But the Lord God called to the man, 'Where are you?' He answered, 'I heard you in the garden, and I was afraid because I was naked, so I hid'" (Genesis 3:8–10). Why did Adam and Eve hide from God? Was it because, as Adam says, 'I was naked'. Yes it was that, but not essentially because of the nakedness itself, but because the nakedness symbolised their consciousness of guilt. That is, their eyes were now open to their wrongdoing and disobedience – they knew not only the good but had experiential knowledge of evil as well. For what was the sin of Adam and Eve? Did the fruit of the tree have some kind of magical properties or power so that the moment they ate it they had this superior knowledge of good and evil? No, there was nothing special about the tree other than the fact that it symbolised God's will or God's command. Adam and Eve's sin lay in the fact that they rejected and disobeyed God's will by doing what He had explicitly forbidden them to do.

The first consequence of this act of disobedience was a sense of guilt and shame and therefore they 'hid from God'. Previously they had been at ease in God's presence and had enjoyed fellowship with Him, but now they dreaded – "I was afraid" – meeting with Him. That is what sin does, it brings about a radical alienation from God. For the believer it means a disruption in our fellowship with Him. But as long as we try to hide from God and seek to evade the reckoning with Him we can know no rest and peace. Francis Thompson's poem, *Hound of Heaven*, expresses it well:

" I fled Him, down the arches of the years;
I fled Him, down the labyrinthine ways
Of my own mind; and in the mist of tears
I hid from Him, and under running laughter.
    . . . .
From those strong Feet that followed, followed after.
But with unhurrying chase, and unperturbed pace,
Deliberate speed, majestic instancy,
They beat – and a Voice beat
More instant than the Feet –
'All things betray thee, who betrayest Me"

The reckoning

At this point we may wonder why God needed to cry out to Adam and Eve: 'Where are you?' Had they been so successful in hiding among the trees that God had no hope of finding them? That's impossible, since God is omniscient – He knows everything. We can never successfully hide anything from God, least of all our sin. Whenever God asks a question in the Bible it is never to seek information but to teach something. In this case it was to reinforce in the minds of Adam and Eve the enormity of their disobedience and to bring them out into the open to confess it. The reckoning had to come, as it will ultimately come for all those who continue to reject God and try to hide from Him. For man has the freedom of will to accept, in obedience, God's rule and purpose for him, or to reject it. That comes out clearly in this passage: "And he said, 'Who told you that you were naked? Have you eaten from the tree from which I commanded you not to eat?'" (Genesis 3:11). Adam and Eve were free agents in choosing between God's command and Satan's lie. What they did, they did knowingly and freely, without any form of compulsion being brought to bear upon them, and therefore they were wholly responsible, in the reckoning with God, for the judgement He brought upon their sin.

The uselessness of excuses

The sad fact is however that in spite of enjoying the gift of personal freedom, man is unwilling to accept the responsibility that goes with it, and always has some excuse for his wicked behaviour; or else he seeks to shift the blame in another direction. "The man said, 'The woman you put here with me – she gave me some fruit from the tree, and I ate it'. Then the Lord God said to the woman, 'What is this you have done?' The woman said, 'The serpent deceived me, and I ate'" (Genesis 3:12–13). Notice how Adam, in an indirect way, even tries to blame God Himself in the first instance. "The woman you put here with me, she gave me …". It was all God's fault really for making the woman in the first place. Men still try to blame God for all kinds of things. I have often wondered about that curious phrase, 'An Act of God' which insurance companies use when no one is directly responsible for an accident – blame it on God!

In modern thinking man looks at the suffering and catastrophe in the world and he says in effect: 'Why doesn't God do something about it? It's all His fault anyway for not making the world better than it is'. But that's just it. He did make the world better than it is. "God saw all that he had made, and it was very good" (Genesis 1:31). It was man himself who messed it all up. Our world is in the moral and spiritual pile-up it is because it chooses to go that way rather than God's way and the blame lies squarely on us. But man refuses to acknowledge his own individual responsibility for his part in the world's wickedness. That is a characteristic of our society – Adam blames Eve and Eve blames the serpent. The fault lies with one's upbringing, or a broken marriage, or the environment, or lack of opportunity, or the people one works with. But no one is prepared to say, "It is my fault, my sin, my responsibility. What I did, I did with my eyes open, knowingly and wilfully and I must reckon with God".

Judgement and the curse

The consequence or judgement which followed from the Fall is generally referred to as the Curse. "So the Lord God said to the serpent, 'Because you have done this, Cursed are you above all the livestock and all the wild animals! You will crawl on your belly and you will eat dust all the days of your life.'" (Genesis 3:14). It is significant that we are told that the serpent was cursed and the ground was cursed because of Adam's sin but that Adam and Eve themselves, whilst they were judged, they were not cursed. That is because they could be restored and forgiven, but the serpent, or rather Satan who had possessed the serpent, could never be restored and forgiven. He would be forever cursed and subjected to degradation and God's wrath, symbolised by the words, 'you will eat dust', until the time of his final destruction (Revelation 20:10).

But the second part of the serpent's curse is even more significant: "And I will put enmity between you and the woman, and between your offspring and hers; he will crush your head, and you will strike his heel." (Genesis 3:15). This is sometimes called the Protoevangelium (first Gospel) because it is the first of a whole series of Messianic prophecies from Genesis to Revelation. In the first place it foretells the antagonism that would exist throughout the ages between the offspring of the woman, meaning all those who belong to God's kingdom through saving faith in the Lord Jesus Christ, and the offspring of Satan, meaning all those who have deliberately taken their stand on the Devil's side by rejecting Christ and His gospel and are the enemies of God. The Lord Jesus refers to these two kinds of people in the world in His parable of the Wheat and Tares. "The field is the world, and the good seed stands for the sons of the kingdom. The weeds are the sons of the evil one" (Matthew 13:38). John likewise says: "… we know who the children of God are and who the children of the devil are" (1 John 3:10). But this warfare and antagonism will one day come to an end, because a decisive blow will be struck which will destroy Satan and his kingdom of evil.

The one who will accomplish this will be Christ the Messiah: "… He will crush your head, and you will strike his heel." Christ was exclusively the offspring of the woman through the miracle of the virgin birth. As Paul puts it: "God sent His Son, born of a woman … that we might receive the full rights of sons" (Galatians 4:4–5). It is the characteristic of the snake or serpent because it crawls in the dust to strike at the heel. This symbolises all the attacks made by Satan in the attempt to destroy Christ and His gospel especially in His death on the Cross. But just as a man's heel can crush a snake's head, so Christ's death on the Cross was the very means God used to finally crush Satan and the powers of evil. The final cry of Christ on the Cross, 'It is finished' was a shout of victory over sin and Satan, and was later confirmed by His glorious resurrection.

Next came the judgement on the woman. "To the woman he said, 'I will greatly increase your pain in childbearing; in pain you will give birth to children. Your desire will be for your husband, and he will rule over you'" (Genesis 3:16). Originally, God had intended that conception and birth should have been a source of joy and blessing for the man and woman. "God blessed them and said to them, 'be fruitful and increase in number'..." (Genesis 1:28). But because of the woman's sin and disobedience that was to change and childbearing would become a source of anxiety and pain. History bears that out, since it is not only in the act of giving birth that the woman experiences pain, but there is also the emotional suffering and heartache associated with motherhood and the bringing up of children because of the effects of sin in society.

And God added further: "Your desire will be for your husband, and he will rule over you". We saw earlier that the woman was intended to be a help to man in a loving relationship under the blessing of God. But Eve had reversed that order when she adopted the leading role in taking the fruit of the tree and in leading Adam into sin with her. God now re-establishes the man's authority over the woman, but because sin has entered into the equation, the relationship would no longer be one of unclouded joy and blessing. Indeed history proves the opposite. Man's rule over woman led to her cruel exploitation and subjugation for centuries and even today she is still treated very harshly in some parts of the world. But when a husband and wife experience salvation in Christ the marriage should once again be the loving relationship God intended. "Wives, submit to your husbands as to the Lord. For the husband is the head of the wife as Christ is the head of the church ... Husbands, love your wives just as Christ loved the church and gave Himself up for her ..." (Ephesians 5:22–25).

Adam's judgement was particularly severe since it involved both the rest of humanity in the future and also the earth over which previously he had had dominion. "To Adam he said, 'Because you listened to your wife and ate from the tree about which I commanded you, 'You must not eat of it.' Cursed is the ground because of you; through painful toil you will eat of it all the days of your life. It will produce thorns and thistles for you, and you will eat the plants of the field. By the sweat of your brow you will eat your food until you return to the ground, since from it you were taken; for dust you are and to dust you will return'" (Genesis 3:17–19).

We repeat what we said earlier about Adam's work in the garden. Then it had been a pleasure, now it was to become a burden. Then, he lived to work, now he would have to work to live. Previously man and nature worked in harmony and co-operation, now man would be pitted against the environment. The operative word then had been 'life' but from now on the principle of decay and death would enter the physical creation. Even man's physical body would return to the dust from which it was taken. Paul refers to the disastrous effects of the Fall when he anticipates our final redemption in Christ when man and creation will again be restored to harmony.

"The creation waits in eager expectation for the sons of God to be revealed. For the creation was subjected to frustration, not by its own choice, but by the will of the one who subjected it, in hope that the creation itself will be liberated from its bondage to decay and brought into the glorious freedom of the children of God" (Romans 8:19–21).

The covering for sin

"Adam named his wife Eve, because she would become the mother of all the living. The Lord God made garments of skin for Adam and his wife and clothed them" (Genesis 3:20–21). The name Eve means 'life' and symbolises the faith of Adam in the promise of God, that from the offspring of the woman, life would come and ultimately salvation. Such faith indicates they had repented of their sin and were pardoned by God, although the consequences remained. This is seen in God's gracious act of making coverings of skin for Adam and Eve to cover their nakedness. Earlier they had attempted to provide their own covering of fig leaves (Genesis 3:7) for their disobedience and sin, but this was inadequate, so God Himself provides a covering for them.

In all this we see a wonderful anticipation of the Gospel of our redemption in Christ. All through history man has attempted to provide his own covering for sin in the hope of receiving pardon and forgiveness from a Holy God. He has attempted to provide his own righteousness through religious ritual, acts of penance and meritorious works. But always God rejected them as inadequate. And just as the skins God provided speak of sacrifice, so the sacrifice of Christ, His own Son, was the only covering for sin acceptable to Him.

"Jesus, Thy blood and righteousness
My beauty are, my glorious dress;
Midst flaming worlds in these arrayed,
With joy shall I lift up my head."

Separation from the tree of life

"And the Lord God said, 'The man has now become like one of us, knowing good and evil. He must not be allowed to reach out his hand and take also from the tree of life and eat, and live for ever'. So the Lord God banished him from the Garden of Eden to work the ground from which he had been taken. After he drove the man out, he placed on the east side of the Garden of Eden cherubim and a flaming sword flashing back and forth to guard the way to the tree of life" (Genesis 3:22–24). Sin always involves separation from God and the loss of the gift of eternal life. The big question is therefore: How can man be reconciled to God and have once more the right to the tree of life? The answer lies with the second Adam, Christ Jesus. "God was reconciling the world to himself in Christ, not counting men's sins against them" (2 Corinthians 5:19). And again: "This is the testimony: God has given us eternal life, and this life is in his Son" (1 John 5:11).

"O loving wisdom of our God!
When all was sin and shame,
A second Adam to the fight,
And to the rescue came."

Home, family and society

The principle of sin and degeneration, which originated in the Garden of Eden is now, in this chapter, transmitted to the life of the home, the family and society in general. Here too we have several 'firsts' or beginnings, including the first birth, the first family, the first act of worship and, most horrifying of all, the world's first murder.

Cain and Abel *

"Adam lay with his wife Eve, and she became pregnant and gave birth to Cain. She said, 'With the help of the Lord I have brought forth a man'. Later, she gave birth to his brother Abel. Now Abel kept flocks and Cain worked the soil" (Genesis 4:1–2). The name Cain means 'possessed' or 'acquired' and was probably derived from Eve's words at the time of the birth "With the help of the Lord I have brought forth a man." This suggests that she was confident that Cain would grow to manhood and may even imply that she believed that he was to be the promised 'offspring' who would overcome Satan and evil in the world. If that was so she was to be bitterly disappointed, for when her second son was born she named him Abel which means 'vanity' or 'ephemeral' which suggests that she could already see, in an almost prophetic manner, how empty and superficial life was going to be in a sinful world. However that may be, Abel's life was certainly ephemeral for he was soon to be murdered by his brother Cain.

The brothers were totally different in character and temperament and we are meant to see in this difference the conflict which God had previously said would develop between the 'offspring' of the woman, represented by Abel, and the 'offspring' of the evil one represented by Cain. This is clear if only from our Lord's description of the younger brother as 'righteous Abel' (Matthew 23:35) and John's reference to Cain as one 'who belonged to the

*For a more detailed study of Cain's character, see my book God Spoke to Them.

evil one' (1 John 3:12). But the inveterate hatred of Satan and the powers of darkness towards the people of God is seen most clearly of all in Cain's murder of his younger brother, and the background against which it was carried out. "Now Cain said to his brother Abel, 'Let's go out to the field'. And while they were in the field, Cain attacked his brother Abel and killed him" (Genesis 4:8). In this wicked act we see how rapidly sin was beginning to dominate man's thinking and behaviour since at this point Cain was only the second man to live on the earth after Adam.

The character of worship

What makes the action of Cain so particularly appalling is that this, the first murder in the history of the human race, should have been associated with the worship of God. "In the course of time Cain brought some of the fruits of the soil as an offering to the Lord. But Abel brought fat portions from some of the firstborn of his flock. The Lord looked with favour on Abel and his offering, but on Cain and his offering he did not look with favour. So Cain was very angry and his face was downcast" (Genesis 4:3–5). There are those who believe that God accepted Abel's offering because it was a blood sacrifice, a lamb from the flock, whereas Cain's came from the produce of the earth which God had previously cursed.

I have never myself been satisfied with that explanation if only because the fruit and the lamb were both the products of God's creation, but furthermore as the form of worship develops in the Old Testament, we find God Himself encouraging mankind to bring Him the first-fruits of harvest as a measure of their gratitude for His providential care (Exodus 23:16). The real explanation lies in what we said earlier, that Abel was righteous and belonged to the Messianic line whereas Cain was of the evil one and the offspring of the serpent. Hebrews says: "By faith Abel offered God a better sacrifice than Cain did. By faith he was commended as a righteous man, when God spoke well of his offerings" (Hebrews 11:4). And John says of Cain's murderous act: "And why did he murder him? Because his own actions were evil and his brother's were righteous" (1 John 3:12).

This tells us something about the way in which we are to worship God; that it is not the Gift but the Giver that is most important, not the act of worship itself but the spirit in which we bring the gift of worship that is truly pleasing to God. Cain was not in the right spirit for worship: "Cain was very angry and his face was downcast". Our Lord had something to say about the spirit of true worship in the Sermon on the Mount. "Therefore, if you are offering your gift at the altar and there remember that your brother has something against you, leave the gift there in front on the altar. First go and be reconciled to your brother; then come and offer your gift" (Matthew 5:23–24). He almost seems to be saying that God considers being in a right spirit for worship is so important that He is prepared to be kept waiting while we make it up with someone we may have fallen out with. And we can surely understand that. How can we hope to know the presence of God in our worship and be truly blessed in our hearts through the prayers that are offered and the preaching of the Word if at the same time, for whatever reason, we are resentful in our spirit, or we are harbouring unkind thoughts, or there is some other sin lurking within which we have not confessed? God has clearly said: "This is the one I esteem: he who is humble and contrite in spirit, and trembles at my word" (Isaiah 66:2).

Cain's resentment

It seems Cain had been brooding on his relationship with Abel and it was having a very negative effect upon him. "Then the Lord said to Cain, 'Why are you angry? Why is your face downcast? If you do what is right, will you not be accepted? But if you do not do what is right, sin is crouching at your door; it desires to have you, but you must master it'. " (Genesis 4:6–7). God tells him that if he does the right thing by making it up with Abel then he will be forgiven, but if not, that same spirit of resentment will be like a lurking beast within waiting to destroy him. And that in fact is what happened. The longer he nursed his anger the stronger it became until it eventually sprang into action and he murdered his brother.

When a spirit of resentment gets hold of us we must deal with it immediately or else it will poison the whole system and may lead us to do something we may regret for the rest of our lifetime. Our Lord also dealt with that point in the same passage in the Sermon on the Mount we referred to earlier. "Settle matters quickly with your adversary who is taking you to court. Do it while you are still with him on the way, or he may hand you over to the judge, and the judge may hand you over to the officer, and you may be thrown into prison. I tell you the truth, you will not get out until you have paid the last penny" (Matthew 5:25–26). The point of the illustration is that the time for reconciliation or for putting matters right in our relationship with others is always NOW, not next week or next month for then it may be too late. The evil beast of sin lurking within may spring and destroy any desire we may have to do the right thing, and we shall find ourselves taken from this world to stand before God the Judge with the spirit of resentment still in our heart.

Cain's judgement

"Then the Lord said to Cain, 'Where is your brother Abel?' 'I don't know' he replied. 'Am I my brother's keeper?'" (Genesis 4:9). Remember what we said earlier about God never asking a question to obtain information but in order to teach something? In this case it was to bring home to Cain the enormity of his sin in killing his younger brother. But his defiant reply was not only an outright lie but it expressed the kind of 'callous indifference' we see so much of today in human relationships. "Am I my brother's keeper?" The worldly answer to that is often 'No! – I have as much as I can do to be my own keeper'. But that can never be the answer of the Christian in the light of the teaching of the Gospel of Christ. We are reminded here of that other question on the same subject of Christian responsibility asked of Jesus by a lawyer: "And who is my neighbour?" Our Lord's answer was the parable of the Good Samaritan (Luke 10:25–37) which makes it perfectly clear that, as a lover of God, we are to act in a neighbourly, loving and helpful way to anyone in trouble or in need.

For let there be no doubt in our minds that all such 'callous indifference' to the humanity of others, whether by murder, violence, injustice or in any other way, is known to God and will be judged by Him as surely as He judged Cain. "The Lord said, 'What have you done? Listen! Your brother's blood cries out to me from the ground. Now you are under a curse and driven from the ground, which opened its mouth to receive your brother's blood from your hand. When you work the ground, it will no longer yield its crops for you. You will be a restless wanderer on the earth'" (Genesis 4:10–12). God is not indifferent to moral wrong-doing on the earth; the blood of Abel cries out to Him on behalf of all those innocent millions in our own century who have suffered humiliation and dehumanisation at the hands of their fellowmen.

But there is a deeper spiritual lesson here. Abel may be regarded as the first martyr in the Bible since he was a man of faith and he died for his faith, "And by faith he still speaks, even though he is dead" (Hebrews 11:4). Furthermore, the Lord Jesus sums up the history of martyrdom in the light of Abel's murder at the hands of Cain, the 'offspring' of the serpent, when he speaks to the enemies of the gospel. "And so upon you will come all the righteous blood that has been shed on earth, from the blood of righteous Abel to the blood of Zechariah … I tell you the truth, all this will come upon this generation" (Matthew 23:35–36). Abel's murder therefore is reminding us that all through history the antagonism between the 'offspring' of the woman and the 'offspring' of the serpent will intensify and the believers and all who love God in Christ must be prepared to suffer, and even die, for the cause of the gospel – "the blood of the martyrs is the seedbed of the Church". But God is mindful of all this and will in his own time vindicate His truth and execute His wrath and judgement on the persecutors of His Church. We have a powerful picture of this truth in the book of Revelation. "When he opened the fifth seal, I saw under the altar the souls of those who had been slain because of the word of God and the testimony they had maintained. They called out in a loud voice 'How long, Sovereign Lord, holy and true, until you judge the inhabitants of the earth and avenge our blood?' Then each of them was given a white robe and they were told to wait a little longer until the number of their fellow-servants and brothers who were to be killed as they had been, was completed" (Revelation 6:9–11).

The 'end time' is certainly a lot nearer now than it was when those words were written, but the wickedness of the serpent's 'offspring' against the Church of God is still not ripe for God's final judgement. But it will come! In the meantime, like Abel and the souls under the altar, we must continue to make our testimony in a sinful world to the truth of God's Word. For this is still the day of God's grace and even for those who continue to reject the gospel of God's mercy, forgiveness is still available. That surely is the meaning of the 'mark' or sign God put upon Cain. "Cain said to the Lord, 'my punishment is more than I can bear. Today you are driving me from the land, and I will be hidden from your presence; I will be a restless wanderer on the earth and whoever finds me will kill me'. But the Lord said to him, 'Not so, if anyone kills Cain he will suffer vengeance seven times over.' Then the Lord put a mark on Cain so that no-one who found him would kill him. So Cain went out from the Lord's presence and lived in the land of Nod, east of Eden" (Genesis 4:13–16). The mark or sign served a two-fold purpose; it was the sign of God's judgement on Cain so that others would know that man cannot sin against God with impunity, but it was also a sign of God's mercy since it served to protect Cain against human vengeance. We might be perplexed at the notion that there was anyone else around who might have wanted to kill Cain, since he was only the second man on the earth after Adam. But we must bear in mind that Adam lived for 930 years and had other sons and daughters (Genesis 5:4–5) and the earth's population at that time was multiplying rapidly.

Development of civilisation
Following the expulsion of Cain from the presence of God we follow the progress of humanity through two distinct lines; the line of Cain, representing the 'offspring' of the serpent, and the line of Seth, born after Abel's death, representing the 'offspring' of the woman and the Messianic promise. The line of Cain over eight generations begins at Genesis 4:17 and ends at verse 24. The line of Seth over ten generations begins at verse 25 and ends at Genesis 5:32.

Line of Cain
"So Cain went out from the Lord's presence and lived in the land of Nod, east of Eden. Cain lay with his wife, and she became pregnant and gave birth to Enoch. Cain was then building a city, and he named it after his son Enoch. To Enoch was born Irad, and Irad was the father of Mehujael, and Mehujael was the father of Methushael and Methushael was the father of Lamech" (Genesis 4:16–18). The locality of Nod is unknown so it is useless to speculate but the old 'chestnut' about where did Cain get his wife is easily answered. She must either have been his sister or some other close relative. We noted earlier that Adam lived for 930 years and had other sons and daughters (Genesis 5:4–5).

More important is the fact that with the line of Cain we have the beginnings of urbanisation. "Cain was building a city and he named it after his son Enoch". This would not have been a city in the modern sense but it does indicate that men were already moving in the direction of a settled way of life. This cuts right across the modern idea that the emergence of man from barbarism to a civilised way of life occurred over a period of hundreds of thousands of years. Moreover, this reference to an urban way of life, so early in the history of the human race, bears out the contention by some anthropologists and ethnologists of the existence of an earlier advanced civilisation which had been wiped off the face of the earth by some catastrophe or other. From the Biblical perspective such a catastrophe would have been the flood. It is interesting in this respect that on television recently a series of programmes appeared called: "Quest for the Lost Civilisation" in which a number of anthropologists and other scholars expressed their deep conviction, based on detailed research, that such an advanced civilisation did in fact exist.

The sophisticated nature of this Cainite civilisation is seen further in the high degree of culture attained by the descendants of Lamech. "Lamech married two women, one named Adah and the other Zillah. Adah gave birth to Jabal; he was the father of those who live in tents and raise livestock. His brother's name was Jubal; he was the father of all who play the harp and flute. Zillah also had a son, Tubal-Cain, who forged all kinds of tools out of bronze and iron. Tubal-Cain's sister was Naamah" (Genesis 4:19-22). In Jabal we have the beginning of nomadism, tent-making and the skills associated with the domestication of flocks and herds. With Jubal we have the beginning of culture and the arts: "He was the father of all who play the harp and flute." Interestingly enough this early reference to music is supported by the archaeological discovery some years ago (Sydney Morning Herald 21 February 1996) in Slovenia south-east Europe, of a five inch flute made by Neanderthal humans. It was said at the time that this discovery that early man could play music had "far-reaching implications for human evolution". But those who accept the authenticity of Genesis already had that information. With Lamech's third son Tubal-Cain we have the beginnings of the manufacture of tools and weapons – "he forged all kinds of tools out of bronze and iron."

It is significant that with this development of civilisation and the products of man's own ingenuity in the form of cattle breeding, trade, the arts and manufacture, although not evil in themselves, were nevertheless the things that began to seduce man away from the true worship of God. For Cain's line, through Lamech, was to become increasingly Godless. "Lamech said to his wives, 'Adah and Zillah, listen to me; wives of Lamech, hear my words. I have killed a man for wounding me, a young man for injuring me. If Cain is avenged seven times, then Lamech seventy-seven times'" (Genesis 4:23–24). Here we have the beginnings of polygamy, which was against God's original intention for man, and the glorification of murder. This is a picture of man proudly boasting of his independence from God and his ability to fashion his own destiny. Lamech regards himself as stronger than God and able to exact a retribution seventy-seven times greater than anything God had promised. The 'offspring' of the serpent was becoming increasingly active in the world and its wickedness and apostasy would culminate finally in the judgement of the Flood.

Line of Seth

"Adam lay with his wife again, and she gave birth to a son and named him Seth, saying, 'God has granted me another child in place of Abel, since Cain killed him'. Seth also had a son, and he named him Enosh. At that time men began to call on the name of the Lord." (Genesis 4:25–26). With the line of Seth we have an entirely different picture from that seen in the line of Cain. Through Seth's descendants the Messianic promise will be continued. It is no longer man's independence of God that is emphasised but rather his reliance upon God, and his recognition of the special relationship he has with the God of his father. "At that time men began to call on the name of the Lord." This probably means the beginning of organised worship and prayer.

As we move into Chapter 5, Adam's descendants through the line of Seth are recorded over ten generations and it is not the most stimulating reading since it is simply a list of names each ending with the refrain: 'and then he died'. But there is one significant thing, and that is the great ages of these antediluvians when they died, from Adam himself who lived for 930 years to Methuselah who lived for almost a thousand years. We cannot be certain

BE FRUITFUL & MULTIPLY

what the explanation is for these long life-spans, but it is interesting to note that in the genealogy recorded in Chapter 11 after the Flood, the life span reduces steadily from Shem who lived 500 years to Terah the father of Abraham who lived a mere 205 years. After this it reduces still further with Abraham himself living only 175 years. The explanation therefore may lie in the fact that the climate and the environment of the earth changed dramatically after the Flood and this had a bearing upon the duration of man's life.

Another insight into this genealogy arises out of the constant refrain: "and then he died". This is a reminder of God's judgement upon man's sin in Adam and of the inevitability of death which comes to everyone whether our life is short or long. Death is something most of us don't like to talk about, and in the modern funeral business great pains are taken to eradicate the starkness and ugliness. Indeed, in the United States the art of Cosmetology – the use of cosmetics – is sometimes taken to absurd lengths in an effort to make the dead person look natural and alive. The truth is however that neither cosmetics nor any other device can rid death of its reality; that is why the New Testament describes it as the last enemy: "The last enemy to be destroyed is death" (1 Corinthians 15:26). But if death is both an enemy and a reality then the best thing we can do is to take the fear out of it before it comes, and that is exactly what the resurrection of our Lord Jesus Christ does. The 'offspring' of the serpent thought it had struck the final blow when Christ died on the Cross; but the last word is always with God. Through the resurrection of Christ, God dispelled the fear of death for the believer and also the power of death through the gift of resurrection life. "Because I live, you also will live" (John 14:19).

Walking with God

Among the names of those listed in Chapter 5 who lived to a great age before they died, there is one exception. "Altogether Enoch lived 365 years. Enoch walked with God; then he was no more, because God took him away" (Genesis 5:23–24). His life was much shorter than the others mentioned for the simple reason that he never actually died. This in itself is quite remarkable and he is one of only two men in scripture to be taken out of this world without meeting with death. The other was the prophet Elijah who was taken up to heaven in a chariot of fire (2 Kings 2:11). I read somewhere of a little girl telling the story of Enoch: "Enoch and God used to take long walks together and one day they walked further than usual. God said, 'Enoch, you must be tired; come into my house and rest.'" That little child had grasped the most important thing about this man, he enjoyed the company and fellowship of God and when the time came he was perfectly happy to spend the rest of eternity with Him.

"Enoch walked with God" – it's one of those haunting phrases that we come across every so often in the Bible. But what does it mean? In both Old and New Testaments the term 'walk' used as a figure of speech means simply to have a close relationship with God in everyday life. God is not someone vague and remote but One whose fellowship and presence we share in every moment of every day in the way that, at the human level, we enjoy the company and conversation of a close friend. Enoch was a godly man in a godless age and it is possible to be that only when one is walking in the way of truth and righteousness, and is close to God. The writer to the Hebrews describes Enoch as a man of faith and 'one who pleased God' (Hebrews 11:5). Jude goes further and in a quotation from the Apocryphal book of Enoch describes him as a prophet. "Enoch the seventh from Adam, prophesied about these men: 'See, the Lord is coming with thousands upon thousands of his holy ones to judge everyone, and to convict all the ungodly of all the ungodly acts they have done in the ungodly way, and all the harsh words ungodly sinners have spoken against him'" (Jude verses 14–15). We may not be able to emulate Enoch and the other great figures of the Bible who were prophets and through whom God did mighty things, because He raised them up for that purpose, but we can emulate them in their walk with God in living a holy life.

The genealogy of Genesis Chapter 5 ends with a reference to that other mighty man of God, Noah, about whom we are going to hear a great deal in the next four chapters. "After Noah was 500 years old, he became the father of Shem, Ham and Japheth" (Genesis 5:32).

The flood and Noah's ark

READ GENESIS CHAPTERS 6 & 7

U p to this point we have followed the development of civilisation through the two lines of Cain and Seth. But now we see the two lines converging and as a result the wickedness of man on the earth becomes ever greater. "When men began to increase in number on the earth and daughters were born to them, the sons of God saw that the daughters of men were beautiful, and they married any of them they chose. Then the Lord said, 'My Spirit will not contend with man for ever, for he is mortal; his days will be a hundred and twenty years.' The Nephilim were on the earth in those days – and also afterwards – when the sons of God went to the daughters of men and had children by them. They were the heroes of old, men of renown" (Genesis 6:1–4).

This is a very difficult passage which commentators interpret in different ways. There are two main explanations which turn on the meaning of the key phrase 'sons of God'. On the one hand it is said to refer to 'angels' as in Job 1:6, Psalm 29:1 and elsewhere, but in this instance they were fallen angels as mentioned in 2 Peter 2:4 and Jude verse 6. Some of these demonic beings, it is said, came to earth and married 'the daughters of men' thus producing the abnormal offspring called Nephilim or 'fallen ones'. The other explanation understands the phrase 'sons of God' to refer to the godly descendants of Seth in the way that it is used of believers in Exodus 4:22, Isaiah 43:6, and Romans 8:14. According to this view intermarriage took place between the godly Sethites and the wicked Cainites in a licentious and promiscuous manner, polygamy having already been introduced by Lamech, and borne out by the remark, "they married any of them they chose".

Whichever of these interpretations we accept, it is clear that the lesson the writer intends to convey remains the same – the eruption of sin and wickedness on the earth was now so intense and universal that it brought God's judgement on the whole human race in the form of the Flood. "Then the Lord said, 'My Spirit will not contend with man for ever, for he is mortal; his days will be a hundred and twenty years'" (Genesis 6:3). Here is a solemn lesson, for God is warning mankind of the limitation of his mercy and grace. Human depravity had degenerated to such an extent that at the end of the hundred and twenty years it was putting itself beyond the possibility of reclamation. "The Lord saw how great man's wickedness on the earth had become, and that every inclination of the thoughts of his heart was only evil all the time. The Lord was grieved that he had made man on the earth, and his heart was filled with pain. So the Lord said, 'I will wipe mankind, whom I have created, from the face of the earth – men and animals, and creatures that move along the ground, and birds of the air – for I am grieved that I have made them'" (Genesis 6:5–7).

This raises the question: Can a man so persist in sin and rebellion where God's patience is concerned that he closes for ever the door of salvation? The answer of the Bible seems to be, yes he can! God withdraws His Spirit from a man not because He is unwilling to save, but because that man continually resists the Spirit's witness and refuses to be saved. We see this limitation on the offer of the gospel in our Lord's instruction: "Do not give dogs what is sacred; do not throw your pearls to pigs" (Matthew 7:6). And in Romans 1 Paul uses the expression three times: "Therefore God gave them over" meaning that because of man's depravity and resistance to His truth God took off the restraints of sin and said in effect: "if you think you can run your life without me then get on with it and see the mess you will make of things". For the truth is we cannot presume on the unlimited patience and mercy of God where sin and rebellion are concerned.

The faith of Noah

The one great exception to the grotesque corruption of the age was Noah. "But Noah found favour in the eyes of the Lord. This is the account of Noah. Noah was a righteous man, blameless among the people of his time, and he walked with God. Noah had three sons: Shem, Ham and Japheth" (Genesis 6:8–10). Noah's faith must have been of an exceptional kind because he found himself in a unique position when God told him to build the ark. There had never been a worldwide flood before, so he had no blueprint to follow for the exercise of the kind of faith God was now asking of him. "So God said to Noah, 'I am going to put an end to all people, for the earth is filled with violence because of them. I am surely going to destroy both them and the earth. So make yourself an ark of cypress wood; make rooms in it and coat it with pitch inside and out. This is how you are to build it: The ark is to be 450 feet long, 75 feet wide and 45 feet high. Make a roof for it and finish the ark to within 18 inches of the top. Put a door in the side of the ark and make lower, middle and upper decks'" (Genesis 6:13–16). Noah was further instructed to take into the ark two of every kind of living creatures, male and female along with his wife and family, and chapter 6 ends with the words: "Noah did everything just as God commanded him".

There are certain things we can learn from the faith of Noah. There is a sense in which the faith of every individual has to be exceptional and suited to his own individual circumstances. Others may have faced a similar situation to our own, and exercised a faith in God that has seen them through. But no situation is exactly the same and just as Noah's faith was unique to his particular situation so our faith has to be uniquely our own, especially in the matter of our salvation. Then again Noah's faith was exceptional because he took God seriously and did not question His Word. When God told him to build his enormous craft he didn't treat it as a fantasy but worked on it for the next 120 years during which time he preached to the people about the coming cataclysm in the Flood. Peter tells us that Noah was "a preacher of righteousness" (2 Peter 2:5). Unlike Noah the rest of mankind did not take God's warning seriously, as our Lord makes clear. "For in the days before the flood, people were eating and drinking, marrying and giving in marriage, up to the day Noah entered the ark; and they knew nothing about what would happen until the flood came and took them all away" (Matthew 24:38–39). People were so absorbed with their materialism and pleasures that they were heedless of the things of the soul. And once again in our own day godlessness in society and absorption with its own comforts and pleasures foreshadows yet another cataclysmic judgement with the coming of Christ and the winding up of history. That surely is the significance of our Lord's further words: "As it was in the days of Noah, so it will be at the coming of the Son of Man" (Matthew 24:37). Do we take God seriously? Hebrews tells us: "By faith

Noah, when warned about things not yet seen, in holy fear built an ark to save his family" (Hebrews 11:7). He took God seriously because he feared God. Indeed he kept working on his ark year after year, in spite of the mocking and jeers he must have endured, because he feared God more than he feared men.

The flood

Between the end of chapter 6 and the opening of chapter 7, more than a hundred years have passed during which time Noah continued working faithfully in building the ark until its completion. Then God spoke to him again. "The Lord then said to Noah, 'Go into the ark, you and your whole family, because I have found you righteous in this generation. Take with you seven of every kind of clean animal, a male and its mate and two of every kind of unclean animal, a male and its mate, and also seven of every kind of bird, male and female, to keep their various kinds alive throughout the earth. Seven days from now I will send rain on the earth for forty days and forty nights, and I will wipe from the face of the earth every living creature I have made.' And Noah did all that the Lord commanded him" (Genesis 7:1–5).

It lies outside the scope and purpose of a devotional commentary like this to even attempt to deal with the many technical questions raised by geology and other sciences relating to the story of the Flood. These include issues such as the dimensions, capacity and stability of the Ark; the source of the rainfall which lasted forty days and forty nights; the extent and depth of the Flood; the meaning of the phrase "Springs of the great deep" (Genesis 7:11); the chronology of the Flood and a number of others. Those wishing to pursue these issues could do no better than to consult the authoritative work "The Genesis Flood and its Scientific Complications" by John C Whitcomb and Henry M Morris (Presbyterian and Reformed Publishing Co 1978).

But if we take the Genesis account of the Flood at its face value then it becomes absolutely clear, from certain statements that are made, that its extent was world-wide and not merely local, as liberal commentators maintain. For instance, the animals taken into the Ark were divided into ceremonially clean and unclean. "Take with you seven of every kind of clean animal, a male and its mate, and two of every kind of unclean animal, a male and its mate" (Genesis 7:2). Some of the clean animals would have been for domestic use and sacrificial purposes; but another stated purpose was, "to keep their various kinds alive throughout the earth". Clearly, this purpose was entirely meaningless if the extent of the Flood was merely local and not universal. Furthermore, we are told that "The waters rose and increased greatly on the earth, and the ark floated on the surface of the water. They rose greatly on the earth, and all the high mountains under the entire heavens were covered. The waters rose and covered the mountains to a depth of more than twenty feet" (Genesis 7:18–20). That has to be accepted as a definite assertion of the universality of the Flood.

God our refuge

The purpose of the Flood was to bring God's judgement upon the depravity and wickedness of mankind. The purpose of the Ark, on the other hand, was to save Noah and his family from the effects of that judgement. "A preacher of righteousness" (2 Peter 2:5) Noah brought a message or warning of judgement upon the corruption of his day. But it was also a message of salvation, since every blow in building the Ark was like a compelling voice urging people to escape the coming wrath. This is vividly illustrated in the expression, "Then the Lord shut him in" (Genesis 7:16). Here was God Himself closing and sealing the door into the Ark thus providing a safe refuge for Noah from the destructive waters.

The force of this illustration was not lost on the apostle Peter who uses it as a picture of our salvation through the waters of baptism. "… God waited patiently in the days of Noah while the ark was being built. In it only a few people, eight in all, were saved through water, and this water symbolises baptism that now saves you also. … It saves you by the resurrection of Jesus Christ, who has gone into heaven and is at God's right hand – with angels, authorities and powers in submission to him" (1 Peter 3:20–22). As the Ark provided by God was the only means of refuge and deliverance from the judgement of the Flood, so Christ is our only hope of refuge and deliverance from God's judgement upon man's sin.

The faithfulness of God

READ GENESIS CHAPTERS 8 TO 11

The closing words of Chapter 7 read: "The waters flooded the earth for a hundred and fifty days". That is a long time to be enclosed within the confined space of the ark surrounded by animals of every description and having to cope with all the problems that must have entailed. I can't help wondering if Noah felt depressed in his spirit at times as he looked out at the grey curtain of rain day after day for the first forty days, and even when the rain stopped there was still the drabness of the surrounding water for a further hundred and ten days. I wonder if he asked himself occasionally: Has God forgotten me?

God remembered

That would have been a natural enough reaction and is something we ourselves may have experienced from time to time, especially when the flood of grief and sickness of bitter disappointment has swept over us and we have found ourselves drifting in a drab and lonely world with none of the certainties we once put our confidence in. Have we then asked ourselves: Has God forgotten me? What a relief therefore to find chapter 8 opening with the words: "But God **remembered** Noah and all the wild animals and the livestock that were with him in the ark, and he sent a wind over the earth and the waters receded. Now the springs of the deep and the floodgates of the heavens had been closed, and the rain had stopped falling from the sky. The water receded steadily from the earth. At the end of the hundred and fifty days the water had gone down, and on the seventeenth day of the seventh month the ark came to rest on the mountains of Ararat. The waters continued to recede until the tenth month, and on the first day of the tenth month the tops of the mountains became visible" (Genesis 8:1–5).

So God had not forgotten after all! But then He never does forget those who belong to Him. It only seems like it at the time. Noah's long and lonely voyage did not end on a note of hopelessness, for a day came when the flood began to abate, the Ark rested on the peak of Ararat and the tops of the mountains became visible. God remained faithful to his servant. We need to take that lesson to heart, for sometimes that is the only thing we have left to go on – the sheer faithfulness and integrity of God. We may forget Him, indeed we often do, but He always remembers us. Paul puts it so clearly: "... if we are faithless, he will remain faithful, for he cannot disown himself" (2 Timothy 2:13). Faithfulness is a part of the very nature of God. Noah must have held on to that during the long grey days and the dark nights: Joseph clung to it in the loneliness of his unjust imprisonment; Jonah believed it in the dark recesses of the great fish. And we must believe it however bleak and discouraging the circumstances. Friends may fail and let us down, our little world may crumble around us, but God remains faithful, unchangeable, everlasting, and He will not forget us.

"Great is Thy faithfulness, O God my father,
There is no shadow of turning with Thee;
Thou changest not, Thy compassions they fail not;
As Thou hast been Thou forever will be."

The importance of little things

The waiting period was still not over for Noah and his family. Although the Ark was now firmly grounded on Mount Ararat many more days had to pass before the waters had receded sufficiently for them to disembark. "After forty days Noah opened the window he had made in the ark and sent out a raven, and it kept flying back and forth until the water had dried up from the earth. Then he sent out a dove to see if the water had receded from the surface of the ground. But the dove could find no place to set its feet because there was water over all the surface of the earth; so it returned to Noah in the ark. He reached out his hand and took the dove and brought it back to himself in the ark. He waited seven more days and again sent out the dove from the ark. When the dove returned to him in the evening, there in its beak was a freshly plucked olive leaf! Then Noah knew that the water had receded from the earth. He waited seven more days and sent the dove out again, but this time it did not return to him." (Genesis 8:6–12). We must not overlook the symbolic significance of the olive leaf.

The time of waiting is always difficult – waiting for news of a loved one, waiting for the results of an examination, waiting for the answer to our prayers. And sometimes our waiting can end in disappointment. It must have been something like that with Noah when he sent out the raven and it didn't return, and later when he sent out the dove the first and second time and it came back to the Ark because it couldn't land anywhere. If only there was the tiniest sign to lift the spirits and lighten the disappointment and signal that the time of waiting was coming to an end. And then it happened! On the second occasion the dove returned with a freshly plucked olive leaf in its beak. Such a small thing in itself but how important to Noah and his family – "Then Noah knew that the water had receded from the earth" (Genesis 8:11). God was speaking to Noah through that olive leaf, telling him that the time of judgement was over and a new era of peace and hope was about to begin.

The God of the Bible is a God of detail, and therefore things that are small and insignificant in themselves are nevertheless used by Him for the working out of His purposes. When Elijah looked for a sign that his prayer for rain had been answered God sent "A cloud as small as a man's hand rising from the sea" (1 Kings 18:44). A small enough token but it was enough for Elijah to know that the crisis was over. Sometimes God uses the most insignificant things to bring people to faith in Christ. I think of the conversion of Zacchaeus (Luke 19) and the fact that he lacked three or four inches in height played such a crucial part in his meeting with the Lord Jesus. A sudden snow storm prevented Spurgeon as a young lad from getting to his own church in Colchester, so he stepped into a little primitive Methodist chapel and was gloriously saved under the message of an unknown lay-preacher. As a boy of seventeen Hudson Taylor, bored to distraction, one day wandered into the storeroom of his father's shop where there was a small library. He idly picked up a gospel tract from a table, read it, and immediately surrendered his life to Christ. John Bunyan aged nineteen, was saved because he happened to overhear a conversation about the things of Christ by a group of women in a street in Bedford. Years later a tinker, Gypsy Smith the evangelist, says in his auto-biography that as a young man he stood before the statue of Bunyan in Bedford and longed to be like him. That was the beginning of his own conversion experience. These were all small things that God used.

Today we are living in a time of 'small things' where the Kingdom of God is concerned. We do not see big congregations in our churches, nor are we experiencing any great movement of the Spirit and sometimes believers, especially pastors, can become discouraged as we wait, endlessly it seems, for God to work again. But there are tokens, little signs here and there that God is at work building His church, lives **are** being changed, new fellowships are being pioneered in the country, and young men are still hearing the call of God into the work of ministry and preaching. Moreover, in our own Christian witness we must not think that anything is too small and insignificant for God to use in making the Lord Jesus known to others – a gospel tract put through a door or in a person's hand, a visit to someone in need, an invitation to an acquaintance or neighbour to a gospel service, an ordinary kindness or a simple word of personal testimony about one's love for Christ. All these God can, and does, use for awakening faith in someone's heart.

A new beginning

We can hardly imagine the indescribable scene of desolation that must have greeted Noah and his family when they eventually came out of the ark. The earth which once teemed with people and wildlife and where there was an abundance of trees and vegetation now presented a hostile and inhospitable environment. "Then God said to Noah, 'Come out of the ark, you and your wife and your sons and their wives. Bring out every kind of living creature that is with you – birds, the animals, and all the creatures that move along the ground – so they can multiply on the earth and be fruitful and increase in number upon it'. So Noah came out, together with his sons and his wife and his sons' wives. All the animals and all the creatures that move along the ground, and all the birds – everything that moves on the earth – came out of the ark, one after another" (Genesis 8:15–19). But in spite of the desolation of the earth, the great thing was that the Flood was now over and there was the possibility of a new beginning for the human race by the grace and mercy of God. Noah knew this, since he himself and his family had experienced that mercy and grace in their own salvation from the catastrophe which had overwhelmed the rest of mankind.

Therefore immediately he leaves the ark, Noah's thoughts turn to God. "Then Noah built an altar to the Lord and taking some of all the clean animals and clean birds, he sacrificed burnt offerings on it. The Lord smelled the pleasing aroma and said in his heart 'Never again will I curse the ground because of man, even though every inclination of his heart is evil from childhood. And never again will I destroy all living creatures, as I have done'" (Genesis 8:20–21). Here was Noah, through the act of worship giving praise and thanksgiving to Almighty God for his deliverance and the opportunity of a new beginning for life on the earth.

This scenario of a new beginning is repeated again and again at the spiritual level whenever a person is regenerated through the power of the Holy Spirit. When our Lord said to Nicodemus 'You must be born again' he was in fact talking about the need for a new beginning. Similarly when the Apostle Paul says, 'Therefore, if anyone is in Christ, he is a new creation; the old has gone, the new has come!' (2 Corinthians 5:17), he too is describing an experience which is a new beginning, a new life in the power of God in the Lord Jesus Christ. Regeneration or being born of the spirit is not merely a reformation or improvement of the old sinful nature to make it spiritually acceptable to God. Man is a sinner from birth and is spiritually dead and he cannot perceive or understand the things of God, "they are foolishness to him" (1 Corinthians 2:14). In order to have the capacity to understand the things of God he has to be quickened by the Holy Spirit on the inside, in his heart and conscience, so as to grasp the truth of salvation and begin the new life in Christ.

But there is another dimension to all this. The best of all new beginnings for the believer is yet to be when this life is over, when history comes to its close and this earth passes away. For we shall then begin our new life in our new risen body in our new heavenly home. This will happen when Christ comes again to establish His eternal kingdom. "But the day of the Lord will come like a thief. The heavens will disappear with a roar; the elements will be destroyed by fire, and the earth and everything in it will be laid bare … But in keeping with his promise we are looking forward to a new heaven and a new earth, the home of right-eousness" (2 Peter 3:10–13).

God's promise

As we come to the end of chapter 8 we have a wonderful promise God made to Noah and to succeeding generations. "As long as the earth endures, seed time and harvest, cold and heat, summer and winter, day and night will never cease" (Genesis 8:22). We notice in the first place that it is a conditional promise – "as long as the earth endures". Peter reminds us that our present world will not endure indefinitely any more than the world of Noah's day. "By water also the world of that time was deluged and destroyed. By the same word the present heavens and earth are reserved for fire, being kept for the day of judgement and destruction of ungodly men" (2 Peter 3:6–7). We are meant to enjoy the material things of this life and the harvest of the earth but we must also realise their limitations. The things of this world are passing away and the Word of God urges us to give more time to the cultivation of the things of the Spirit, for these will endure for ever. "Heaven and earth will pass away, but my words will never pass away" (Matthew 24:35).

We notice secondly that it is a promise of the reliability of God. "… seed time and harvest, cold and heat, summer and winter, day and night will never cease". The world God has created has a rhythm in it; it is not chaotic and capricious but orderly and reliable. The constant march of the seasons, the quiet rest of darkness and the coming of the dawn all follow one another without break or intermission. And this element of reliability and dependability in creation is a reflection of God's own nature. In a confused and uncertain day such as ours is, it is good to know that we can rest on the total dependability of God. The Psalmist said: "The Lord is my rock, my fortress and my deliverer; my God is my rock in whom I take refuge" (Psalm 18:2). The Bible assures us that we can rely on God's love – "Never will I leave you; never will I forsake you". (Hebrews 13:5). We can rely upon His promises – "For no matter how many promises God has made, they are 'Yes' in Christ" (2 Corinthians 1:20). We can rely on His eternal purpose – "And he made known to us the mystery of his will according to his good pleasure, which he purposed in Christ, to be put into effect when the times will have reached their fulfilment – to bring all things in heaven and on earth together under one head, even Christ" (Ephesians 1:9–10).

Man's dominion renewed

In the first seven verses of chapter 9, man's dominion over creation is re-established in Noah and his family although carrying with it certain limitations and warnings. "Then God blessed Noah and his sons, saying to them, 'Be fruitful and increase in number and fill the earth. The fear and dread of you will fall upon all the beasts of the earth and all the birds of the air, upon every creature that moves along the ground, and upon all the fish of the sea; they are given into your hands. Everything that lives and moves will be food for you. Just as I gave you the green plants, I now give you everything'" (Genesis 9:1–3). Things however were no longer the same. Sin had now entered into the human situation and the harmony which had previously existed between man and the animal world had now disappeared, since creation itself had fallen. The elements of fear and hostility would now characterise the relationship between man and the animals, and meat would become part of man's food. And there are warnings too. "But you must not eat meat that has its life-blood still in it. And for your life-blood I will surely demand an accounting. I will demand an accounting from every animal" (Genesis 9:4–5).

In this prohibition concerning the 'life-blood' God is teaching the sacredness of life, but at a deeper spiritual level the idea of atonement is also being taught here. In the development of the Old Testament sacrificial system, the meat of the animal was intended for food, but the life-blood through sacrifice on the altar symbolised in a substitutionary manner the guilty life of the sinner. This doctrine of Atonement reaches its true fulfilment in the substitutionary sacrifice of Christ. "But now he (Christ) has appeared once for all at the end of the ages to do away with sin by the sacrifice of himself" (Hebrews 9:26). But the warning about the sacredness of life goes further and involves man himself. "And from each man, too, I will demand an accounting for the life of his fellow man. Whoever sheds the blood of man, by man shall his blood be shed; for in the image of God has God made man. As for you, be fruitful and increase in number; multiply on the earth and increase upon it" (Genesis 9:5–7). Here we have the beginning of human government and the exercise of judicial authority for future generations. God is not giving man the right to engage in vengeance killing but is establishing in human society the authority for judicial execution, or capital punishment, for murder. Because this was a divine command and not simply part of the Mosaic law it still stands under the Gospel dispensation, as is clear from Romans 13:1–7 where Paul talks about the believer's attitude towards the governing authorities. "Do you want to be free from fear of the one in authority? Then do what is right and he will commend you. For he is God's servant to do you good. But if you do wrong, be afraid, for he does not **bear the sword** for nothing" (Romans 13:3–4).

God's covenant

"Then God said to Noah and to his sons with him: 'I now establish my covenant with you and with your descendants after you and with every living creature that was with you … every living creature on earth. I establish my covenant with you: Never again will all life be cut off by the waters of a flood; never again will there be a flood to destroy the earth" (Genesis 9:8–11). The threefold features of this covenant were: that it was Unconditional; God did not ask for any pledge of obedience; it was Eternal as seen in such phrases as 'your descendants after you' and 'never again'; and it was Universal, all mankind was included in it as well as the animal world. The assurance contained in the promise that man would never again be destroyed by a flood must have brought great comfort to Noah and his family having themselves come through such a traumatic experience.

But God went further and gave Noah a sign, something he could actually see and which would be a reminder of His gracious promise. "And God said, 'This is the sign of the covenant I am making between me and you and every living creature with you, a covenant for all generations to come: I have set my rainbow in the clouds, and it will be the sign of the covenant between me and the earth'" (Genesis 9:12–13). It is difficult to know if this was the first appearance of the rainbow or whether it had existed previously and God now gave it a new spiritual significance. Such signs, illustrative of some great spiritual truth, are found elsewhere in the Bible. The Passover Lamb was the sign of deliverance from Egypt: Circumcision was the sign of God's covenant with Israel; Baptism is the sign of dying and rising with Christ and the Bread and Wine of the Lord's Supper the sign of His body and blood. The rainbow was a particularly fitting sign of God's saving grace, and it appears again with the same meaning in Revelation 4:3 around the throne of God, and in Revelation 10:1 around the head of Christ.

Noah's shame

The closing verses of chapter 9 do not make the happiest reading: "Noah, a man of the soil, proceeded to plant a vineyard. When he drank some of its wine he became drunk and lay uncovered inside his tent. Ham, the father of Canaan, saw his father's nakedness and told his two brothers outside. But Shem and Japheth took a garment and laid it across their shoulders; then they walked in backward and covered their father's nakedness. Their faces were turned the other way so that they would not see their father's nakedness" (Genesis 9:20–23). One would much rather that this account of Noah's fall and shame had not been recorded since it casts a cloud over his otherwise godly life. But the Bible is an honest book and reveals even the saints of God in all their weaknesses as well as their strengths, so that we may learn the lessons God would teach us. "For everything that was written in the past was written to teach us, so that through endurance and the encouragement of the Scriptures we might have hope" (Romans 15:4).

It is a sad contradiction that the first mention of drunkenness in the Bible should be associated with one of its greatest saints. For whatever views one may hold on the question of alcohol there is no doubt that the Bible strongly condemns drunkenness as a sin. "Woe to those who rise early in the morning to run after their drinks, who stay up late at night till they are inflamed with wine" (Isaiah 5:11). In Romans 13 Paul includes drunkenness in his list of the most shameful of evils: "Let us behave decently, as in the day time, not in orgies and drunkenness, not in sexual immorality and debauchery, not in dissension and jealousy" (Romans 13:13). It was this verse God used to convict Augustine of his debauched life and to bring about his conversion which he tells us about in his 'Confessions'. Under the influence of drink a person can lose all their inhibitions and engage in forms of behaviour they would be thoroughly ashamed of in a sober condition. It seems that is what happened with Noah. For whatever reason, he threw off his clothes and lay down on his bed in a drunken stupor. He was without excuse. He fell, and fell badly.

That was the condition in which Ham found him, and according to some commentators engaged in some kind of homosexual act. But the passage doesn't say that. It simply says: "Ham, the father of Canaan, saw his father's nakedness and told his two brothers outside". The implication is that Ham's sin was the lewd pleasure he experienced in seeing his godly father in such a shameful condition and his eagerness to tell his brothers about it. He gloated over his father's predicament and derived some kind of malicious satisfaction from it. There is surely something to be learned from all this. In the first place it is a warning to us against taking any kind of perverse pleasure in another Christian's fall from a state of grace, even when it is the result of their own wilfulness or stupidity. It is so easy to be self-righteous in such a situation and to feel the same thing could never happen to us. Couldn't it? The scriptures tell us: "So, if you think you are standing firm, be careful that you don't fall!" (1 Corinthians 10:12). This is not to condone or overlook wilful sin in a fellow believer, it simply means we should feel sorrow for the harm done to the reputation of the gospel rather than delight in the other's downfall. And that is where the response of Shem and Japheth was so different from that of their brother Ham. They "took a garment and laid it across their shoulder, then they walked in backward, and covered their father's nakedness". That was much more in keeping with the spirit of the New Testament: "Brothers, if someone is caught in a sin, you who are spiritual should restore him gently. But watch yourself, or you also may be tempted" (Galatians 6:1).

A curse and blessing on the nations

When Noah awoke from his drunken stupor he was led, in spite of his own shameful downfall to make the most remarkable prophetic statement. "When Noah awoke from his wine and found out what his youngest son had done to him, he said, 'Cursed be Canaan! The lowest of slaves will he be to his brothers'. He also said, 'Blessed be the Lord, the God of Shem. May Canaan be the slave of Shem. May God extend the territory of Japheth; may Japheth live in the tents of Shem, and may Canaan be his slave'. After the flood Noah lived 350 years. Altogether, Noah lived 950 years, and then he died" (Genesis 9:24–29). In this prophecy Noah is foretelling the destinies of the descendants of his three sons, and it should be studied in connection with the genealogies of Shem, Ham and Japheth given in chapter 10. Noah's prophecy concerning Ham has been interpreted by some as a justification for the subjugation of the black peoples in particular and by others as a more general confirmation of their own special brand of racial superiority. This is definitely wrong, and does violence to the Word of God. Nevertheless, both the prophecy and the 'Table of Nations' in chapter 10 contain a great deal of important detail concerning the ethnological and geographical aspects of the different nations and peoples of the world, which call for the kind of close study that lies outside the scope of this commentary. Our main concern is with the spiritual character of Genesis as it portrays men and women in relation to God, and that leads us straight into chapter 11 and the scattering of the nations over the face of the earth.

The Tower of Babel

What we have in chapter 11 is a more detailed account of the events that actually took place in chapter 10 when the earth was divided during the time of Peleg. "Two sons were born to Eber: One was named Peleg, because in his time the earth was divided;" (Genesis 10:25). This division of mankind into national groupings seems to have been God's original intention (Acts 17:26) but men resisted it. "Now the whole world had one language and a common speech. As men moved eastward, they found a plain in Shinar and settled there. They said to each other, 'Come let's make bricks and bake them thoroughly'. They used brick instead of stone, and tar instead of mortar. Then they said, 'Come let us build ourselves a city, with a tower that reaches to the heavens, so that we may make a name for ourselves and not be scattered over the face of the whole earth'" (Genesis 11:1–4).

Who, or what, lay behind this attempt to build "a tower that reaches to the heavens, so that we may make a name for ourselves" – and what does it signify? Chiefly it represents the rebelliousness of the sinful human heart in its desire to dethrone God and deify man. The moving force was Nimrod, mentioned in chapter 10 and coming from the line of Ham. "Cush was the father of Nimrod, who grew to be a mighty warrior on the earth. He was a mighty hunter before the Lord; that is why it is said, 'Like Nimrod, a mighty hunter before the Lord'. The first centres of his kingdom were Babylon,

Erech, Akkad and Calneh, in Shinar" (Genesis 10:8–10). He was a man of great ability and military prowess determined to establish his own form of centralised government at Babel, later to be called Babylon, and all in direct opposition to God's purpose that man should "be fruitful and increase in number and fill the earth".

But Nimrod and the forces of rebellion failed, for man cannot oppose God and hope to win. "But the Lord came down to see the city and the tower that the men were building. The Lord said, 'If as one people speaking the same language they have begun to do this, then nothing they plan to do will be impossible for them. Come, let us go down and confuse their language so they will not understand each other.' So the Lord scattered them from there over all the earth, and they stopped building the city. That is why it was called Babel – because there the Lord confused the language of the whole world. From there the Lord scattered them over the face of the whole earth" (Genesis 11:5–9).

From this point onwards in the Bible, Babylon represents the anti-God world system which in its pride and arrogance leads man to think that he can dethrone God and has no need of His laws and commandments. It occurs in Daniel where the statue in Nebuchadnezzar's dream, symbolising the kingdoms of Babylon, Persia, Greece and Rome, is brought crashing down by the rock "not cut by human hands" symbolising the kingdom of God (Daniel 2:34 fol.). Likewise, in Revelation we have a picture of the irrevocable finality of God's judgement upon Babylon and the anti-God culture and philosophy she represents: "Woe! Woe, O great city, O Babylon, city of power! In one hour your doom has come!" (Revelation 18:10). So what is all this saying? It is telling us that nothing man builds in his own strength, and in defiance to God's sovereignty, including the political systems of our own day, can last forever. Hitler's Third Reich which he claimed would last a thousand years, Lenin's Soviet system which lasted a mere seventy years, and our own mighty British Empire have all come and gone. … So it will be with all human systems until the day comes when "The kingdom of the world has become the kingdom of our Lord and of his Christ, and he will reign for ever and ever" (Revelation 11:15).

In the remaining verses of Genesis chapter 11 attention is concentrated on tracing the line of Shem down to Terah the father of Abram. From this point we are no longer concerned with the human race so much as with a single individual through whom God will accomplish His saving purpose for mankind. For the next fourteen chapters Abram will remain centre stage.

God's call to Abram

With God's call to Abram we come to a turning point in the history of mankind, for he was to be the cornerstone of the new spiritual humanity God was going to bring into being, beginning with the formation of the nation Israel. Here was a man who was right at the centre of God's choice. Why God should have chosen Abram we cannot say, for he came from a pagan background in the Ur of the Chaldeans (Genesis 11:31) and his father Terah was an idolater. "Long ago your forefathers, including Terah the father of Abram and Nahor, lived beyond the River and worshipped other gods" (Joshua 24:2). But we have to accept that God is sovereign in His choices, whether in the area of service or in the greater matter of our salvation. Paul says: "For he chose us in him before the creation of the world to be holy and blameless in his sight" (Ephesians 1:4). Why God should have chosen any of us for salvation will always remain a mystery, but when in our own heart we experience that salvation through Christ we are glad that He did so and we are humbled by it. When God's choice fell on Abram therefore to play such a vital role in the outworking of His great purposes for mankind, He knew that he was the right man for the task. Speaking of Abram and God's choice Nehemiah says: "You found his heart faithful to you" (Nehemiah 9:8).

The call

"The Lord had said to Abram, 'Leave your country, your people and your father's household and go to the land I will show you'" (Genesis 12:1). According to Stephen in Acts 7:2, God's revelation to Abram and the call which followed took place when he was still in Mesopotamia and it involved a threefold directive. First, he had to leave his country. It is quite wrong, I believe, to say with one writer that Abram was "a rough simple, venerable Bedouin-like sheep master" (Lockyer, All the men of the Bible). That gives a totally false impression of his background, for we know from archaeological discoveries that Ur of the Chaldeans had attained a very high degree of civilisation with many fine buildings and a vigorous commercial life. It was this progressive culture that Abram was called to leave in the service of God, and that was no small undertaking. Would we be willing so easily to give up our comfortable sophisticated life-style for service among some primitive people if God were to make a similar demand upon us? Second, he had to leave his own people, and that meant turning his back on the cultural and social patterns of which he was so much a part. They were his 'kind' of people, speaking his language, following the same customs and traditions, and with whom he had relationships that were instinctively dear to him. Third, he had to leave his "father's household". This must have meant his immediate family and close relations; those whom he loved and who represented all that was familiar and most precious to him. In all this we learn that the call into God's service can be a costly business, which was the very thing our Lord was anxious to impress upon those who would be His disciples (Luke 14:28 fol).

The promise

But the cost involved in the call was nowhere as great as the promise that accompanied it. "I will make you into a great nation and I will bless those who bless you; ... and whoever curses you I will curse; and all people on earth will be blessed through you" (Genesis 12:2–3). We can never lose out by responding in faith to God's call however great the cost or sacrifice involved; if only because the greatest of all blessings is to be in line with God's will for us. But Abram was blessed in an especially profound manner. He did indeed become a great nation through the formation of Israel and its subsequent history as the chosen people of God. And all people on earth have indeed been blessed through Abram, since from Israel came the Messiah, the Lord Jesus Christ and His Gospel of salvation which is preached to all nations. Paul sums up the blessing and privileges belonging to Israel in this way: "Theirs is the adoption as sons; theirs the divine glory, the covenants, the receiving of the law, the temple worship and the promises. Theirs are the patriarchs, and from them is traced the human ancestry of Christ, who is God over all, for ever praised! Amen" (Romans 9:4–5).

And when we study the history of God's ancient people up to the present day, who can doubt that they hold a unique place among the nations of the world. For in spite of their violent past, their persecution and their dispersion over the earth for almost two thousand years, they have not only retained their identity, but in our own time have established themselves as a national political unit back in their ancient homeland.

Abram's obedience

"So Abram left as the Lord had told him; and Lot went with him. Abram was seventy-five years old when he set out from Haran. He took his wife Sarai, his nephew Lot, all the possessions they had accumulated and the people they had acquired in Haran, and they set out for the land of Canaan, and they arrived there" (Genesis 12:4–5). Abram might have put up all kinds of solid arguments and convincing reasons why it was totally impractical to expect him to leave all the certainties of his present position for the uncertainties to which God was calling him. For at this point he didn't even know where he was going. Hebrews says: "By faith Abraham … obeyed and went even though he did not know where he was going" (Hebrews 11:8). He was setting out on a great pilgrimage of faith and the only certainty he had was the knowledge that God was with him and He knew the way.

And a large part of our Christian pilgrimage is like that. "We live by faith, not by sight" (2 Corinthians 5:7). God asks us to trust and obey even when we do not understand the way He is taking us. Trust is a fundamental principle, not only in religion, but in life as a whole and without it some of the loveliest things in life would be lost. What kind of a marriage relationship is it without trust? What a nerve-racking flight it would be if you couldn't trust the pilot of the aircraft! Without trust in one another progress through life would become impossible. To a much greater degree this is certainly true of our spiritual life; without obedience based on trust in God there can be no going forward. But if trust is all we have, then like Abram we have all we need.

The journey from Haran to Canaan would have been long and arduous, more than four hundred miles, but Abram arrived safely with his family and possessions. "Abram travelled through the land as far as the site of the great tree of Moreh at Shechem. The Canaanites were then in the land, but the Lord appeared to Abram and said, 'To your offspring I will give this land'. So he built an altar there to the Lord, who had appeared to him" (Genesis 12:6–7). This was one of several divine appearances or theophanies given to Abram and other people in the Bible, and usually it was at some critical juncture in their lives. Where Abram was concerned it certainly came at the right time, for it confirmed that this was in fact the land to which God had said He would lead him and which He would give to his descendants. However, it would be 430 years before that promise would be fulfilled in Moses and the Exodus, and in the meantime Abram had to carry on believing that God would be true to His word.

Apart from the altar which he had built at Shechem, Abram built another altar at Bethel. "From there he went on towards the hills east of Bethel and pitched his tent, with Bethel on the west and Ai on the east. There he built an altar to the Lord and called on the name of the Lord. Then Abram set out and continued towards the Negev" (Genesis 12:8–9). These altars would have had a deep spiritual significance. First, as centres of worship they represented his profound thankfulness to God for continued guidance and help. Second, they represented to all and sundry Abram's 'claiming' Canaan as God's land in the way the early explorers would plant the flag of the mother nation on some newly discovered territory. Third, it was a clear witness to the pagan Canaanites that Abram worshipped the true and the living God.

Down to Egypt

In living the Christian life we may be certain of one thing – Satan will not be idle in manipulating the different situations of life to undermine our faith. Abram was not long in Canaan before he was faced with a particularly difficult challenge. "Now there was a famine in the land, and Abram went down to Egypt to live there for a while because the famine was severe" (Genesis 12:10). Some commentators maintain that this decision in itself was sinful since God had promised to bless Abram and therefore, he was wrong to take matters into his own hands by going down to Egypt. I do not accept that myself since there is no indication whatever that God was displeased with him. Furthermore it was an eminently sensible thing to do since the famine was 'severe' and with a family to support, Egypt's food supply held out a welcome prospect. It was not the situation, nor the decision Abram made in the light of that circumstance, that was wrong, but the manner in which he allowed Satan to manipulate the situation that caused him to sin.

"As he was about to enter Egypt, he said to his wife Sarai, 'I know what a beautiful woman you are. When the Egyptians see you, they will say, 'this is his wife'. Then they will kill me but will let you live. Say you are my sister, so that I will be treated well for your sake, and my life will be spared because of you'" (Genesis 12:11–13). Here was the unacceptable face of Abram's faith and in no way can we defend it. Not only was he guilty of lying, but he was thoroughly selfish in thinking only of his own safety, and he was perfectly prepared to put Sarai in danger of being sexually abused. Pharaoh had every intention of taking her into his harem and he paid Abram a good price in return. "And when Pharaoh's officials saw her, they praised her to Pharaoh, and she was taken into his palace. He treated Abram well for her sake, and Abram acquired sheep and cattle, male and female donkeys, menservants and maidservants and camels" (Genesis 12:15–16).

The whole episode leaves us with a sickening sense of disappointment that such a great man should have fallen so badly. But that is the reality of sinful human nature. We cannot condone Abram's action or seek to excuse it, and we have to accept the possibility that we can be guilty of the same. We all have our own shabby little schemes for furthering our own interests, and all too often we are prepared to sacrifice the noblest values of faith, truth and integrity on the altar of expediency. But the experience of Abram also serves to emphasise in a graphic way our great need of God's power and grace to save us from ourselves. For the whole miserable episode would have ended in complete disaster had not God in His mercy, and in the fulfilment of His own sovereign purpose, intervened to deliver Abram from the mess he had got himself into. "But the Lord inflicted serious diseases on Pharaoh and his household because of Abram's wife Sarai. So Pharaoh summoned Abram. 'What have you done to me?' he said. Why didn't you tell me she was your wife? Why did you say, 'She is my sister,' so that I took her to be my wife? Now then, here is your wife. Take her and go!' Then Pharaoh gave orders about Abram to his men, and they sent him on his way, with his wife and everything he had" (Genesis 12:17–20).

There are two significant points here. First, what are we to make of the fact that Abram profited materially from his miserable behaviour? Shouldn't he have been punished? Well, we shall see later that there was a price to pay and that his ill-gotten gains brought only trouble and dissension to his family life. More important is the lesson that behind Abram's failure and the events in Egypt God was in control. God had a purpose to fulfil in Abram and nothing would be allowed to frustrate that purpose. "... behind the dim unknown, standeth God within the shadows keeping watch above His own" (James Russell Lowell "The present crisis"). Second, we are reminded how easily the believer can lose his testimony in the eyes of the world. For that is what happened to Abram. He must have felt particularly ashamed and humiliated to be rebuked by the pagan Pharaoh for his behaviour. This is a picture of the world rebuking the Church of God, and it is something that happens all too often. Today – especially in the life of our own nation – the Church, in the eyes of so many ordinary men and women, has lost its spiritual credibility and authority and its message falls on deaf ears.

Abram and Lot

READ GENESIS CHAPTERS 13 AND 14

As we move into chapter 13 we get the feeling that Abram had been severely shaken by his experience in Egypt and that he knew he had to put matters right with God. For on arriving back in Canaan he made straight for Bethel, which to him was a sacred spot. "So Abram went up from Egypt to the Negev, with his wife and everything he had, and Lot went with him. Abram had become very wealthy in livestock and in silver and gold. From the Negev he went from place to place until he came to Bethel, to the place between Bethel and Ai where his tent had been earlier and where he had first built an altar. There Abram called on the name of the Lord" (Genesis 13:1–4).

When we fall out of fellowship with God because of our own stupidity and sinfulness we do not have to remain there. There is always a way back from Egypt to Bethel, from the place of shame and failure to the sacred spot of restoration and forgiveness. The important thing is not to delay putting matters right with God, for the longer we leave it the deeper becomes our sense of self-condemnation and failure or, on the other hand, we become hardened in our rebellion and backsliding. God desires only to restore and forgive, but we must take the initiative in seeking that. "If we confess our sins, he is faithful and just and will forgive us our sins and purify us from all unrighteousness" (1 John 1:9).

When believers fall out

Although Abram had made his peace with God, the experience in Egypt nevertheless left its mark, as sin always does. To begin with it seems to have had a disillusioning effect upon the younger man Lot, for he no longer had the same respect for the godly character of Abram he had had previously, and tension developed between them. "Now Lot, who was moving around with Abram, also had flocks and herds and tents. But the land could not support them while they stayed together, for their possessions were so great that they were not able to stay together. And quarrelling arose between Abram's herdsmen and the herdsmen of Lot. The Canaanites and Perizzites were also living in the land at that time" (Genesis 13:5–7). As we trace the history of Lot through the next few chapters we find him to be a sad and pitiable character. He began well enough when he set out on the pilgrimage of faith in the company of his godly Uncle Abram. Indeed Peter describes him as a righteous man. Speaking of the judgement on Sodom he says: "… (God) rescued Lot, a righteous man who was distressed by the filthy lives of lawless men – (for that righteous man, … living among them day after day, was tormented in his righteous soul by the lawless deeds he saw and heard)" (2 Peter 2:7–8). But the pull and attraction of the old life, which epitomised Sodom, was too much for Lot and he was gradually drawn into its orbit with fatal consequences for his spiritual life. He ended his life in a mountain cave outside the city, isolated and lonely and in a drunken stupor (Genesis 19:30 fol).

But we cannot ignore the strong possibility that Abram's moral lapse in Egypt was the beginning of Lot's backsliding and is a reminder to older Christians of the influence they can exert, for good or ill, upon younger believers. Neither Lot, nor those like him, can be excused for allowing themselves to be seduced by the glamour of the world's life-style, for each is responsible for his or her soul. But it helps young Christians to remain firm in their faith, when they can look to mature believers in the local church as role models to be followed.

When mammon comes in

The prime factor in the deteriorating relations between Abram and Lot was their material prosperity. "… their possessions were so great that they were not able to stay together. The quarrelling arose between Abram's herdsmen and the herdsmen of Lot". The land was not big enough for both of them, and yet this was the very land God Himself had brought them to, so that His people in the future might live there in peace and unity. What a miserable business it is when believers fall out over the love of money and possessions. Not that material things in themselves are bad, but the love of mammon means that God has to compete with all the other things in our lives in order to get His way with us. No wonder our Lord gave such grave warnings about the dangers of riches; "For where your treasure is there your heart will be also" (Matthew 6:21). We may at the outset be in control of our possessions, but if we are not careful little by little they can get a grip on us, they entice our heart away from the things of God so that something vital drops out of our spiritual experience and worldliness sets in.

Moreover the behaviour of Abram and Lot was worsened by the fact that "The Canaanites and Perizzites were also living in the land at that time" (Genesis 13:7). There the writer is telling us that they were dishonouring the Name of God by their quarrelling, and is a reminder to us that a pagan world is watching and observing our behaviour and rightly expects us, as believers, to be different from the general run of things.

Lot's choice

It seems on the face of it that Lot was chiefly to blame since it was Abram who took the first step to resolve the situation, and it is evident from what follows that Lot was already in the grip of a covetous and greedy spirit. "So Abram said to Lot, 'Let's not have any quarrelling between you and me, or between your herdsmen and mine, for we are brothers. Is not the whole land before you? Let's part company. If you go to the left, I'll go to the right; if you go to the right, I'll go to the left'" (Genesis 13:8–9). That was a very generous proposition and shows what a big-hearted man Abram really was at bottom. Lot, on the other hand, needed no urging to take up the offer since he had an eye on the main chance, and in his scheming greedy imagination he could see how the fertile pastures of the Jordan plain would fatten his flocks and herds, and make him richer than he already was. "Lot looked up and saw that the whole plain of the Jordan was well watered like the garden of the Lord. ... So Lot chose for himself the whole plain of the Jordan and set out towards the east. The two men parted company: Abram lived in the land of Canaan, while Lot lived among the cities of the plain and pitched his tents near Sodom. Now the men of Sodom were wicked and were sinning greatly against the Lord" (Genesis 13:10–13).

Some of the choices we make in this life are crucial for the direction our lives will take in the future; in relation to God and our service for Him. This was certainly true of Lot's choice. His eye was not on God but on his future prosperity, and his decision to live near Sodom was to prove disastrous for himself and his family. As believers, when we make our plans and choices about our work, moving home, choosing schools for our children and all the other things that affect the future of ourselves and family, we ought to have an eye on God and not only on the material considerations involved. Let us take God into our plans and decision-making and ask him to give us grace and wisdom to do whatever is pleasing to Him and for the benefit of our spiritual lives.

But in spite of Lot's greed and lack of consideration for the feelings of his uncle, Abram did not lose out. God spoke very graciously to him and reaffirmed the promise of future greatness and blessing. "The Lord said to Abram after Lot had parted from him, 'Lift up your eyes from where you are and look north and south, east and west. All the land that you see I will give to you and your offspring for ever. I will make your offspring like the dust of the earth, so that if anyone could count the dust, then your offspring could be counted. Go, walk through the length and breadth of the land, for I am giving it to you.' So Abram moved his tents and went to live near the great trees of Mamre at Hebron, where he built an altar to the Lord" (Genesis 13:14–18). What was Lot's fertile plain and fat sheep compared with a promise like that! God is no man's debtor. If we honour Him, He will honour us. The difference between the two men is evident. Lot lacked holiness and represents the worldly Christian. God had a place in his life but was not at the centre. Abram on the other hand, with all his weaknesses, represents the consecrated life – the believer who wants to put God first.

The first war

As we move into chapter 14 we have the first recorded war in the Bible. It involved a powerful confederacy of four kings from the north-eastern part of Canaan against five lesser kings of the plain of Jordan on whom they had imposed tribute for twelve years but who ultimately rebelled. "At this time Amraphel king of Shinar, Arioch king of Ellasar, Kedorlaomer king of Elam and Tidal king of Goiim went to war against Bera king of Sodom, Birsha king of Gomorrah, Shinab king of Admah, Shemeber king of Zeboiim and the king of Bela (that is, Zoar)" (Genesis 14:1–2). War is an unmitigated evil that has plagued mankind all through history. The reason for that is simple; war is a consequence of man's sin and rebellion towards God and as long as we live in this sinful world it will continue to set man against man, nation against nation and ideology against ideology. Our Lord confirms that fact. "When you hear of wars and rumours of wars, do not be alarmed. Such things must happen, but the end is still to come" (Mark 13:7). James says the same thing: "What causes fights and quarrels among you? Don't they come from your desires that battle within you?" (James 4:1). Whether we are talking of individuals or nations, conflict and war arises out of our evil desires. The essential difference between national conflicts or wars and the personal conflicts between men is only a matter of degree, the root cause in both instances is the same. If we choose to satisfy our own desires rather than pursue God's will then the inevitable consequence is violence and destruction. Therefore whilst war, because of a sinful world, may at times be necessary and unavoidable we must never as believers seek to justify it, or defend it, or glorify it in any way. It is to be deplored.

Among the spoils carried off by the northern confederacy were Lot and his family. "They also carried off Abram's nephew Lot and his possessions, since he was living in Sodom" (Genesis 14:12). Notice the continual spiritual decline of Lot for he was now actually living in Sodom and was part of its life and activity instead of simply living near the city as we are told earlier (Genesis 13:12). One of the most dreadful aspects of war is its effect upon the innocent, in this case Abram, for at this time he was living quietly in Hebron on good relations with the local chieftains Mamre, Eshcol and Aner (Genesis 14:13). But he now finds himself being dragged into this war because of his concern for Lot. "When Abram heard that his relative had been taken captive, he called out the 318 trained men born in his household and went in pursuit as far as Dan. During the night Abram divided his men to attack them and he routed them. ... He recovered all the goods and brought back his relative Lot and his possessions, together with the women and the other people" (Genesis 14:14–16).

We may wonder how Abram managed to beat a powerful confederacy of four kings with only 318 men? Perhaps the answer is that God was with him in a special way as He was with Gideon and his army of 300 (Judges 7). On the other hand we are told that the local chieftains mentioned in verse 13 were "allied with Abram" so that his fighting force would have been considerably more than the men of his own household. But more important was Abram's greatness of heart in going to the rescue of Lot in spite of the shabby treatment he had received from him earlier. There was a complete absence of resentment on Abram's part and we can only put it down to his strong and godly character. It reminds us of Paul's words; "We who are strong ought to bear with the failings of the weak …" (Romans 15:1). Remember Peter tells us that Lot was a righteous man. That is, he was a believer, but a weak and worldly believer, like those Christians we all know who only seem to make progress in their spiritual life when they have someone stronger than themselves to lean on. They need a spiritual crutch, a prop to keep them from collapsing. Every local church is a mixed bag of weak and strong Christians. It is sad, but that is the reality of the situation; and if we are among the strong then it is not enough simply to tolerate the weak but, as Paul says, to "bear with their failings" and to seek to strengthen them where we can.

Mysterious Melchizedek

On his return from the battle Abram was met by two kings: "After Abram returned from defeating Kedorlaomer and the kings allied with him, the king of Sodom came out to meet him in the Valley of Shaveh … Then Melchizedek king of Salem brought out bread and wine. He was priest of God Most High, and he blessed Abram, saying, 'Blessed be Abram by God Most High, Creator of heaven and earth. And blessed be God Most High, who delivered your enemies into your hand'" (Genesis 14:17–20). Here we have one of the most intriguing and fascinating characters in the Bible who is still the subject of much disagreement among evangelical scholars. Who was Melchizedek? He was both a king and a priest, the name means 'king of righteousness' and the title king of Salem means 'king of peace'. The bread and wine he brought to Abram may have been an ordinary meal or it may have had some ritual significance connected with his priesthood. 'Salem' is a shortened form of Jerusalem and raises the question – How did such a godly man come to be king of a pagan Canaanite city? Furthermore; he seems to have had a unique relationship with the true God for he speaks of Him as God Most High, the Creator of heaven and earth.

Then again Abram's attitude towards this mysterious figure is equally fascinating. He receives his blessing, thus recognising Melchizedek's spiritual superiority and actually gave him a tithe (or tenth) of the spoils. What are we to make of all this and what does it have to teach us? This is one of those passages where we need the help of other parts of the scriptures to throw light upon it. In Psalm 110, which is a Messianic Psalm, David speaks prophetically of Christ and says: "The Lord has sworn and will not change his mind: 'You are a priest for ever, in the order of Melchizedek'" (Psalm 110:4). At the very least David is pointing us to a connection between Melchizedek and the Lord Jesus Christ as our King and High Priest. But it is the writer to the Hebrews who develops this theme in his inspired commentary on David's statement. He says of Melchizedek: "Without father or mother, without genealogy, without beginning of days or end of life, like the Son of God he remains a priest for ever" (Hebrews 7:3). He is saying that Melchizedek appeared to Abram as a type or prefiguration of Christ in His eternal existence, without beginning or end, and of his never-ending priesthood. The lessons arising out of the comparison are clear.

(a) As Melchizedek priest of God Most High stood between God and Abram in blessing, so Christ our High Priest stands as intercessor between God and ourselves.

(b) As king of righteousness and king of peace, Melchizedek points to the righteousness and peace that are ours through the atoning high-priestly work of Christ.

(c) As Melchizedek received tithes from Abram, so Christ, as our High Priest and Head of the Church, has a right to the tithes and offerings of His people. If it is objected that tithing is part of the old dispensation whereas we live in the new dispensation of Grace, then it follows we ought to give even more freely in return for the greater blessing of our salvation through Christ. Tithing is not a ceiling, but a foundation for giving. Or, as it has been said: God demands our tithes but deserves our offerings.

A noble refusal

The whole episode ends on a high note where Abram is concerned when the king of Sodom offers him a share in the spoils of battle. "The king of Sodom said to Abram, 'Give me the people and keep the goods for yourself'. But Abram said to the king of Sodom, 'I have raised my hand to the Lord, God Most High, Creator of heaven and earth, and have taken an oath that I will accept nothing belonging to you, not even a thread or the thong of a sandal, so that you will never be able to say, 'I made Abram rich'. I will accept nothing but what my men have eaten and the share that belongs to the men who went with me – to Aner, Eschol and Mamre. Let them have their share'" (Genesis 14:21–24).

Reading that surely make us feel proud of Abram as God's man. Faced with the temptation and opportunity of enriching himself through the offices of a pagan king he firmly rejects it. I wonder if the hard lesson of Egypt, when he accepted riches from the pagan Pharaoh and later paid a heavy price, was still in his mind? In any case he had not engaged in the battle for personal advantage or profit but to help his nephew Lot. Nevertheless the temptation to live one's life on the principle of the 'market-mind', where everything has its price, is a very real one especially in a materialistic age like ours. But more importantly Abram had already taken an oath "to the Lord God most high" that he would not be obligated to the powers of paganism, not even for the thong of a sandal, and he intended keeping to that oath or vow he had made.

Vows and promises can be easily made and just as easily broken, as the increasing divorce rate in the country clearly testifies. But believers too can be very careless when it comes to making vows and promises not realising that the words we speak are a reflection of our hearts. Becoming a member of our local church, being baptised, or having our children dedicated or christened all involve promises of faithfulness and commitment for which God will hold us responsible.

God's covenant with Abram

READ GENESIS CHAPTERS 15 AND 16

After the excitement and elation generated by his victory in battle and his experience with Melchizedek, we find Abram in a much more reflective and pensive mood with the opening of chapter 15. "After this, the word of the Lord came to Abram in a vision: 'Do not be afraid, Abram. I am your shield, your very great reward'" (Genesis 15:1).

The word of the Lord

This is the first time the expression 'The word of the Lord' is used in the Bible and it pays to spend a few moments to reflect upon it. I wonder if we fully realise what a tremendous privilege it is to hear the word of the Lord or to receive it in the message of the Gospel in some way or other. It came to Abram in the form of a vision but there are many other ways in which God communicates His word to us. Today the word of the Lord comes to people through preaching and worship services, through tape and video recordings, through books and films and magazine articles, but all too often people turn a deaf ear to it. They will listen to the meaningless mouthings of some pop singer, but are heedless of God speaking to them in His word about the great issues of life and death. It shows the spiritual deadness of the human heart apart from God Himself. As Paul says: "The man without the Spirit does not accept the things that come from the Spirit of God, for they are foolishness to him and he cannot understand them, because they are spiritually discerned" (1 Corinthians 2:14). It is only God Himself, by His Spirit, who can awaken in a person that sense of God-consciousness that enables him to listen to the Word of the Lord and take it seriously. That is why we must keep on preaching it or seeking to communicate it to people because God will honour it. Romans chapter 10 puts it so clearly: "And how can they hear without someone preaching to them? ... Consequently, faith comes from hearing the message, and the message is heard through the Word of Christ" (Romans 10:14–17).

There is also a personal aspect to all this. The word of the Lord came to Abram personally, it singled him out and spoke directly to his heart. It was as if God said to him: "Abram, I have something special to say which is for your heart only in the situation in which you find yourself". And it is a wonderful experience when that happens to a person, for God still speaks directly out of His word to individuals in a personal manner, and directed to their own particular situation. One can be sitting in a congregation listening to the word of the Lord in the preaching, or reading a passage in the Bible or in a Christian book, when suddenly one is aware that what is being said has a specific and personal relevance to oneself, and without any shadow of doubt know that this is the authentic voice of God speaking to your own heart. It happens that way often in the matter of salvation. A person is suddenly convicted of their sin as the Word of God is preached and in an instant is brought to repentance and faith in Christ. The crowds listening to Peter preaching the word of God on the day of Pentecost reacted in that way. "When the people heard this, they were cut to the heart and said to Peter and the other apostles, 'Brothers what shall we do?' Peter replied, 'Repent and be baptised, every one of you, in the name of Jesus Christ so that your sins may be forgiven'" (Acts 2:37–38).

Abram's response

So what was Abram's situation at this time that needed God to speak to him a direct personal word? It seems that after the excitement of the battle, and the Melchizedek experience, for whatever reason Abram was a bit fearful and depressed. Perhaps he was afraid of some kind of retaliation from the northern confederacy of kings he had defeated earlier. But he was certainly in need of encouragement and God gave it to him. "Do not be afraid, Abram. I am your shield, your very great reward" (Genesis 15:1). But more than anything else, Abram was discouraged and depressed because he had now been in Canaan for several years and as yet he had seen no evidence that God's earlier promise of becoming a great nation would be fulfilled. In fact he was still without a child of his own. "But Abram said, 'O sovereign Lord, what can you give me since I remain childless and the one who will inherit my estate is Eliezer of Damascus?' And Abram said, 'You have given me no children; so a servant in my household will be my heir'" (Genesis

15:2–3). It seemed such a hopeless and impossible situation. He and Sarai were both that much older, with little prospect of having children of their own, and it seems on the face of it that Abram had reconciled himself to the fact that his servant Eliezer would be the only heir he would have.

I am sure many of us would sympathise with Abram because we ourselves have experienced periods when we have felt discouraged and depressed. It is not an uncommon experience among God's people. Elijah had reached a very low point when he fled to the wilderness and prayed that God would let him die. "'I have had enough Lord,' he said. 'Take my life; I am no better than my ancestors'" (1 Kings 19:4). Jeremiah felt alone and dejected in the face of resentment and ridicule from his own people. "Cursed be the day I was born! May the day my mother bore me not be blessed!" (Jeremiah 20:14).

Here were men, like Abram, who were godly and of deep faith and, in expressing their feelings in this way, were really acting out of character. But when, as believers, we get into a similarly low spiritual state, for whatever reason, I don't think we ought to feel guilty about it and dig ourselves still deeper into a hole of depression. The truth is we are not machines or robots but human beings with emotions and feelings and capable of being hurt by the harsh realities of life. What we must not do is allow Satan to exploit our feelings of discouragement by dwelling upon it until it becomes an obsession leading to a sense of total defeatism and despair. That I believe is wrong, and we must ask God to help us deal with it before it gets to that point.

God's promise. Abram's faith

God is very gracious and understanding with us in our low moments as He was with Abram. "Then the word of the Lord came to him: 'This man will not be your heir, but a son coming from your own body will be your heir.' He took him outside and said, 'Look up at the heavens and count the stars – if indeed you can count them.' Then he said to him, 'So shall your offspring be'. Abram believed the Lord, and he credited it to him as righteousness" (Genesis 15:4–6). This was just the assurance Abram needed and it put new heart into him. His response is evidence of that. "Abram believed the Lord, and he credited it to him as righteousness". This is a tremendously important statement since it is the first mention in the scriptures of imparted righteousness, or salvation through believing faith in God's promise rather than by works.

For what was it Abram believed? He believed the promise God had given that he would have a son and heir from his own body, and that his descendants would be as numerous as the stars in the sky, and would lead eventually to the coming of the Messiah, the Lord Jesus Christ, through whose Gospel of salvation all the nations on earth would be blessed. And it was on the basis of his faith alone that God credited Abram as righteous and gave him the gift of salvation. In the fourth chapter of Romans, Paul uses this example of Abram's believing to expound more fully the doctrine of justification by faith: "What then shall we say that Abraham, our fore-father, discovered in this matter? If, in fact, Abraham was justified by works, he had something to boast about – but not before God. What does the Scripture say? 'Abraham believed God, and it was credited to him as righteousness'" (Romans 4:1–3). Paul then goes on to apply the same principle of imparted righteousness to all Christians. "The words 'it was credited to him' were written not for him alone, but also for us, to whom God will credit righteousness – for us who believe in him who raised Jesus our Lord from the dead. He was delivered over to death for our sins and was raised to life for our justification" (Romans 4:23–25).

God's covenant

We generally think of Abram as the very epitome of faith. And he was indeed a man of great faith as we have already seen. But even his strong faith didn't come all at once. It took time, and there were occasions, as we shall see in the next chapter of Genesis (16), when his weakness in this regard led to serious consequences. He believed firmly in God's promise that he would have a son, but he was not so sure about the promise of possessing the land, and he asked God to give him some visible sign of confirmation. "He also said to him, 'I am the Lord, who brought you out of Ur of the Chaldeans to give you this land to take possession of it'. But Abram said, 'O Sovereign Lord, how can I know that I shall gain possession of it?'" (Genesis 15:7–8).

Is it wrong for the believer to ask God for some sign or confirmation of His leading? I don't think so entirely. After all, it is not that we do not believe that God leads and guides us in the situations of life, but that we want the certainty of knowing that it is His guidance, and not simply our own subjective feelings. And God surely understands this. When Gideon put out his fleece (Judges 6:36 fol) God gave him the confirmation he asked for. When Mary replied to the angel's announcement of the coming birth of Christ she asked: "How will this be, ... since I am a virgin?" (Luke 1:34); the explanation was given. When Thomas said he wanted confirmation that the Lord had risen, it was given to him: "Then he said to Thomas, 'Put your finger here; see my hands. Reach out your hand and put it into my side'". But then the Lord added: "Stop doubting and believe" (John 20:27). We learn from all this that asking for a sign or confirmation, whilst not indicating a lack of faith nevertheless is an indication of spiritual immaturity, and what God really wants of us is that we should learn to "walk by faith and not by sight". But God is very patient with our weakness.

So Abram received his visible confirmation in the form of a Divine Covenant carried out according to the custom of his day. "So the Lord said to him, 'Bring me a heifer, a goat and a ram, each three years old, along with a dove and a young pigeon'. Abram brought all these to him, cut them in two and arranged the halves opposite each other; the birds, however, he did not cut in half. Then the birds of prey came down on the carcasses, but Abram drove them away. As the sun was setting, Abram fell into a deep sleep, and a thick and dreadful darkness came over him ... When the sun had set and darkness had fallen, a smoking fire pot with a blazing torch appeared and passed between the pieces" (Genesis 15:9–12 and 17).

Bible scholars are not that well informed about the symbolism of covenantal rites and ritual in the Old Testament, but in this instance some of the elements are perfectly clear. It involved blood sacrifice; and spiritually points forward to the everlasting covenant based on the substitutionary sacrifice of the Lord Jesus Christ. The thick darkness and sense of dread that came upon Abram symbolised the awesome presence of the God of the covenant. Likewise the brazier and flaming torch represented the holy character of God. Lastly, it was the custom for the parties involved in the covenant to walk between the pieces (Jeremiah 34:18–19) thus ratifying the agreement; but in this instance only God passed through since this was a covenant of grace in response to Abram's believing faith. This again therefore is a prophetic foreshadowing of the salvation that is ours through Christ.

The word of the covenant

But in addition to the ritual and ceremony God spoke to Abram a definite word of promise, "Then the Lord said to him, 'Know for certain that your descendants will be strangers in a country not their own, and they will be enslaved and ill-treated four hundred years. But I will punish the nation they serve as slaves, and afterwards they will come out with great possessions. You, however, will go to your fathers in peace and be buried at a good old age. In the fourth generation your descendants will come back here, for the sin of the Amorites has not yet reached its full measure' ... On that day the Lord made a covenant with Abram and said, 'To your descendants I give this land, from the river of Egypt to the great river, the Euphrates'" (Genesis 15:13–16 and 18).

There are several important points here. Firstly it teaches us that God keeps His promises, for Israel did indeed spend 430 years (Exodus 12:40) – (400 is a round number) in slavery in Egypt; the Egyptians were indeed divinely punished at the Red Sea (Exodus 14) and when the Exodus took place under Moses, the Israelites did in fact come out with great possessions (Exodus 12:35–36), and Abram did live a long life and have a peaceful end (Genesis 25:7). Secondly, God's mercy and patience towards sinful mankind is seen in His reason for delaying the return of the Israelites to Canaan until the fourth generation – "for the sin of the Amorites has not yet reached its full measure". The Canaanite tribes were extremely wicked and their religious practices were not only idolatrous, but included prostitution and child sacrifice. However, God delayed his judgement so as to give them an opportunity for repentance. Peter gives the same reason to those in his day who scoffed at the seeming delay of the Second Coming of Christ and the day of judgement. "The Lord is not slow in keeping his promise, as some understand slowness. He is patient with you, not wanting anyone to perish, but everyone to come to repentance" (2 Peter 3:9). Thirdly, history testifies to the veracity of God's word. The statement "To your descendants I give this land, from the river of Egypt to the great river, the Euphrates" began its fulfilment in the conquest of Canaan under Joshua and reached its final extent in the reigns of David and Solomon (1 Kings 4:24, and 2 Chronicles 9:26). Furthermore, although the boundaries of Israel contracted over the centuries and eventually the Jewish people lost their land altogether in the great dispersion, nevertheless in our own day, history, after two thousand years, has witnessed their return once again to the land of Israel. All this helps to explain the tenacity with which the modern state of Israel defends its borders and it yet remains to be seen whether those borders will again be extended to their original limits.

Hagar and Ishmael

We need to read chapters 15 and 16 together because there is a very real sense in which they cover the same theme. In the covenant He made with Abram, God gave the double promise concerning possession of a child and possession of the land. We also said earlier that Abram did not come to strong faith all at once, and that his weakness in this respect sometimes led to serious consequences. That is what we see happening in this chapter. "Now Sarai, Abram's wife, had borne him no children. But she had an Egyptian maidservant named Hagar, so she said to Abram, 'The Lord has kept me from having children. Go, sleep with my maidservant; perhaps I can build a family through her.' Abram agreed to what Sarai said. So after Abram had been living in Canaan ten years, Sarai his wife took her Egyptian maidservant Hagar and gave her to her husband to be his wife. He slept with Hagar and she conceived" (Genesis 16:1–4).

The only one to come out of this incident with any sense of integrity is Hagar, since being a slave she would have had no say in the matter and was more sinned against than sinning. That is evident in the gracious manner God deals with her later in the story. But there are certain lessons here, not the least of which was the attempt by Sarai and Abram to do God's thinking for Him. They were equally to blame in this. Sarai desperately wanted a child and tried to solve the problem in her own way in spite of the promise God had given to Abram. The consequences were disastrous since they both knew it was wrong for Abram to have more than one wife. The outcome was jealousy and friction in the home, making life intolerable for both of them. "When she (Hagar) knew she was pregnant, she began to despise her mistress. Then Sarai said to Abram, 'You are responsible for the wrong I am suffering. I put my servant in your arms, and now that she knows she is pregnant, she despises me. May the Lord judge between you and me'" (Genesis 16:4–5). Why can we not learn to accept that God knows what He is doing even if we have to wait for it? This incident may have a special relevance today with the tremendous focus on attempting to solve the problem of childlessness through medical technology, and that not always successfully, whereas at the other end of the spectrum thousands of babies are aborted every year for the most trivial of reasons! What a sad and confused mixture of moral and spiritual values that represents. And we dare to be of the opinion that we can do God's thinking for Him!

Before coming to the consequences of Abram's part in all this let us see what happened to Hagar. First of all she was driven from home. "'Your servant is in your hands,' Abram said. 'Do with her whatever you think best'. Then Sarai ill-treated Hagar so she fled from her" (Genesis 16:6). But we go on to read that God found her in the wilderness and spoke graciously to her, for He is as mindful of the Hagars of this world as He is of the Abrams. She was at the bottom of the pile – a slave, and you can't get lower than that, but God had a gracious word and a mighty promise to give her. "The angel of the Lord also said to her: 'You are now with child and you will have a son. You shall name him Ishmael, for the Lord has heard of your misery. He will be a wild donkey of a man; his hand will be against everyone and everyone's hand against him, and he will live in hostility towards all his brothers'. She gave this name to the Lord who spoke to her: 'You are the God who sees me,' for she said, 'I have now seen the One who sees me.' That is why the well was called Beer Lahai Roi; it is still there between Kadesh and Bered ... Abram was eighty-six years old when Hagar bore him Ishmael" (Genesis 16:11–16).

In spite of its traumatic nature, Hagar's experience seems to have brought her very close to God for she said "I have now seen the One Who sees me" and she returned to Abram's household with a much lighter heart. It was as if God was compensating her for the injustice she had received, and it also teaches us that we are to look for the hand of God in all the experiences of life. What is most significant, however, was the far reaching effects of Abram's action for the future seen in what God says about

Ishmael. He would be a "wild donkey of a man" roaming the deserts and becoming the father of the nomadic Arab peoples and through his descendants would "live in hostility towards all his brothers" the Jews. Abram was not aware of it but in his fathering of Ishmael, as well as Isaac the promised son later on, he was laying the foundation for that inveterate hatred and political unrest between Arab and Jew which has come down through history to the present day.

The sign of the covenant

READ GENESIS CHAPTERS 17 AND 18

Thirteen years have now passed since the incident involving Hagar and the birth of Ishmael, and during that time nothing is heard about Abram. And then, with the opening of chapter 17, God again appears to him to confirm the covenant He had made earlier. "When Abram was ninety-nine years old, the Lord appeared to him and said, 'I am God Almighty; (El Shaddai) walk before me and be blameless. I will confirm my covenant between me and you and will greatly increase your numbers'" (Genesis 17:1–2). The remainder of the chapter is divided into four sections devoted to a more detailed explanation of the covenant and the promises contained within it. In verses 3–8, Abram's name is changed to Abraham (father of many) indicating that he would become the "father of many nations", and the promise given that the land will become the "everlasting possession" of his descendants. In verses 9–14 the command is given for Abraham and his household to be circumcised as a sign of the covenantal relationship. In verses 15–22 God expressly declares that Sarai alone is to bear the promised son Isaac and her name would be changed to Sarah (Princess) as an indication of that. But Ishmael would also be blessed and become the father of a great nation. Finally, verses 23–27 record Abraham's obedience in carrying out the conditions of the covenant on the very day God confirmed it.

The rite of circumcision

The one additional element in this explanation of the covenant from what has gone before is the command concerning circumcision. This was to be the external sign that Abraham and his descendants had been chosen by God and belonged wholly to Him. "My covenant in your flesh is to be an everlasting covenant. Any uncircumcised male, who has not been circumcised in the flesh, will be cut off from his people; he has broken my covenant" (Genesis 17:13–14). The rite itself was not peculiar to the Jewish people but was widely practised by other nations (Jeremiah 9:25–26). But God gave it a sacredness and meaning that was new and different, just as He had with the sign of the rainbow given in His promise to Noah (Genesis 9:13).

We need such external signs in the devotional life, if only as reminders to us of God's grace. This is sometimes called the sacramental principle and, within the context of the New Covenant, applies especially to Baptism and the Lord's Supper. But circumcision, just like any other sacramental sign, was much more than the external rite itself. Its real meaning lay in the inward experience of faith and obedience that accompanied it and expressed in God's word to Abram, "I am God Almighty, walk before me and be blameless". Paul refers to this inward aspect of circumcision when he says of Abraham: "And he received the sign of circumcision, a seal of the righteousness that he had by faith while he was still uncircumcised" (Romans 4:11). The tragedy was that in the development of Jewish history the inwardness of the rite of circumcision became entirely lost and men became content to believe that, because they were circumcised, they were therefore saved.

And the same thing happened, and does happen, with the sacrament of baptism. All too often it has become simply a traditional form, a rite that people undergo believing that somehow it affords them entrance into God's Kingdom and the blessing of salvation. And this is true both of infant baptism, where the child is said to become a member of the family of God through regeneration, and believer's baptism where the baptised may make a profession of salvation by mouth but without experiencing it in the heart. The outward form or rite must not therefore be ignored or treated as unimportant, but unless it is the expression of inward faith and obedience in God and His Word it becomes degraded and meaningless.

The changed name
One very interesting sidelight on this chapter is the new name given both to Abram and to Sarai. He is called Abraham (Father of nations) and she is called Sarah (Princess) because she would become the mother or queen of many nations. Names are important in the Bible because they are often, not always, more than just a label and are seen to express the character of the

person, or at least the hopes and sentiments associated with the name. For example the name Isaac (laughter) was to be given to the promised son because of the joy he would bring to his parents. But the Bible also changed names to show that something new and wonderful had taken place in a person's life. Hence the new name Abraham, signified the new regenerative powers within himself on being told that he would have a son even when he and Sarah were well past the child-bearing age. "Abraham fell face down; he laughed and said to himself, 'Will a son be born to a man a hundred years old? Will Sarah bear a child at the age of ninety?'" (Genesis 17:17). His was not the laugh of contempt and unbelief, but of sheer joy and wonder at the miracle that was to take place. Other instances of a change in name signifying a change of direction and purpose in a person's life are Jacob who was called Israel (a prince with God), Simon who was called Peter (Rock), and Saul who was called Paul.

It is neither fanciful nor unscriptural to see, in this process of the changed name, a picture of what happens when a person comes to faith in the Lord Jesus Christ. He too undergoes a wonderful and miraculous change in the direction of his life and in the depths of his own character and temperament. He is in Paul's words "a new creation, the old has gone, the new has come!" (2 Corinthians 5:17). And there is a new name to signify that change which is from unbeliever to believer, from a child of the devil to a child of God. In the book of Revelation we have a wonderful picture of a new name being given by the Spirit to those who remain faithful and are victorious in the Christian life. "To him who overcomes, I will give some of the hidden manna. I will also give him a white stone with a new name written on it, known only to him who receives it" (Revelation 2:17).

The divine visitors

Moving into chapter 18 we have yet another appearance of God to Abraham which seems to have taken place shortly after the appearance in connection with the covenant and the sign of circumcision. God had then said: "But my covenant I will establish with Isaac, whom Sarah will bear to you by this time next year" (Genesis 17:21). The same time-scale is now repeated in this second appearance in Genesis 18:10: "I will surely return to you about this time next year, and Sarah your wife will have a son". But the appearance itself is quite different because Abraham finds himself confronted by three divine beings in the form of men. "The Lord appeared to Abraham near the great trees of Mamre while he was sitting at the entrance to his tent in the heat of the day. Abraham looked up and saw three men standing nearby. When he saw them, he hurried from the entrance of his tent to meet them and bowed low to the ground. He said, 'If I have found favour in your eyes, my Lord, do not pass your servant by. Let a little water be brought and then you may all wash your feet and rest under this tree. Let me get you something to eat, so you can be refreshed and then go on your way – now that you have come to your servant.' 'Very well' they answered, 'do as you say'" (Genesis 18:1–5).

I get the impression as I read this passage that Abraham didn't see the men approaching in the distance but that they suddenly appeared. He "looked up and saw three men standing nearby". I also get the feeling from Abraham's response and the lavish hospitality (Genesis 18:6) he provided that, although he was unaware at first of the divine nature of the visitors, it quickly dawned on him the moment they began to speak. "'Where is your wife Sarah?' they asked him. 'There in the tent' he said. Then the Lord said, 'I will surely return to you about this time next year, and Sarah your wife will have a son'" (Genesis 18:9–10). The moment one speaks of angels and angelic appearances some people, including believers, get distinctly uncomfortable, because they find it difficult to believe that angels come to earth and especially, as in this case, that they look and act like ordinary human beings. Yet the Bible has many references of angels coming to earth as God's messengers. Joshua, Gideon, Daniel, Mary and Zechariah all received messages from angels. And when you reflect on it, it is no more difficult to accept angels in human form than it is to accept the appearance of the risen Lord in his human body. He too ate and drank with His disciples to show them that he was not insubstantial spirit. And yet his body was different because it was a glorified body, able to appear to the disciples in the upper room even when the doors were locked (John 20:19).

There are other insights into all this. Abraham clearly recognised one of the visitors as superior to the other two and addresses him as 'my Lord'. It seems certain that what we have here is a preincarnate appearance of the Lord Jesus, and the consistent use of the term 'Lord' in verses 13, 17, 20, 26 and 33 bears this out. The writer to the Hebrews probably had this incident in mind when he said: "Do not forget to entertain strangers, for by so doing some people have entertained angels without knowing it" (Hebrews 13:2), and wanted believers to learn from it the lesson of Christian hospitality. There is a real sense in which our homes can indeed become an extension of our Christian life and witness and can be greatly blessed of God in furthering the work of the gospel.

The message of joy

The purpose of the visit was to bring a message of joy to Abraham by confirming the coming birth of the promised son Isaac. "Then the Lord said, 'I will surely return to you about this time next year, and Sarah your wife will have a son'. Now Sarah was listening at the entrance to the tent, which was behind him. Abraham and Sarah were already old and well advanced in years, and Sarah was past the age of child bearing. So Sarah laughed to herself as she thought, 'After I am worn out and my master is old, will I now have this pleasure?' Then the Lord said to Abraham, 'Why did Sarah laugh and say, "Will I really have a child, now that I am old?" Is anything too hard for the Lord? I will return to you at the appointed time next year and Sarah will have a son'. Sarah was afraid so she lied and said, 'I did not laugh'. But he said, 'Yes you did laugh'"(Genesis 18:10–15).

In chapter 17 Abraham also laughed when he first heard about the coming birth of Isaac (Genesis 17:17), but since he was not rebuked in any way we said it was a laugh of joy at the wonder of such a miracle taking place. For there are different kinds of laughter – the laughter of exhilaration and happiness at God's goodness like that of the exiles on their return from Babylon: "Our mouths were filled with laughter, our tongues with songs of joy" (Psalm 126:2); the laughter of mockery and contempt; the cynical laughter of the man whose philosophy is, "eat, drink and be merry for tomorrow we die"; the dirty laughter of the prurient mind and, as in Sarah's case, the laughter of unbelief. But as if that were not bad enough she then compounded her fault by lying about it to the Lord! But her scepticism and doubt are met with the direct question: "Is anything too hard for the Lord?" To which the answer must clearly be no, for He is the Mighty Sovereign God the Maker of heaven and earth; the One who enacts the law whereby the child is conceived in the womb. Abraham and Sarah might be old and Sarah well beyond the child bearing age but that doesn't matter, it is God they are dealing with and not man. And that must always be the answer of faith to an unbelieving and sceptical world "For nothing is impossible with God" (Luke 1:37).

The message of judgement

But there was another purpose to the angel's visit, to bring the message of God's judgement upon the cities of Sodom and Gomorrah. "When the men got up to leave, they looked down towards Sodom, and Abraham walked along with them to see them on their way. Then the Lord said, 'Shall I hide from Abraham what I am about to do? Abraham will surely become a great and powerful nation, and all nations on earth will be blessed through him. For I have chosen him, so that he will direct his children and his household after him to keep the way of the Lord by doing what is right and just, so that the Lord will bring about for Abraham what he has promised him.' Then the Lord said, 'The outcry against Sodom and Gomorrah is so great and their sin so grievous that I will go down and see if what they have done is as bad as the outcry that has reached me. If not, I will know'. The men turned away and went towards Sodom, but Abraham remained standing before the Lord" (Genesis 18:16–22).

We are back here to the question raised earlier in connection with the Flood in chapters 6–7 namely, the danger of reaching a point of no return where the patience and forgiveness of God are concerned. The people of Sodom and Gomorrah had seemingly reached that point because their sin and corruption were so nauseating in God's sight that it was His intention to wipe the two cities from off the face of the earth. In the moral and spiritual deterioration of life in our own nation today we may be drawing closer than we think to crossing that line between God's patience with sin and his judgement upon it. For it is not the blasphemous and profane behaviour of our society that is its most disturbing feature but the almost total rejection of God that pervades the lives of so many. That is the ultimate blasphemy; the arrogant assertion that they have no need of God and can live independently of His providential love and care. They treat God as of no account in the scheme of things, and that brings them dangerously close to that hidden boundary between His patience and His wrath.

This was the message God wanted to share with Abraham. "Shall I hide from Abraham what I am about to do?" He needed to know it so that he could pass on to his family and his descendants after him the warning that God was not to be trifled with and that they were to "keep the way of the Lord by doing what is right and just" (Genesis 18:19). And that is still a vital ingredient in the message we must give to our children and which the Church today must preach to society at large.

Intercessory prayer

When dealing with Abraham's intercessory prayer for the cities of Sodom and Gomorrah we must not forget that his own nephew Lot and his family were living there. "Then Abraham approached him and said: 'Will you sweep away the righteous with the wicked? What if there are fifty righteous people in the city? Will you really sweep it away and not spare the place for the sake of the fifty righteous people in it? Far be it from you to do such a thing – to kill the righteous with the wicked, treating the righteous and the wicked alike. Far be it from you! Will not the Judge of all the earth do right?'" (Genesis 18:23–25). The prayer continues in the following verses until God finally says that even if only ten righteous are found in the city, He will not destroy it. "When the Lord had finished speaking with Abraham, he left, and Abraham returned home" (Genesis 18:33).

Intercessory prayer for others is a powerful ministry and a great privilege, and the Bible encourages us to engage in it. Samuel was so acutely aware of the importance and the need to pray for his people that he regarded it as a sin not to do so: "As for me, far be it from me that I should sin against the Lord by failing to pray for you" (1 Samuel 12:23). At the close of the book of Job we have a wonderful picture of Job interceding on behalf of the friends who had treated him so shamefully: "My servant Job will pray for you, and I will accept his prayer and not deal with you according to your folly. ... After Job had prayed for his friends, the Lord made him prosperous again and gave him twice as much as he had before" (Job 42:8–10). In the New Testament James urges believers to "pray for each other so that you may be healed" (James 5:16). The healing may be either physical or spiritual. Paul was very dependent on the intercessory prayers of his fellow-believers, and at the end of his letters, often urges it on them: Ephesians 6:19; Colossians 4:18; 1 Thessalonians 5:25; Philemon verse 22. Intercessory prayer was one of the most powerful weapons in the armoury of the early church. They prayed for each other in times of persecution and danger and we have a wonderful example of this in Acts 12 when Peter was in prison awaiting execution: "So Peter was kept in prison, but the church was earnestly praying to God for him" (Acts 12:5). Herod and the governing authorities mistakenly thought they were simply up against a few ignorant fishermen like Peter and the other disciples, but in fact they were confronted by the mighty power of God that was being harnessed by the intercession of the other believers, with the result that Peter was delivered. And not only is intercessory prayer a powerful weapon but it is also a secret weapon in the Christian's armoury. We may have a loved one we long to see coming into the experience of God's salvation but they resist any attempt to talk to them about it. But they cannot stop us praying for them and need not even be aware that we are doing so.

But there are other things we can learn from Abraham's intercession. He had the right approach to God. On the one hand he was bold and persistent but he never forgot that it was God he was speaking to, and he recognised His righteous character. "Will not the judge of all the earth do right?" (Genesis 18:25). On the other hand he was deeply conscious of his own unworthiness in coming before God. "Then Abraham spoke up again: 'Now that I have been so bold as to speak to the Lord, though I am nothing but dust and ashes" (Genesis 18:27). We learn from this that there is a right balance to be struck in the matter of prayer, intercessory or otherwise. On the one hand the scriptures teach us to be bold and confident in our praying: "Therefore, brothers, since we have confidence to enter the Most Holy place by the blood of Jesus, by a new and living way opened for us through the curtain, that is his body..." (Hebrews 10:19–20). It is right for us to have the confidence of faith in our praying and like Abraham to even be persistent in pleading our case, since it shows God that we are deeply in earnest. But at the same time we must never be tempted to forget our relationship with God. He is the Creator, we are the creatures. He is "the Judge of all the earth"; we are "nothing but dust and ashes". Being the "friend of

God", as Abraham was, is not the same thing as being "familiar with God".

Another insight into this passage concerns the whole question of persistence in our intercession. Abraham didn't ask just once, but six times he interceded for the city of Sodom, and each time the Lord encouraged him to go further with expressions like, "If I find", "I will spare", "I will not destroy it". In two of His parables, The Friend at Midnight and the Persistent Widow (Luke 11:5 and 18:1) our Lord taught exactly the same lesson about the need to persevere in our praying. In spite of his sleepiness, and the likelihood of disturbing the whole family, the neighbour will answer the persistent knocking of his friend and give him the bread he needs. Similarly, the unjust judge in the second parable gave way in the end to the widow's persistent plea for justice. It is not that we must continue battering the door of heaven until God hears us, since He always hears the prayers of His children. But by our very intensity and persistence in praying we are showing God how deeply earnest we are and that we believe that He will in the end answer us in a way best suited to our needs. After all, God did more for Abraham than he asked for. We shall see in chapter 19 that there were not even ten righteous people in Sodom, but God in mercy saved the four people nearest to his servant before destruction came on the city.

The destruction of Sodom and Gomorrah

READ GENESIS CHAPTER 19

D uring the time Abraham was engaging in intercessory prayer the two angels who had accompanied the Lord were making their way to Sodom, and chapter 19 opens with their arrival at the city.

Lot's continuing deterioration

"The two angels arrived at Sodom in the evening, and Lot was sitting in the gateway of the city. When he saw them, he got up to meet them and bowed down with his face to the ground" (Genesis 19:1). Mention of Lot "sitting in the gateway of the city" has distinct technical overtones, for in Old Testament times the 'gateway' was the place where the city elders or magistrates met to settle disputes and engage in judicial matters. It seems therefore that we have here a further indication of Lot's spiritual deterioration since he had now become accepted as a city elder or magistrate in Sodom, and was part of its way of life. At the same time however he had not entirely forgotten his spiritual roots and according to Peter he "was tormented in his righteous soul by the lawless deeds he saw and heard" in Sodom (2 Peter 2:8). But that is always the unhappy position of the backslider; he lives in the grey no-man's-land between the claims of God on his life and the claims of the world. He is not fully at home with God's people, but neither is he at total peace in the company of unbelievers. And that discontent and unhappiness will continue until he is restored to full fellowship with God through repentance.

We also see that Lot's spiritual sensitivity was not entirely blunted since he insisted the visitors should enjoy the hospitality and safety of his own home. They wanted to remain outside but his own knowledge of the city told him how dangerous that could be. "'My lords,' he said, 'please turn aside to your servant's house. You can wash your feet and spend the night and then go on your way early in the morning'. 'No', they answered, 'we will spend the night in the square'. But he insisted so strongly that they did go with him and entered his house. He prepared a meal for them, baking bread without yeast, and they ate" (Genesis 19:2–3). Clearly Lot was deeply uneasy about his position in Sodom, and when he eventually realised the identity of his two visitors, we wonder if he felt any sense of guilt and shame as he reflected on his present situation and the initial choice that led up to it. When he made that original decision to live in the region of Sodom and to separate from his Uncle Abraham, he thought it was a smart move that would increase his wealth and social standing, but he was now about to pay the consequences.

Sodom's depravity

Those consequences came in the first instance in the form of collective homosexual rape attempted by the men of Sodom. "Before they had gone to bed, the men from every part of the city of Sodom – both young and old – surrounded the house. They called to Lot, 'Where are the men who came to you tonight? Bring them out to us so that we can have sex with them'. Lot went outside to meet them and shut the door behind him and said, 'No, my friends. Don't do this wicked thing. Look, I have two daughters who have never slept with a man. Let me bring them out to you, and you can do what you like with them. But don't do anything to these men, for they have come under the protection of my roof'. 'Get out of our way,' they replied. And they said, 'This fellow came here as an alien, and now he wants to play the judge! We'll treat you worse than them'. They kept bringing pressure on Lot and moved forward to break down the door. But the men inside reached out and pulled Lot back into the house and shut the door. Then they struck the men who were at the door of the house, young and old, with blindness so that they could not find the door" (Genesis 19:4–11).

This is an ugly scene and one which has left an indelible mark in history in the term 'sodomy' which comes from it and which was partly, if not wholly, the reason why Sodom's wickedness and depravity were so 'grievous' (Genesis 18:20) in God's sight and brought down His judgement. We have come a long way since that time and one would have thought that we might have taken the lesson of Sodom to heart, but the opposite is the case and today's society not only accepts homosexual practice as natural but the latest move has been to lower the age of consent to sixteen! And the saddest thing of all has been the way in which so many who claim to be Christians, including some evangelicals, have gone along with this kind of thinking.

But there is no doubt whatever in any straightforward understanding of the Bible's teaching, homosexual behaviour is strongly condemned. In Leviticus 18:22 and 20:13 homosexual practice is described as 'detestable' and incurred the death penalty. Homosexual practice was common among the Canaanites and, from time to time, infected the religious life of Israel in the form of male prostitution, and was severely dealt with (1 Kings 15:12; 22:46; 2 Kings 23:7).

In the New Testament Paul's denunciation of homosexual behaviour is equally explicit. Because mankind had rejected the Creator and worshipped instead the creation, God took the restraints off sin as an act of judgement. "Because of this God gave them over to shameful lusts. Even their women exchanged natural relations for unnatural ones. In the same way the men also abandoned natural relations with women and were inflamed with lust for one another. Men committed indecent acts with other men, and received in themselves the due penalty for their perversion" (Romans 1:26–27). By his use of the terms 'natural' and 'unnatural' Paul is clearly referring to the creation order God established in Genesis in the heterosexual relationship of Adam and Eve. This also explains our Lord's silence on the subject of homosexuality. He took a much deeper and broader view of sexual relationships emphasising the marriage relationship within the creation order. "For this reason a man will leave his father and mother and be united to his wife, and the two will become one flesh? So they are no longer two, but one. Therefore what God has joined together let man not separate" (Matthew 19:5–6). The marvellous provision God has made within marriage for sexual intercourse and procreation is both natural, and His will and intention for mankind, and anything else is contrary to that.

From what has been said two things follow: First, the Bible does not condemn homosexual feelings, but homosexual **behaviour**. Second, in spite of Paul's explicit condemnation of homosexual behaviour, it is clear from what he says to the Corinthian believers they too can be saved and redeemed and brought into a new life in Christ. "Do you not know that the wicked will not inherit the kingdom of God? ... Neither the sexually immoral nor idolaters, nor adulterers, nor male prostitutes, nor homosexual offenders ... And that is what some of you were. But you were washed, you were sanctified, you were justified in the name of the Lord Jesus Christ and by the Spirit of our God" (1 Corinthians 6:9–11).

Before leaving this section we cannot overlook the bizarre behaviour of Lot in his willingness to hand over his two daughters to the mob to be sexually abused! "Look, I have two daughters who have never slept with a man. Let me bring them out to you, and you can do what you like with them" (Genesis 19:8). This was a terribly wicked thing to do and we cannot pass it by, saying he was trying to protect his guests and obey the rules of hospitality. You cannot prevent one sin by committing another. The only conclusion we can come to is that the evil of Sodom had so infected his soul that it had confused his moral judgement and blunted his finer feelings.

The deliverance

In spite of his weakness God was very gracious and merciful to Lot, and gave him the opportunity – along with his family – to escape the coming judgement upon Sodom. "The two men said to Lot, 'Do you have anyone else here – sons-in-law, sons or daughters, or anyone else in the city who belongs to you? Get them out of here, because we are going to destroy this place. The outcry to the Lord against its people is so great that he has sent us to destroy it'. So Lot went out and spoke to his sons-in-law who were pledged to marry his daughters. He said, 'Hurry and get out of this place, because the Lord is about to destroy the city!' But his sons-in-law thought he was joking" (Genesis 19:12–14). It is not surprising that his warning to his sons-in-law had no effect since his previous way of life had been so like theirs that his words meant nothing. Why should the world believe what the Christian man or woman has to say about the worth of the Gospel if it is not seen in the kind of life they live?

"With the coming of dawn, the angels urged Lot saying, 'Hurry! Take your wife and your two daughters who are here, or you will be swept away when the city is punished.' When he hesitated the men grasped his hand and the hands of his wife and of his two daughters and led them safely out of the city, for the Lord was merciful to them. As soon as they had brought them out, one of them said, 'Flee for your lives! Don't look back, and don't stop anywhere in the plain. Flee to the mountains or you will be swept away!'" (Genesis 19:15–17). Even in the face of its imminent destruction Lot was clearly reluctant to leave the prosperity and material comfort of his way of life in Sodom. He may have been "distressed by the filthy lives" of its inhabitants (2 Peter 2:7) but he had done little about it in the past. And right up to the last moment he attempts a compromise by begging to be allowed to settle in the nearby city of Zoar rather than flee to the isolation of the mountains. "He said to him, 'Very well, I will grant this request too; I will not overthrow the town you speak of. But flee there quickly because I cannot do anything until you reach it' (That is why the town was called Zoar)" (Genesis 19:21–22).

The destruction

"By the time Lot reached Zoar, the sun had risen over the land. Then the Lord rained down burning sulphur on Sodom and Gomorrah – from the Lord out of the heavens. Thus he overthrew those cities and the entire plain, including all those living in the cities – and also the vegetation in the land. But Lot's wife looked back, and she became a pillar of salt" (Genesis 19:23–26). The destruction of Sodom is often explained as the result of natural physical phenomena – an enormous volcanic upheaval accompanied by an earthquake and possibly an electrical storm. This is supported by the unusual geological formations found in the area of the Dead Sea and the fact that it forms part of the 'Great Rift' which runs through the Nile valley into Africa. This may well have been the case and in no way does it contradict the present account that it was also God's judgement. It is the timing of the event that is important. After all, if we believe God is the God of creation then He can use natural phenomena for His own purposes.

Furthermore, we must not overlook the fact that our Lord also refers to Sodom's destruction as the judgement of God. Speaking of His own second coming and the judgement that will accompany it He says: "It was the same in the days of Lot. People were eating and drinking, buying and selling, planting and building. But the day Lot left Sodom, fire and sulphur rained down from heaven and destroyed them all. It will be just like this on the day the Son of Man is revealed" (Luke 17:28–30). What our Lord stresses is the godlessness of the people of Sodom; their total absorption with the material and physical aspects of life to the exclusion of God and the things of the soul. And He is warning us that the same features will characterise society in the days leading up to His coming. And we can see it happening today. As a society we are becoming increasingly materialistic and pagan as history runs down to its termination point when Christ will come back to this world to sum up all things, and to judge the living and the dead. Having reminded us of this, our Lord then reinforces the point with the expression, "Remember Lot's wife!" (Luke 17:32).

Why remember Lot's wife? Because she looked back with wistful longing to the life of Sodom she was having to leave behind. Our Lord uses her destruction in the judgement on Sodom as a warning against failing to break with the old life of worldliness, and to commit ourselves wholly to the life of the Spirit. For He goes on to say: "Whoever tries to keep his life will lose it, and whoever loses his life will preserve it" (Luke 17:33). Lot's wife valued the life of Sodom above everything else and tried to hang on to it, with the result that she lost her life and her soul in the catastrophe that overtook the city.

Lot's final disgrace

What we have already read about Lot and his experience in Sodom was bad enough, but the saga of his spiritual deterioration goes one step further and reveals him in an even more lurid light. "Lot and his two daughters left Zoar and settled in the mountains, for he was afraid to stay in Zoar. He and his two daughters lived in a cave. One day the older daughter said to the younger, 'Our father is old, and there is no man around here to lie with us, as is the custom all over the earth. Let's get our father to drink wine and then lie with him and preserve our family line through our father' … So both of Lot's daughters became pregnant by their father. The older daughter had a son and she named him Moab; he is the father of the Moabites of today. The younger daughter also had a son, and she named him Ben-Ammi; he is the father of the Ammonites of today" (Genesis 19:30–38).

What a pathetic, miserable way to end one's days! Years before, Lot as a young man, had known the high calling of God when he had set out on the great pilgrimage of faith in the company of his Uncle Abraham. And we must imagine him now, living in a mountain cave, old, isolated and lonely having lost his spiritual integrity and adding to it all an act of incest committed with his two daughters whilst in a drunken stupor. Can anything be said that would lessen in any way the depravity of this incident? Well, it might be argued that the daughters had to get their father drunk in the first place, because they knew he would not willingly have agreed to have sex with them. But any man with an atom of common sense knows that this is not an absolute defence of Lot's character since, however befuddled by drink, he would have known what he was doing when it came to engaging in sexual intercourse – especially since he had sobered up after the first time and still repeated the sin. As for the daughters, they had no hope of getting husbands in the future; and the text points out that their motive was to "preserve our family line through our father" (Genesis 19:32). We certainly cannot condone what they did, but at least it was not simply an act of lust but a case of doing the wrong thing from a genuine desire to preserve life through future generations. Moreover we must make allowance for their background, and the kind of life they had become accustomed to in Sodom, and for which Lot himself was responsible.

Following this incident we hear nothing more about Lot and he passes off the pages of the Bible without even his death being recorded. As to his final salvation only God knows, but he strongly reminds me of the man the Apostle Paul had in mind when he said: "he will suffer loss; he himself will be saved, but as one escaping through the flames" (1 Corinthians 3:15).

Repeating an old sin

READ GENESIS CHAPTER 20

The very fact that the incident recorded in this chapter appears at all in the Bible is, in itself, a testimony to its honesty and realism in not disguising the faults and weaknesses of even its greatest characters, like Abraham who appears in a very poor light. "Now Abraham moved on from there into the region of the Negev and lived between Kadesh and Shur. For a while he stayed in Gerar, and there Abraham said of his wife Sarah, 'She is my sister'. Then Abimelech king of Gerar sent for Sarah and took her" (Genesis 20:1–2).

Here is Abraham, and to a lesser extent Sarah, repeating the very same sin of which they had been guilty some twenty years earlier when they went down to Egypt (Genesis 12:10 fol). Only this time it was even more deplorable since, during those years, Abraham had experienced God's care and guidance in many wonderful ways. God had entered into a personal covenant with him (Genesis chapter 15); had promised him a son by Sarai (Genesis 17:15 fol); had answered his prayer concerning Lot in Sodom (Genesis 18 and 19) and in general had shown him that he could trust Him absolutely for care and protection in any situation. But, like so many of us, Abraham was still fearful and lacking faith at times, and was prone to depend more upon his own schemes and devices than upon God. As he approached Philistine territory in his wanderings he was afraid that in such a godless place his life would be in danger because of Sarah, and he reminded her of the pact they had entered into many years before (Genesis 20:13), that whenever they entered strange territory she was to say she was his sister. His sin on this occasion therefore, was not committed on the spur of the moment but had long been a deliberate policy, which he and Sarah had agreed to follow.

The persistence of sin

If there is one thing that stands out in this passage, it is that the principle or law of sin is not entirely eradicated within the believer's life as long as he is living in this world. Like Abraham, the Christian finds that again and again the old sinful nature pushes itself up to the surface of his life causing him to give way to temptation and to act in a way totally contrary to God's commandments, even to the extent of repeating some old sin or habit he thought he had conquered once and for all. This inner conflict between, on the one hand, the genuine desire to please God by living a holy life and, on the other hand, the relentless persistence of evil, is the practical side of sanctification. Positionally, in God's sight we are already "sanctified in Christ Jesus" (1 Corinthians 1:2), but on the practical side here below, we still struggle after a holy character. The classic passage in the New Testament describing this inward struggle is Romans 7. "So I find this law at work: When I want to do good, evil is right there with me. For in my inner being I delight in God's law; but I see another law at work in the members of my body, waging war against the law of my mind and making me a prisoner of the law of sin at work within my members. What a wretched man I am! Who will rescue me from this body of death? Thanks be to God – through Jesus Christ our Lord!" (Romans 7:21–25). Paul is surely telling us that whilst we struggle with sin in this life it is not a hopeless battle. Our proness to sin is no longer inevitable, for we have the power of Christ working through the Holy Spirit within us, counteracting its effect in our lives, and enabling us to live triumphantly.

But there is another aspect of this struggle, which emerges from Abraham's attempt to save his own life at the expense of allowing Abimelech the king of Gerar to take Sarah into his harem. It was the same sin repeated, and since it was a deliberate policy to pass Sarah off as his sister, it suggests that he was open to doing it again and again. In short, his fear in this regard was a particular weakness in his character, and that too is something many of us have in common with him. Again and again we show a tendency to fall before the onslaught of Satan at the very point where we have fallen previously. This, I believe, is partly the explanation of Hebrews 12:1 which speaks of the "sin that so easily entangles" (AV "easily besets"). This seems to suggest sins to which we, individually and personally, are exposed because of some peculiar weakness in our character, and which we are therefore liable to repeat again and again. This is a danger point, and Satan knows it and will attack us at that point repeatedly. It may be a quick temper, an old habit, a gossipy tongue, sexual laxity, a critical spirit, or whatever. We need therefore to recognise this weakness in our spiritual and moral life and to be especially on our guard.

God's intervention

Where would we be without God's merciful intervention in our lives to save us from our own stupidity and disobedience? Again and again we read of this happening in the Bible. In this instance God intervened to save Abraham from his own folly, to save Sarah from being sexually exploited and, above all, to prevent His own sovereign purpose, in the coming birth of Isaac the promised son, from being frustrated. Indeed, Sarah might even have been pregnant with Isaac at this very time. "But God came to Abimelech in a dream one night and said to him, 'You are as good as dead because of the woman you have taken; she is a married woman.' Now Abimelech had not gone near her, so he said, 'Lord will you destroy an innocent nation? Did he not say to me, "She is my sister", and didn't she also say, "He is my brother"? I have done this with a clear conscience and clean hands.' Then God said to him in the dream, 'Yes I know you did this with a clear conscience, and so I have kept you from sinning against me. That is why I did not let you touch her. Now return the man's wife, for he is a prophet, and he will pray for you and you will live. But if you do not return her, you may be sure that you and yours will die'" (Genesis 20:3–7).

Had God not intervened to save the situation the results would have been disastrous, and Isaac, instead of being the promised son through whom the messianic line was to be continued, might well have been regarded as the child of Abimelech. That would have suited Satan, who all through the Bible seeks to frustrate the purpose of God and the prophetic promise of the coming Messiah, the Lord Jesus Christ. But God did not allow that to happen. Abraham may have been weak and failed God, but God did not fail Abraham. It may well be that Satan, and the forces of evil, are able through human weakness and man's sin to frustrate the plan of God in the short term, but ultimately God is in control, and as this passage shows neither the wilfulness and disobedience of His servant Abraham, nor the collusion of Sarah, nor the desires of a pagan king, determined the outcome of this incident but God Himself.

How God breaks through

It was through a dream that God broke through to the consciousness of Abimelech and warned him of the consequences of his action in abducting Sarah. This is significant, since here was a pagan king with no knowledge of God, but he was quickly brought to an understanding of who God was through the instrumentality of a dream. "Early the next morning Abimelech summoned all his officials, and when he told them all that had happened, they were very much afraid" (Genesis 20:8). In the light of this, we must be careful not to put limits on God's power to make His will known to us by dismissing all talk of dreams and visions as fanciful, and no more than a person's own subjective and speculative experience. After all, the Bible is full of instances of God breaking through to men and women through the medium of dreams. God revealed Himself to Jacob in a dream at Bethel; the young Joseph was given dreams by God, and so was Solomon when he became king. The coming birth of Jesus was told to Joseph in a dream, and it was through a dream the Magi were warned not to return to King Herod.

These few instances, and there are many others, are sufficient therefore to show us that God can use whatever means He chooses to make known His will to us. Granted, dreams and visions are no longer the accepted method by which God speaks to us, since we now have the written word in the full canon of scripture, and the revelation of God in the Person of the Lord Jesus Christ. But that is not to say God cannot, even today, use other methods when it pleases Him, to speak a personal word to us. And sometimes if He cannot break through to us when we are awake and busy with all the other encumbering concerns of life He will even disturb our sleep. The important thing is that we keep our minds and hearts sensitive to the movement of the Holy Spirit, so that if God does break through we shall not miss His voice, or doubt within ourselves that He has in fact spoken to us.

Rebuked by the world

The one person to come out of this sorry incident with any integrity was Abimelech the pagan king! "Then Abimelech called Abraham in and said, 'What have you done to us? How have I wronged you that you have brought such great guilt upon me and my kingdom? You have done things to me that should not be done'. And Abimelech asked Abraham, 'What was your reason for doing this?'" (Genesis 20:9–10). Well, we have seen clearly enough why Abraham did what he did, and his half-hearted excuse that Sarah was really his half-sister does not lessen in any way the wrong he did to Abimelech. This is a sad and shameful picture of the pagan justly rebuking the man of God, or the worldly man rebuking the Christian. And when it happens, it is a deeply humiliating experience and brings the gospel into disrepute. For this one brief moment Abraham had lost his testimony in the eyes of Abimelech, and that can happen to any one of us when we act out of character as a Christian in the eyes of the world.

It also happens when the Church loses her credibility with the secular man and woman because it no longer appears to be taking its own message seriously, but fiddles around with secondary issues and trivialities and fails so often to bring to people's notice the great truths of the Gospel, and to give the guidance in spiritual and moral matters that is so sorely needed. But having said that, we must not run away with the idea that the worldly man who, in his integrity, appears in a better light than the Christian is somehow closer to God. That is not so. Abraham, for all his faults, was God's man whilst Abimelech, for all his innocence and generosity, was a pagan. God does not love us, use us, or deliver us because of our integrity of character and good behaviour, but because we have been redeemed through the precious blood of Christ and belong wholly to Him. Abraham could pray for Abimelech, but Abimelech could not pray for Abraham. "Then Abraham prayed to God, and God healed Abimelech, his wife and his slave girls so they could have children again, for the Lord had closed up every womb in Abimelech's household because of Abraham's wife Sarah" (Genesis 20:17–18). We cannot be certain what the illness was from which Abimelech was healed, but the context seems to suggest that God had made him impotent so that he was unable to have sexual relations with Sarah or with his wife and slave girls. The opposite was true however with regard to Abraham and Sarah. He was old and she was well past the child bearing age and yet God seems to have rejuvenated them both miraculously so that they were capable of having Isaac. This may also help to explain why Sarah was still attractive enough physically to gain the attentions of Abimelech.

The promised son

With the birth of Isaac, recorded in this chapter, we come to a significant advance in the history of the patriarchs, for he was the promised offspring through whom the line of the Messiah was to be continued. Twenty-five years had passed since God called Abraham from Ur of the Chaldeans and had said to him: "I will make you into a great nation and I will bless you; I will make your name great, and you will be a blessing. I will bless those who bless you, and whoever curses you I will curse; and all peoples on earth will be blessed through you" (Genesis 12:2–3). During those long years of waiting for the promise to be fulfilled Abraham's faith had been sorely tried, and at one point, in connection with the birth of Ishmael, it had failed him completely. But with God's assurance that He would establish His covenant with the coming birth of Isaac (Genesis 17:19) Abraham's faith returned, and with the opening of this chapter we see his confidence rewarded.

God's power to perform

It is easy to make a promise, however grand, but it is infinitely more difficult to fulfil it. The reason we fail so often to keep the promises we make is not our lack of sincerity but our inability to fulfil them. We cannot perform what we promise. That is never true where God's promises are concerned, as the opening verses make clear. "Now the Lord was gracious to Sarah as he had said, and the Lord did for Sarah what he had promised. Sarah became pregnant and bore a son to Abraham in his old age, at the very time God had promised him. Abraham gave the name Isaac to the son Sarah bore him. When his son was eight days old, Abraham circumcised him, as God commanded him. Abraham was a hundred years old when his son Isaac was born to him" (Genesis 21:1–5). Notice the emphasis placed upon God's power to perform: "… as he had said", "the Lord did for Sarah what he had promised", "at the very time God had promised him".

Whichever way you look at it, the birth of Isaac was a supernatural act made possible only by the power of an omnipotent sovereign God. Abraham was well aware that he and Sarah could have no expectation of having a child at their advanced age, nevertheless, once God had given him His word on the matter, he believed that His power was equal to the performance, and that He could make the impossible possible. The apostle Paul comments on Abraham's confidence in God's Word: "Without weakening in his faith, he faced the fact that his body was as good as dead – since he was about a hundred years old – and that Sarah's womb was also dead. Yet he did not waver through unbelief regarding the promise of God, but was strengthened in his faith and gave glory to God, being fully persuaded that God had power to do what he had promised" (Romans 4:19–21).

The key phrase there is "... being fully persuaded that God had power to do what he had promised". As believers we must never be afraid to face the reality of life's situations. There are times in our lives when things look black and hopeless and incapable of ever being changed for the better, and we have to face up to that fact, and not pretend to ourselves in some vague way that everything will turn out all right in the end. That kind of superficial optimism will never gird us sufficiently to face triumphantly the struggles of life, and since that is the only resource of the non-Christian it often leads him to a sense of hopelessness and despair. But the believer looks beyond the reality of the impossible, and through faith is persuaded that God has the power to make it possible.

In the accounts of the miraculous conception both of Isaac, the son of the covenant, and of the Lord Jesus, who was the fulfilment of the covenant, the same assurance was given by God of His power to perform. Sarah's laugh of unbelief at the mention of her bearing a son was met with the angel's direct question, "Is anything too hard for the Lord?" (Genesis 18:14). Now however the situation has radically changed, and Sarah laughs with confidence and joy that God has performed what He had promised. The child was named Isaac (Laughter) and "Sarah said, 'God has brought me laughter, and everyone who hears about this will laugh with me.' And she added, 'Who would have said to Abraham that Sarah would nurse children? Yet I have borne him a son in his old age'" (Genesis 21:6–7).

Likewise when Mary received the announcement of the coming birth of Christ she too raised the question of the impossibility of it happening. "'How will this be', Mary asked the angel, 'since I am a virgin?'" But she received the same answer, "Nothing is impossible with God" (Luke 1:34 and 37). All this raises the question, do we really believe that God is sovereign and omnipotent? If we do, then it follows that, however hopeless and seemingly impossible the situation facing us, we know that God can turn things around, for he has the power to perform, and it is in **that** that we put our faith and trust.

Relevant to salvation

This truth concerning God's power to perform is especially relevant in the matter of our salvation. When the rich young ruler turned away from Jesus because he couldn't face the challenge to give up his riches to obtain eternal life, our Lord said: "How hard it is for the rich to enter the kingdom of God!" This shocked the disciples who exclaimed: "Who then can be saved?" (Mark 10:23 and 26). They still had, in their thinking, the notion that the rich were especially blessed of God, so what hope had they of obtaining salvation? To which Jesus replied: "With man this is impossible but not with God; all things are possible with God"; In this way he was making it perfectly clear that salvation is entirely dependent upon the power of God to perform and is impossible for man to bring about, whether through his riches, or by reason of his merit, or any human achievement.

We dare not forget this, or else we shall despair of certain people ever being saved. Here is a man, shall we say, to whom we have spoken many times about the needs of his soul, only to be met with total indifference or even hostility. Furthermore, we know him to be a covetous man, totally earthbound in his thinking and dominated by the material concerns of this life. We may be tempted to feel therefore that it is impossible that his life could ever be changed to a God-ward direction so that he should experience salvation. And it would indeed be impossible if it were left to the man himself, or to our own powers of persuasion, for we cannot renew his heart or break the power of sin in his life. But God can do it – "all things are possible with God".

"Faith is the grasping of Almighty Power,
The hand of man laid on the arm of God,
The grand and blessed hour
In which the things impossible to me
Become the possible, O Lord, through Thee."

Ishmael's hostility

Back in chapter sixteen, we considered Sarah and Abraham's attempt to deal with the problem of their childlessness through his marriage to Hagar and the birth of Ishmael, and we said then that the consequences of their action would be disastrous since they were attempting to do God's thinking for Him. The truth of that statement can now be seen in what happened following the birth of Isaac. "The child grew and was weaned, and on the day Isaac was weaned Abraham held a great feast. But Sarah saw that the son whom Hagar the Egyptian had borne to Abraham was mocking, and she said to Abraham, 'Get rid of that slave woman and her son, for that slave woman's son will never share in the inheritance with my son Isaac'. The matter distressed Abraham greatly because it concerned his son" (Genesis 21:8–11). What an unhappy state of affairs. And yet it was bound to happen. Ishmael was now about sixteen years old and had enjoyed first place in his father's affections. But now the situation had changed with the entry of Isaac into the family, and he felt ignored and resentful, and was not slow to make his hostility known. We can't condone his attitude, but we can understand it. Sarah in turn was equally resentful of Ishmael since she saw him as a threat to Isaac's inheritance, and she made it perfectly clear to Abraham that she wanted him and his mother out of the house.

We can only imagine how Abraham must have felt as he saw this scenario of hatred and jealousy developing. After all, he was mainly responsible for what was happening, and all because he had failed to let God be God. He was certainly filled with a profound sadness as the text makes clear. "The matter distressed Abraham greatly because it concerned his son" (Genesis 21:11). Ishmael was as much his son as Isaac, and he loved him dearly. So there he was, confused and uncertain, not knowing what to do, but feeling himself pressurised on the one hand by Sarah's insistence that he get rid of the boy, and on the other hand by his deep love for Ishmael and the knowledge that it was his own wilful disobedience that had brought about the situation in the first place.

Isn't that a perfect picture of the kind of confused mess we get ourselves into when we ignore God's direction in our lives and take matters into our own hands? And isn't it a great blessing that God is very merciful when this happens and helps us straighten out the situation, as He did with Abraham. "But God said to him, 'Do not be so distressed about the boy and your maidservant. Listen to whatever Sarah tells you, because it is through Isaac that your offspring will be reckoned. I will make the son of the maidservant into a nation also, because he is your offspring'" (Genesis 21:12–13). Abraham was to follow Sarah's decision without approving of her hostile attitude. It was a case of her doing the right thing but from the wrong motive, and we cannot approve of that. But more importantly it shows God's sovereignty in His over-ruling of our human circumstances for the fulfilment of His purpose.

The Apostle Paul interprets the whole incident as an allegory of the conflict between law and faith in the purpose of God's salvation. "For it is written that Abraham had two sons, one by the slave woman and the other by the free woman. His son by the slave woman was born in the ordinary way, but his son by the free woman was born as the result of a promise. These things may be taken figuratively, for the women represent two covenants" (Galatians 4:22–24). Paul then develops at some length the thought that Hagar and her son stand for those under the Law, which enslaves and cannot save, whereas Sarah and Isaac stand for those under the covenant of Grace and enjoy freedom and salvation in Christ. Law and grace cannot dwell together, therefore Sarah was right to insist on Ishmael's ejection, for the eternal inheritance is for believers only as the children of promise (Galatians 4:30). This teaches us that the Christian is called to live a life separate from the world.

The promise of Ishmael

It must have been with a heavy heart that Abraham sent Hagar and Ishmael on their way in obedience to God's instruction. "Early the next morning Abraham took some food and a skin of water and gave them to Hagar. He set them on her shoulders and then sent her off with the boy. She went on her way and wandered in the desert of Beersheba" (Genesis 21:14). It seems, on the face of it, a pretty mean provision Abraham made for the two of them as they faced a journey in the desert – just bread and water. But that is to overlook the fact that Ishmael too, in a sense, was a child of promise. Back in chapter seventeen God had assured Abraham that He had plans for Ishmael and that He would bless him; "I will make him fruitful and will greatly increase his numbers. He will be the father of twelve rulers, and I will make him into a great nation" (Genesis 17:20). Abraham was confident in his own mind therefore that God would look after Hagar and her child, and that was how it turned out as the following verses show.

"When the water in the skin was gone, she put the boy under one of the bushes. Then she went off and sat down nearby, about a bow-shot away, for she thought, 'I cannot watch the boy die'. And as she sat there nearby she began to sob. God heard the boy crying, and the angel of God called to Hagar from heaven and said to her, 'What is the matter, Hagar? Do not be afraid; God has heard the boy crying as he lies there. Lift the boy up and take him by the hand, for I will make him into a great nation'. Then God opened her eyes and she saw a well of water. So she went and filled the skin with water and gave the boy a drink. God was with the boy as he grew up. He lived in the desert and became an archer. While he was living in the Desert of Paran, his mother got a wife for him from Egypt" (Genesis 21:15–21). Later, in chapter twenty five, we have a list of Ishmael's twelve sons all of whom became powerful princes or tribal chiefs leading to the formation of the Arab people of Northern Arabia. This was to be the long-term consequence of Abraham's failure and wrong-doing in marrying Hagar in the attempt to provide a substitute for the promised son. The hostility it generated between Sarah and Hagar, and Isaac and Ishmael, was continued through the long history of their descendants right down to the political tensions existing in Israeli-Arab relations today. It all goes to show the far-reaching effects of sin and how foolish we are to think we can plan things better than God. Whenever I listen to the pundits on television discussing the Middle East political situation, I cannot help thinking they would have a far better understanding of what is happening there if they knew the Old Testament and, in particular, the story of Sarah and Hagar.

The peace treaty

The final section of this chapter, verses 22–34, records the making of a peace treaty between Abraham and Abimelech, the Philistine king of Gerar mentioned in chapter 20. "At that time Abimelech and Phicol the commander of his forces said to Abraham, 'God is with you in everything you do. Now swear to me here before God that you will not deal falsely with me or my children or my descendants. Show to me and the country where you are living as an alien the same kindness that I have shown to you'. Abraham said, 'I swear it' … So Abraham brought sheep and cattle and gave them to Abimelech, and the two men made a treaty" (Genesis 21:22–24 and 27). The important thing to note here is the heathen king's appraisal of God's servant: "God is with you in everything you do".

Abimelech could see that Abraham had now become powerful and prosperous and that it was in his interests to enter into a non-aggression pact with him. But more importantly he could see that Abraham was a man of integrity and faithfulness and greatly blessed of God, and to have him as a friend would be a definite advantage. It is still the case in today's world that the unbeliever recognises the reality of the Christian's faith by the integrity and honesty he brings to his daily work and behaviour, and it therefore becomes a true witness to the Gospel. Nor should we overlook the fact that it was a 'peace treaty' Abraham made with Abimelech. Abraham was not an aggressive personality. This is evident from the fact that—in spite of a great wrong that had been done to him when a well he had dug at Beersheba was stolen by Abimelech's men—he still only wanted peace. "Then Abraham complained to Abimelech about a well of water that Abimelech's servants had seized. But Abimelech said, 'I don't know who has done this. You did not tell me, and I heard about it only today' … So that place was called Beersheba, because the two men swore an oath there. After the treaty had been made at Beersheba, Abimelech and Phicol the commander of his forces returned to the land of the Philistines. Abraham planted a tamarisk tree in Beersheba, and there he called upon the name of the Lord the Eternal God" (Genesis 21:25–33).

"Make every effort to live in peace with all men", so writes the author of Hebrews 12:14, and in our Lord's teaching and the New Testament as a whole there is a strong emphasis on peace and peacemaking. Never was the need for peacemakers greater than today, for ours is a world of continual war and strife. Social disorder in the form of vandalism, crime and violence has infected virtually every city, town and village in the country and all the efforts made to deal with it seem to fail. It all points surely to the greatest need of all, which is for man himself to be at peace with God in his own heart. James in his epistle deals with the causes and cure of strife when he asks: "What causes fights and quarrels among you? Don't they come from your desires that battle within you? You want something but don't get it. You kill and covet, but you cannot have what you want. You quarrel and fight. You do not have, because you do not ask God" (James 4:1–2). His point is that concentrating on the outward circumstances alone will not solve the problem of conflict in the world, or in society, or in human relationships, but we have to deal with the root of the problem which lies in the sinful human heart, and only God's power in Christ can achieve that.

The supreme test

READ GENESIS CHAPTER 22

The years passed and Abraham and Sarah had great joy in watching the son of their old age grow into a young man. It is difficult to follow the chronology exactly, but by the time of the event recorded in this chapter Isaac must certainly have been about seventeen or eighteen years of age.

The sacrifice of Isaac

"Some time later God tested Abraham. He said to him, 'Abraham!' 'Here I am,' he replied. Then God said, 'Take your son, your only son Isaac, whom you love, and go to the region in Moriah. Sacrifice him there as a burnt offering on one of the mountains I will tell you about'" (Genesis 22:1–2). For years Abraham had not received any word from God, and now, when He finally speaks, it was to give him a message that would test his faith to the very limit. We can only imagine his inner feelings, and any doubts he might have had about God's love for him in the light of such an instruction. Isaac was the light of his eyes and here was God actually asking him to put him to death. Abraham was well aware that the gods of the surrounding pagan nations demanded human sacrifice, but wasn't his God the true and sovereign God and therefore different from all others?

Did thoughts like these go through Abraham's mind, I wonder? In the next verse (3) we read: "Early the next morning Abraham got up and saddled his donkey. He took with him two of his servants and his son Isaac. When he had cut enough wood for the burnt offering, he set out for the place God had told him about." Some commentators make great play of the fact that there is no hint of reluctance on Abraham's part to obey God's word. And that is true, he was indeed perfectly obedient, and willing to meet the test with which God was now confronting him. But that doesn't mean that we should discount the possibility, indeed probability, that he suffered deep emotional pain and inner writhing of the soul as he struggled to understand why God should ask him to sacrifice the son in whom was enshrined the promise for the ages to come. So what does this say to us, and what are the lessons we can learn from this event?

Faith must be tested

When God puts our faith to the test, as He did with Abraham, it is not because He needs to know how strong or weak it is, but that we need to know. It can certainly be a painful process, physically, emotionally or spiritually, as it was with Abraham and Job, but it is necessary for our growth in the Christian life. This is the point James makes in the opening verses of his letter. "Consider it pure joy, my brothers, whenever you face trials of many kinds, because you know that the testing of your faith develops perseverance. Perseverance must finish its work so that you may be mature and complete, not lacking anything." (James 1:2–4). James is saying that, when trials and difficulties face us in this life, we are not to give way to a victim mentality by reproaching God, but that we should view them as a testing ground for faith enabling us to become mature Christians. How else can we discover if we are making progress in our spiritual lives?

For the sad truth is that we can live in a fantasy world of self-approval where our Christian discipleship is concerned, and therefore God exposes us to the cutting edge of the sufferings and challenges of life so that we may discover whether our faith in His grace and power is a reality and not an illusion.

Our love for God

In the request God made of His servant there is a strong emphasis on how precious Isaac was to Abraham, and how deep was the love of the father for his son. "Take your son, your only son, Isaac, whom you love ..." Are we meant to learn from this that Abraham was in danger of loving Isaac more than he loved God? Or at least that he was tending to devote more and more of his time and thought to the care of Isaac than to the service of God? And God was now reminding him of that by asking him to sacrifice what was most precious in his life, and that He, God, must come first and will not take second place to anyone or anything else. And we can be open to the same danger of allowing someone or something that we love deeply to come right into the centre of our affections at the expense of our love for God. And when that happens God may well ask us to surrender that object of our affections as a proof or test of our love for Him.

The story of Hannah is very instructive in this respect. She received from God in answer to prayer what was to become the most treasured possession in her life with the birth of Samuel. But then she did a most remarkable thing. In her prayer she had already vowed that if God would give her a son she would give him back to the Lord to serve Him in His sanctuary for the rest of his life (1 Samuel 1:11). This was a remarkable act of self-sacrifice, and if anything speaks to us of the place God held in Hannah's heart this must surely be it. Would we be willing if God were to ask us to give up our most precious possession as a proof of our love for Him, and of the central place He has in our lives?

Are we willing?

It may well be that God will never ask us to make any great demanding sacrifice for Him in our Christian life. But it would surely gladden God's heart if we were to show Him that we are willing to make that sacrifice should it ever be asked of us. It is clear from this story that God never intended that Abraham should actually slay Isaac, only that he should show himself willing, in obedience to God's request. "When they reached the place God had told him about, Abraham built an altar there and arranged the wood on it. He bound his son Isaac and laid him on the altar, on top of the wood. Then he reached out his hand and took the knife to slay his son. But the angel of the Lord called out to him from heaven, 'Abraham, Abraham!' 'Here I am,' he replied. 'Do not lay a hand on the boy,' he said. 'Do not do anything to him. Now I know that you fear God, because you have not withheld from me your son, your only son.'" (Genesis 22:9–12). And in the closing verses of the chapter the angel speaks to Abraham a second time to commend him for his willingness and obedience in response to God's request:

"…through your offspring all nations on earth will be blessed, because you have obeyed me" (Genesis 22:18).

There are two things here. First, Abraham was living in the midst of a pagan society in which the idol gods demanded human sacrifice.

Abraham's willingness to offer Isaac was a witness to those nations that he loved his God as much as they loved theirs. Let's face it, in our materialistic society we see the willingness with which people give enormous amounts of time, money and effort to the worship of their idols in the form of pleasure, sport, sex, politics, careers, hobbies, home and family. And when we compare that with the meagre amount of time, effort and money some Christians give in their service for Christ we are forced to conclude that the willingness just isn't there, and therefore the witness is weak and ineffective.

Second, Abraham's willingness was not only a witness to the surrounding pagans by showing how much he, Abraham, loved God, but also how much God loved Abraham! The pagan gods, in the minds of their worshippers, could be satisfied with nothing less than the actual offering of the human victims. Abraham's God, on the other hand, had no desire for the blood of human sacrifice, but accepted the willing obedience of his servant in place of the deed. God said: "Do not lay a hand on the boy. ... Do not do anything to him. Now I know that you fear God, because you have not withheld from me your son, your only son" (Genesis 22:12). Abraham was willing to offer God his very best, and God in His love and mercy set His seal on that willing obedience. Are we willing? That is all God asks of us.

Unique faith

In verse 5, we have from the mouth of Abraham one of the most remarkable statements of faith in the power and promises of God to be found anywhere in the whole Bible. "He said to his servants, 'Stay here with the donkey while I and the boy go over there. We will worship and then we will come back to you'". He was confident that on his return Isaac would be with him. How this would be possible he would not have been able to say, but in spite of all his doubts and fears and inner turmoil he knew with certainty that God would be true to His word and Isaac would be restored. How else could the covenant promise, centred in Isaac, be fulfilled? This was not only great faith, triumphant faith, it was UNIQUE faith since there had never been a resurrection before, so that Abraham had no precedent to fall back on. The writer to the Hebrews picks this up in his commentary on the passage: "By faith Abraham, when God tested him, offered Isaac as a sacrifice. He who had received the promises was about to sacrifice his one and only son, even though God had said to him, 'It is through Isaac that your offspring will be reckoned.' Abraham reasoned that God could raise the dead, and figuratively speaking, he did receive Isaac back from death" (Hebrews 11:17–19).

There is a sense in which every believer's faith in the power of God needs to be unique, that is unique to oneself. When we find ourselves in a difficult situation and look to God to help us we may recall the experience of other Christians who have had a similar trial, but the circumstances are never exactly the same. Our situation is particular to us, and we have to meet it with our particular brand of faith. Like Abraham in the matter of Isaac's sacrifice we have no blue print we can follow. It must be our own particular unique faith in the unlimited power and fidelity of Almighty God.

Jehovah-Jireh (God will provide)

Some Christian writers place a great deal of emphasis on typology when expounding the great narratives of the Old Testament, and can sometimes be guilty of going to exaggerated lengths in their attempt to see anticipations of the person and work of Christ. For example when we read in verse 6: "Abraham took the wood for the burnt offering and placed it on his son Isaac," they interpret it as a type of Christ carrying His Cross for the sacrifice on Calvary. But having said that, it is clear that the account of Abraham offering up Isaac is, in many ways, the foreshadowing of the salvation provided by God (Jehovah-Jireh) through the sacrifice of the Lord Jesus Christ.

When we read, "Then God said, 'Take your son, your only son, Isaac, whom you love...'", we immediately think of God's gift to us expressed in such verses as, "He who did not spare his own Son, but gave him up for us all" (Romans 8:32), and "For God so loved the world that he gave his one and only Son ..." (John 3:16).

As they made their way together to the place of sacrifice Isaac spoke to his father. "'The fire and the wood are here,' Isaac said, 'but where is the lamb for the burnt offering?' Abraham answered, 'God himself will provide the lamb for the burnt offering, my son'" (Genesis 22:7–8).

Abraham's reply to Isaac was literally fulfilled when he "looked up and there in a thicket he saw a ram caught by its horns. He went over and took the ram and sacrificed it as a burnt offering instead of his son. So Abraham called that place, 'The Lord Will Provide.' And to this day it is said, 'On the mountain of the Lord it will be provided'" (Genesis 22:13–14).

"God Himself will provide a lamb", so said Abraham and his words point forward to the sacrifice God provided for our salvation in the "Lamb of God who takes away the sin of the world" (John 1:29). And the ram caught in a thicket, which Abraham offered instead of his son, is a clear picture of Christ as a substitutionary sacrifice for our sin. But what of Isaac in all this? We said earlier that he must have been seventeen or eighteen years of age at this time and therefore strong enough to have easily over-powered his elderly father. But he didn't do that and nowhere in the story is there the slightest suggestion that Isaac was an unwilling victim. He was of the same mind as his father in obeying the Divine command and it fore-shadows the voluntary nature of our Lord's sacrifice as expressed in that wonderful passage in Philippians: "Who being in very nature God, did not consider equality with God something to be grasped, but made himself nothing, taking the very nature of a servant, being made in human likeness. And being found in appearance as a man he humbled himself and became obedient to death – even death on a cross!" (Philippians 2:6–8).

But when all the similarities and types in the account of Abraham's offering of Isaac have been exhausted, it is the one outstanding contrast that is most significant. Abraham, at the last, was spared his son, whereas God on the other hand "did not spare his own Son, but gave him up for us all". And for that we give to God our heartfelt thanksgiving and praise.

A bride for Isaac

READ GENESIS CHAPTERS 23 AND 24

B efore considering chapter 24, which is the longest in Genesis, we must look briefly at the death of Sarah recorded in chapter 23. "Sarah lived to be a hundred and twenty-seven years old. She died in Kiriath Arba (that is, Hebron) in the land of Canaan, and Abraham went to mourn for Sarah and to weep over her" (Genesis 23:1–2). This statement of Sarah's death is brief and to the point and the remainder of the chapter consists of a long description of the negotiations Abraham entered into with the inhabitants of Canaan for the purchase of a burial site. Sarah had lived a long and godly life and, apart from the incident involving Hagar, was deeply devoted to Abraham, as is clear from the statement by Peter (1 Peter 3:5–6).

The main lesson in the passage arises out of Abraham's decision not to bury Sarah in her homeland of Mesopotamia but in Canaan. In the protracted negotiations with the Hittites he was determined not to rent a burial site, or to receive one as a gift, but to make it his own possession through legal purchase. "Afterwards Abraham buried his wife Sarah in the cave in the field of Machpelah near Mamre (which is at Hebron) in the land of Canaan. So the field and the cave in it were legally made over to Abraham by the Hittites as a burial site" (Genesis 23:19–20). Through this legal transaction Abraham was expressing in a very positive way his absolute faith in God's promise that Canaan was his new homeland and would become the possession of his descendants for ever. Later, Abraham himself was buried in the cave of Machpelah (Genesis 25:9), as were Isaac (Genesis 35:27–29), Leah and Rebekah (Genesis 49:30–31), and Jacob (Genesis 50:13).

The ongoing purpose

Chapter 24 contains one of the loveliest stories in the Old Testament. On the one hand it is simply a warm and tender love story involving the securing of a wife for Isaac, but from the spiritual perspective it is far more, and shows how the on-going purpose of God is connected to the thread of ordinary events in human history. The chapter opens with Abraham expressing his deep concern for the fulfilment of the divine promise through Isaac. "Abraham was now old and well advanced in years, and the Lord had blessed him in every way. He said to the chief servant in his household, the one in charge of all that he had, 'Put your hand under my thigh. I want you to swear by the Lord, the God of heaven and the God of earth that you will not get a wife for my son from the daughters of the Canaanites, among whom I am living, but will go to my country and my own relatives and get a wife for my son Isaac'" (Genesis 24:1–4).

Isaac was the heir of promise and it was unthinkable that he should have a wife from among the pagan Canaanites, for then there would be no promised offspring. The preservation of the worship of the true God was everything and therefore the wife-to-be had to come from among Abraham's own people. So important was this that Abraham made his servant swear to it by taking a solemn oath. The placing of the hand under the thigh is generally considered to be a reference to the procreative system and its connection with the promised offspring, whilst the oath itself was sworn in the name of "the God of heaven and the God of earth" thus showing that Abraham did not conceive of God as a mere local deity. And when the servant asks if he is to take Isaac out of Canaan if the bride-to-be refuses to leave her own people, Abraham is equally emphatic that this must not happen, and he expresses his own total confidence that the Sovereign God of heaven and earth will ensure the success of the mission. "'Make sure you do not take my son back there,' Abraham said. 'The Lord, the God of heaven, who brought me out of my father's household and my native land and who spoke to me and promised me on oath, saying, 'To your offspring I will give this land' – he will send his angel before you so that you can get a wife for my son from there. If the woman is unwilling to come back with you, then you will be released from this oath of mine. Only do not take my son back there'. So the servant put his hand under the thigh of his master Abraham and swore an oath to him concerning this matter" (Genesis 24:6–9).

Separation

What can we learn from this passage? Well, apart from the clear lesson arising out of Abraham's faith and obedience concerning God's promise, it focuses our thinking on the need for believers to be a separated people. Abraham and his descendants were God's covenant people and it was God's intention for Israel, as a nation, to live a life that was different from the culture and idolatry of the surrounding pagan nations of Canaan. This was adhered to during the lives of the patriarchs so that later Joseph advised his brethren, when he brought them down to Egypt, to tell Pharaoh they were shepherds, knowing as he did that the Egyptians detested and despised shepherding (Genesis 46:31–34). In this way he was ensuring that God's people would be allowed to live a separate life in the region of Goshen and not be assimilated into the Egyptian culture.

Later in their history the Israelites however failed to separate themselves from the practices and idolatry of their pagan neighbours, with the result that God brought His judgement upon them in the form of Nebuchadnezzar's conquest of Jerusalem, the destruction of the temple, and the deportation of the people into exile. All that is a warning to us. For as Christian believers we are also called to a life of separation, not in the sense of cutting ourselves off from normal social interaction with other people, but by resisting the allure of secular society with its godless ways and values. If we do not keep a tight reign on our pleasures and enjoyments, and discipline ourselves to maintain our Christian distinctives, we shall quickly find that the corrosives of worldliness will eat away the marks of God's grace in our lives. For, let's face it, there is an increasing encroachment of the spirit of worldliness in many churches today, including those of an evangelical persuasion. This was the concern Paul had in mind when he warned the Corinthian Christians to separate from the corrupting associations of the pagans of their day. "Do not be yoked together with unbelievers. For what do righteousness and wickedness have in common? Or what fellowship can light have with darkness? What harmony is there between Christ and Belial? What does a believer have in common with an unbeliever? What agreement is there between the temple of God and idols? For we are the temple of the living God. As God has said: 'I will live with them and walk among them, and I will be their God, and they will be my people. Therefore come out from them and be separate, says the Lord'" (2 Corinthians 6:14–17).

We may find it difficult to live this life of separation because there is a natural tendency in all of us to dislike being different from others. Furthermore, it is always easier to conform to prevailing attitudes than it is to resist the current of popular opinion. But that is what the gospel urges us to do, and God's power in Christ enables us to do it, for He has transformed us in the renewing of our minds. "Do not conform any longer to the pattern of this world, but be transformed by the renewing of your mind. Then you will be able to test and approve what God's will is – his good, pleasing and perfect will" (Romans 12:2).

The journey

Following his master's instructions the servant (Possibly Eliezer of Genesis 15:2) set out on the long journey northwards of some five hundred miles from Hebron, where Abraham lived, to the town of Nahor in the region of Haran. "Then the servant took ten of his master's camels and left, taking with him all kinds of good things from his master. He set out for Aram Naharaim and made his way to the town of Nahor." (Genesis 24:10). The journey itself is passed over in silence, but from the point of arrival at Nahor there is a lot of fascinating detail focusing on the servant's godly attitude and sense of responsibility in seeking to carry out his delicate mission. There is also a large section (verses 34–49) which is more or less a repetition of the main narrative as the servant explains to Laban the purpose of his visit, and how God had led him on the journey.

For some commentators the vivid detail of the narrative leads them to see in it a good deal of typological teaching which I think can be overdone. For example the servant represents the Holy Spirit in the world seeking a bride for Christ; the bride (Rebekah) is the Church comprising those who receive Christ; Rebekah's decision to marry Isaac represents those who must say yes or no to Christ, and if they decide for Him they must leave the things of the world in the way Rebekah had to leave her home in Nahor (The Genesis Record. Henry M. Morris page 401). Another commentator sees it differently. Abraham the father is like God the Father seeking a bride (the Church) for His Son; the bride was thought of before she herself knew it, just as believers are chosen before the foundation of the world (Ephesians 1:4); the testimony of the servant concerning the purpose of his journey is like the Holy Spirit proclaiming through Christian preachers the glory of Christ; the power and success of the servant's message represents the power of the gospel to draw men to Christ (Genesis, W H Griffith Thomas page 215).

It might be argued that this kind of typology, because it is mainly applicatory rather than interpretative, is therefore perfectly legitimate from a spiritual standpoint. But for my own part I prefer to stay with the main theme of the narrative which tells us something about prayer and God's guidance.

Prayer and guidance

Most Christians would accept without question the truth of divine guidance because it is so clearly taught in the bible. When Abraham set out on his journey from Ur of the Chaldeans he believed God would lead the way – "go to the land I will show you". When Moses and the Israelites left Egypt for the Promised Land, God led the way in the pillar of cloud by day and the pillar of fire by night. When the Wise Men set out on their journey to find the Christ Child they were led by the star which they had seen in the east. But although there are many examples of divine guidance in the Bible, and plenty of teaching about God's general guidance, we are still left with certain questions. How does God guide us in definite situations and how are we to discern His guidance?

One thing we learn from this story is the importance of prayer in the matter of God's leading. When the servant arrived at the town of Nahor the first thing he did was to pray. "He made the camels kneel down near the well outside the town; it was towards evening, the time the women go out to draw water. Then he prayed, 'O Lord, God of my master Abraham, give me success today, and show kindness to my master Abraham. See, I am standing beside this spring, and the daughters of the townspeople are coming out to draw water. May it be that when I say to a girl, 'Please let down your jar that I may have a drink', and she says, 'Drink, and I'll water your camels too' – let her be the one you have chosen for your servant Isaac. By this I will know that you have shown kindness to my master'" (Genesis

24:11–14). We notice that not only did he pray for guidance because his task was such a difficult one but he actually laid down a plan by which God might guide him and show him which of the girls would be a suitable bride for Isaac. This is a marvellous example of specific detailed praying. The servant was not doing God's thinking for Him, or suggesting that God should stick to the plan laid down, but by mentioning specific details he was showing his deep earnestness and his confidence that God could, and would, meet his definite need. Scripture is clear that, whereas there is place for general prayer that God will bless and guide us in life, and times when we do not even know what to pray for (Romans 8:26), there are also those occasions when vague generalities are not good enough and we need to be precise and specific in the requests we make, especially in the matter of God's leading. Wasn't this in Paul's mind when he says: "Do not be anxious about anything, but in everything, by prayer and petition, with thanksgiving present your requests to God" (Philippians 4:6).

But there is another facet to this truth about guidance. The servant not only prayed, he planned. He used his own intelligence and sanctified common sense. The planning began when he set out on the journey, "taking with him all kinds of good things from his master" (Genesis 24:10). These 'good things' were intended to impress Rebekah's family with the status of Abraham and how Isaac would one day inherit his father's wealth. "So he said, 'I am Abraham's servant. The Lord has blessed my master abundantly, and he has become wealthy. He has given him sheep and cattle, silver and gold, menservants and maidservants, and camels and donkeys. My master's wife Sarah has borne him a son in her old age, and he has given him everything he owns'" (Genesis 24:34–36). Later, the abundance of God's blessing is shown in the lavish gifts given to the family. "Then the servant brought out gold and silver jewellery and articles of clothing and gave them to Rebekah; he also gave costly gifts to her brother and to her mother." (Genesis 24:53). Planning is also seen in the servant's decision to halt at the well outside the town at the very time the women would come out to draw water. What better way to make contact with whichever girl was the bride-to-be?

Prayer, planning and guidance all go together. God has given us brains and he means us to use them! In the matter of God's leading we are not meant to sit around waiting for the miraculous to happen. We make our plans, use our ingenuity and initiative but we take God into our arrangements, and seek His blessing upon them if they are in line with his will. That is what John tells us to do. "This is the assurance we have in approaching God: that if we ask anything according to his will, he hears us. And if we know that he hears us – whatever we ask – we know that we have what we asked of him" (1 John 5:14–15). In the parable of the Shrewd Manager (Luke 16) our Lord commends his keen-wittedness and foresight and concludes with the words: "For the people of this world are more shrewd in dealing with their own kind than are the people of the light" (verse 8). He means that God's people must be as inventive and enterprising in the life of the Spirit, whether seeking guidance or anything else, as worldly people are in the management of their secular affairs.

There is still one other lesson about God's guidance which emerges from this lovely story. We can find it very difficult at times, when seeking God's leading, to know exactly what His will is. But even when we have planned and prayed and know for certain what He wants us to do, or where He wants us to go, there is still the difficulty of putting God's will into effective action, especially if there is a personal cost involved. Immediately following his prayer, indeed before he had actually finished, the servant knew for certain the direction God was leading him and he acted upon it without any doubts or hesitation. "Before he had finished praying, Rebekah came out with her jar on her shoulder. She was the daughter of Bethuel son of Milcah, who was the wife of Abraham's brother Nahor. The girl was very beautiful, a virgin; no man had ever lain with her. She went down to the spring, filled her jar and came up again. The servant hurried to meet her and said, 'Please give me a little water from your jar.' 'Drink, my lord,' she said, and quickly lowered the jar to her hands and gave him a drink. After she had given him a drink, she said, 'I'll draw water for your camels too, until they have finished drinking.' So she quickly emptied her jar into the trough, ran back to the well to draw more water, and drew enough for all his camels. Without saying a word, the man watched her closely to learn whether or not the Lord had made his journey successful. When the camels had finished drinking, the man took out a gold nose ring weighing a beka and two gold bracelets, weighing ten shekels. Then he asked, 'Whose daughter are you? Please tell me, is there room in your father's house for us to spend the night?'"(Genesis 24:15–23). Later in the story, after the servant had informed the family of God's leading, Rebekah too acted upon it when asked to make her decision, "Then they said, 'Let's call the girl and ask her about it.' So they called Rebekah and asked her, 'Will you go with this man?' 'I will go', she said" (Genesis 24:57–58).

That was a brave decision on Rebekah's part, for it meant leaving the security of home and family to live in a strange country and to be the bride of a man she had never met. But she had no doubt that God was leading the way and she was prepared to go even though the decision was costly. Are we prepared for that when seeking God's leading in our own lives? When He makes His will known, through whatever means, it may not be what we had hoped for. Personal sacrifice may be asked for, or the loss of home, or family, or private ambition, and we suddenly discover we are unable to follow where God is leading. So let us be careful about seeking God's guidance in our personal lives or we might end up grieving the Holy Spirit, instead of pleasing Him as happened with Rebekah. "Isaac brought her into the tent of his mother Sarah, and he married Rebekah. So she became his wife, and he loved her; and Isaac was comforted after his mother's death" (Genesis 24:67).

Abraham, God's friend

READ GENESIS CHAPTER 25:1–18

In this section we have recorded the final years in the life of Abraham, including his marriage to Keturah following the death of Sarah. "Abraham took another wife, whose name was Keturah. She bore him Zimran, Jokshan, Medan, Midian, Ishbak and Shuah. Jokshan was the father of Sheba and Dedan; the descendants of Dedan were the Asshurites, the Letushites and the Leummites. The sons of Midian were Ephah, Epher, Hanoch, Abida and Eldaah. All these were the descendants of Keturah" (Genesis 25:1–4). I find this one of the most puzzling passages in the life story of Abraham. Not because he married again, since this is perfectly understandable if he were lonely after the loss of Sarah, but because no information is given about the marriage itself or about the character and background of Keturah. Unlike Sarah she is not mentioned in the New Testament, and, most astonishing of all, she was able to bear Abraham six sons in spite of his great age. We can only assume that the rejuvenation of Abraham's body by God's power, which enabled him at the age of a hundred to father Isaac, must have continued for at least another forty years or so – so great is God's healing power.

The concept of nationhood

Keturah and her sons did not, however, enjoy anything like the status of Sarah and Isaac, as is evident from the arrangements Abraham made in guarding the inheritance of Isaac as the promised son. "Abraham left everything he owned to Isaac. But while he was still living, he gave gifts to the sons of his concubines (Hagar and Keturah?) and sent them away from his son Isaac to the land of the east. Altogether, Abraham lived a hundred and seventy-five years. Then Abraham breathed his last and died at a good old age, an old man full of years; and he was gathered to his people. His sons Isaac and Ishmael buried him in the cave of Machpelah near Mamre. …There Abraham was buried with his wife Sarah. After Abraham's death,

God blessed his son Isaac, who then lived near Beer Lahai Roi" (Genesis 25:5–11). There are certain things worth noting here.

The statement that Abraham sent the sons of Keturah "to the land of the east" is generally considered to refer to the region of Arabia, so that they, together with the twelve tribal rulers descended from Ishmael listed in verses 13–16, formed the foundation of the Arab peoples of today and that helps to explain why the Islamic and Jewish traditions both claim Abraham as their father. The twelve tribal rulers descended from Ishmael were also a fulfilment of the prophetic promise God had earlier made to Abraham. "And as for Ishmael, … I will make him fruitful and will greatly increase his numbers. He will be the father of twelve rulers, and I will make him into a great nation" (Genesis 17:20). This concept of nationhood is a biblical principle therefore, and a very important one at that, not to be given up lightly. The Apostle Paul confirms this in his statement in Acts 17:24–26. "The God who made the world and everything in it is the Lord of heaven and earth … he himself gives all men life and breath and everything else. From one man he made every nation of men, that they should inhabit the whole earth; and he determined the times set for them and the exact places where they should live". This passage seems to have a particular relevance at a time when we are having to consider the future of our own nation in relation to closer ties with Europe.

In making his statement Paul seems to have had in mind the Table of Nations given in Genesis chapter 10 which ends with the words: "from these the nations spread out over the earth after the flood". This tells us that it was God's intention that nations should have their national character in the same way as individuals have their own distinct characteristics. The account of the Tower of Babel (Genesis 11), with its emphasis upon different languages and its concluding words, "From there the Lord scattered them over the face of the whole earth", (verse 8) seems to confirm this. It is this difference between the races, nations and peoples of the world that gives variety and colour to our human existence, and since it was God ordained it is something we ought to treasure.

Life beyond death?

Another thing worth noticing in this passage occurs in verse 8. "Then

Abraham breathed his last and died at a good old age, an old man and full of years; and he was gathered to his people". The expression 'gathered to his people' cannot possibly refer to his burial in the cave of Machpelah alone, since only Sarah was buried there. Nor can it mean the graves of his ancestors, because they were far away in Ur of the Chaldeans. It has to reflect a hope, dimly conceived perhaps, of a life beyond death and the grave. Speaking of Abraham, the writer to the Hebrews says, "For he was looking forward to the city with foundations, whose architect and builder is God" (Hebrews 11:10). That city is heaven itself, or the 'new Jerusalem' of Revelation 21, or 'Abraham's side' to where the angels carried the beggar at his death in our Lord's parable of the Rich Man and Lazarus (Luke 16).

Clearly then, a belief in life after death was foundational to Abraham's faith, but it was a dim perception. As the writer to the Hebrews makes clear, where the ultimate realities are concerned, Abraham and his fellow patriarchs "only saw them and welcomed them from a distance. And they admitted that they were aliens and strangers on earth" (Hebrews 11:13). We can say that they hoped and believed in faith that the 'better country' would ultimately be theirs, but they did not have the absolute certainty that we have in the fuller revelation given in the Lord Jesus Christ. It is only the Christian believer who can answer Job's question, 'If a man dies, will he live again?' (Job 14:14); with the positive affirmation Christ himself gives to us in those glorious words: "I am the resurrection and the life. He who believes in me will live, even though he dies; and whoever lives and believes in me will never die" (John 11:25–26).

Reconciliation

Yet another spiritual insight into this passage focuses on the words, "His sons Isaac and Ishmael buried him in the cave of Machpelah near Mamre ..." (Genesis 25:9). Does this mean that the hostility and estrangement which had existed between the brothers was now put aside and they were reconciled to each other? If so, it would not be the first time that the death of a parent or loved one has exercised a healing influence in family relationships. The truth is that death can have a softening effect upon the human spirit. In the presence of the vastness of eternity we are made to reflect upon the brevity of our earthly life, that it is no more than 'a mist that appears for a little while and then vanishes' (James 4:14) and in that awareness, the triviality of the petty squabbles and tawdriness of the things that so often spoil our lives and destroy our relationships is borne in upon us.

And that is no bad thing when you think of it, for many of us are tempted to cram our lives with much of the trivia of this world whilst ignoring, or at least neglecting, the imperishable things that foster the well-being of our souls and spirits. And if, in the goodness of God, it takes some crisis, such as the death of a loved one whom we respected and cherished, to make us change our priorities in this way, then it is not without meaning and value.

The life of Abraham

Now that we have come to the end of Abraham's life, perhaps this is the point at which we can make some attempt to assess the significance of his contribution in the outworking of the divine purpose of God's people. For there is no doubt that he is an outstanding figure not only in the redemptive history of Israel, but for the spiritual life of the world. In confirming the covenant with Isaac, God Himself makes clear His estimate of Abraham: "because Abraham obeyed me and kept my requirements, my commands, my decrees and my laws" (Genesis 26:5).

Abraham's name occurs again and again in both Old and New Testaments and is frequently associated with the Divine title. In the revelation given to Moses out of the burning bush God says: "I am the God of your father, the God of Abraham …" (Exodus 3:6). Elijah opens his great prayer on Mount Carmel with the words: "O Lord God of Abraham…" (1 Kings 18:36). When Isaiah impresses upon the people that God will complete the work of redemption he reminds them that that work was begun when Abraham was redeemed from the paganism and idolatry of Ur of the Chaldeans. "Therefore this is what the Lord, who redeemed Abraham, says to the house of Jacob" (Isaiah 29:22). And when he later speaks to the people of the greatness of their spiritual heritage he urges them to "Look to the rock from which you were cut and to the quarry from which you were hewn; look to Abraham, your father, and to Sarah who gave you birth" (Isaiah 51:1–2).

The New Testament likewise confirms the testimony of the Old Testament writers to Abraham's greatness. Matthew, in his genealogy of

Jesus, refers to Him as 'the son of Abraham' (Matthew 1:1). Jesus Himself, when speaking to the Jews of their spiritual blindness and refusal to accept the gospel, contrasts their position with that of faithful Abraham. "'Abraham is our father', they answered, 'If you were Abraham's children', Jesus said, 'then you would do the things Abraham did'" (John 8:39). When teaching about the evangelisation of the Gentiles Jesus illustrates from the life of Abraham: "I say to you that many will come from the east and the west, and will take their places at the feast with Abraham, Isaac and Jacob in the kingdom of heaven" (Matthew 8:11). And then there is that remarkable statement by our Lord: "Abraham rejoiced at the thought of seeing my day; he saw it and was glad" (John 8:56). In receiving the promise Abraham anticipated with joy the coming of the Messiah when all nations would be blessed through the gospel. For Stephen the call of Abraham in an idolatrous country was so phenomenal that he describes it as a personal revelation or appearance of God's glory. "The God of glory appeared to our father Abraham while he was still in Mesopotamia, before he lived in Haran" (Acts 7:2). Paul, James, and the writer to the Hebrews all have a lot more to say about Abraham to which we shall refer shortly.

In the spiritual and moral advance recorded in the Old Testament, Abraham was a 'creative force', a pioneer and adventurer whose daring in leaving the stability of life in Ur of the Chaldeans for the uncertainties of a pilgrimage into the unknown, was the result of his deep conviction in the reality and power of God. In that regard he speaks to all Christians today, for the temptation faces all of us to remain in our 'comfort zones', complacent and satisfied when God may be calling us to show something of an adventurous and daring spirit in the cause of the gospel. After all, where would the Christian Church be today without the pioneers of the Christian faith, those who threw all caution to the winds and 'went out' knowing only that Christ was with them? At a lower level perhaps we should ask ourselves: When did I last do anything that was daring and costly for the cause of the gospel? Or, to put it another way: Am I content only to give to God what is the acceptable minimum of my time, money, energy, gifts, abilities etc. That is the challenge to come out of Abraham's life, and there are two main features he exemplifies which might help us to face that challenge. His profound faith in God and his intimacy with God.

His faith in God

In the Bible Abraham is set forth as the very embodiment of faith. The writer to the Hebrews describes the life of faith for the Christian by reference to the experiences of the men and women of the Old Testament, and makes use of a number of illustrations from the life of Abraham (Hebrews 11:8–19). He wants to show that Abraham accomplished all that he did because he believed God with all his heart and mind, and was willing to stake everything on the power of God to see him through. It was because he believed that he left Ur of the Chaldeans and lived as a stranger in a foreign country. Because he believed he allowed Lot to make the first choice of the land, knowing as he did that God would take care of his own interests. Because he believed he waited years for God's promise to be fulfilled in the birth of Isaac. Because he believed he was able to meet the great crisis in his life in the offering up of Isaac, in spite of any nagging doubts he might have had.

But what kind of faith was it that Abraham possessed? Paul and James emphasise the two sides of Abraham's faith as leading to righteousness and justification on the one hand, and faith leading to active obedience in good works on the other. In Romans 4:3, Paul quotes Genesis 15:6 where we are told: "Abraham believed God and it was credited to him as righteousness". It was on the basis of his faith that God regarded Abraham as righteous and gave him the gift of salvation, and in the same way God credits us as righteous through our faith in the atoning death of Christ. James on the other hand is concerned to show that genuine faith, like that of Abraham, will always lead to action and godly living, and he illustrates his point by reference to Abraham's active obedience to God's request to offer up Isaac. "Was not our ancestor Abraham considered righteous for what he did when he offered his son Isaac on the altar? You see that his faith and his actions were working together, and his faith was made complete by what he did" (James 2:21–22).

His intimacy with God

Abraham has the rare distinction of being the only person in the Old Testament to be called 'God's friend' – in the prayer of Jehoshaphat king of Judah, 2 Chronicles 20:7; in Isaiah's appeal to Israel, Isaiah 41:8; and in

James' reference to Abraham's faith, James 2:23. It speaks to us of the close intimate relationship he had with God. For God not only spoke to him, but actually appeared to him in theophanies and visions. And it was not only that God spoke to Abraham but Abraham entered into deep conversation with God, as in Genesis 15 when God gave him the promise of a son, and Genesis 18 when he pleaded with God for Sodom.

How close are we to God? Theophanies and visions, such as charac-terised the lives of Abraham and other Old Testament saints, are no longer the norm by which God makes Himself known, since we now have the fullness of His revelation in the Bible and in the Lord Jesus Christ. But there can still be the danger that our understanding of that revelation can be largely a head knowledge rather than a close, intimate, inward relationship with our heavenly Father that enables us to talk things through with Him in the way we can discuss intimate things with a dear friend, but not with someone with whom we have only a nodding acquaintance. After all, the Lord Jesus did say: "I no longer call you servants, because a servant does not know his master's business. Instead, I have called you friends, for everything that I learned from my Father I have made known to you" (John 15:15). And He said this to the disciples knowing their deficiencies and weaknesses, just as Abraham was God's friend in spite of those occasions when he was weak and deficient in faith, such as the experience in Egypt when he lost his testimony for a while. But it only reinforces the truth that God's love for us in Christ is so deep and condescending that, in spite of our unfriendliness towards Him at times, He still wants us to enjoy intimate fellowship with Him as His friends.

Jacob and Esau

READ GENESIS CHAPTER 25:19–34

In the second part of this chapter we continue the story of Isaac and his marriage to Rebekah. "This is the account of Abraham's son Isaac. Abraham became the father of Isaac, and Isaac was forty years old when he married Rebekah, daughter of Bethuel the Aramean from Paddan Aram, the sister of Laban the Aramean. Isaac prayed to the Lord on behalf of his wife, because she was barren. The Lord answered his prayer, and Rebekah became pregnant." (Genesis 25:19–21).

Isaac and Rebekah

The information given about Isaac is remarkably brief and nothing like as detailed as that given about his father Abraham or his son Jacob. It is as if his life is recorded simply to show that he is the link in the chain of promise between Abraham and Jacob, who was to become the father of the twelve tribes of Israel. What kind of man was Isaac? From what we are told he seems to have lived a quiet uneventful life up to the age of 180, and was buried by his sons Esau and Jacob in the family tomb at Mamre (Genesis 35:28). Like his father Abraham before him, his faith was sorely tried when, after twenty years of marriage, he and Rebekah failed to produce a child. This must have been a bitter disappointment especially since Isaac knew well enough that the promised offspring was to come through him. But he did the right thing, he prayed about it, and the "Lord answered his prayer and his wife Rebekah became pregnant".

I see a double lesson here. Through the long delay prior to Rebekah's pregnancy God was not only testing Isaac's faith, but He was also teaching him that the continuation of the promised offspring was not dependent in the first instance upon natural means, but upon His own sovereign power and grace. There is also the lesson that things go better with prayer. We all have problems of one kind or another, and whilst we should always be open to whatever help we can get from others, we ought never to leave out the dimension of prayer. Praying a thing through, whatever else it does, will always leave us with a more positive attitude to our problem and enable us to handle it more efficiently. Rebekah knew something of this, because although, in answer to Isaac's prayer, she could now expect the child she had longed for, she suddenly discovered that she was carrying twins, and this brought its own problem. "The babies jostled each other within her, and she said, 'Why is this happening to me?' So she went to inquire of the Lord" (Genesis 25:22). She knew this disturbance within her womb was something extraordinary and not the normal movement felt in pregnancy. In her perplexity therefore she too did the sensible thing and talked it through with God.

The problem stated

"The Lord said to her, 'Two nations are in your womb, and two peoples from within you will be separated; one people will be stronger than the other, and the older will serve the younger'" (Genesis 25:23). How God spoke to Rebekah we are not told, whether directly in an audible voice or by means of a vision or theophany. But the prophetic announcement was clear; two nations or peoples are mentioned as well as two individuals, and Rebekah was being made aware that the birth of her twins would have far reaching consequences for the future in the struggle which had already started in the womb. The two nations, Edom and Israel, that would develop from the sons would be hostile to each other, and the older son, contrary to accepted custom, would serve the younger. In this last statement, God was making it clear to Rebekah that the Messianic line and promise would continue through Jacob rather than through Esau as the elder son, and it also helps to explain Rebekah's preference for Jacob as the twins grew to manhood. (Genesis 25:28).

God's sovereignty

"When the time came for her to give birth, there were twin boys in her womb. The first to come out was red, and his whole body was like a hairy garment; so they named him Esau. After this, his brother came out, with his hand grasping Esau's heel; so he was named Jacob. Isaac was sixty years old when Rebekah gave birth to them" (Genesis 25:24–26). We may wonder why God should have chosen Jacob, before the birth occurred, to inherit the divine promise rather than Esau. We can only put it down to God's sovereign choice in the same way that He chose Abraham, and called him from the idolatrous background of Ur of the Chaldeans, to become the cornerstone of the new humanity He was to bring into being. The Apostle Paul refers to the birth of Esau and Jacob in expounding the doctrine of election in the work of salvation.

"Rebekah's children had one and the same father, our father Isaac. Yet, before the twins were born or had done anything good or bad – in order that God's purpose in election might stand: not by works but by him who calls – she was told, 'The older will serve the younger'. Just as it is written, 'Jacob I loved, but Esau I hated'" (Romans 9:10–13). We see from this that our salvation depends entirely upon God's grace, and there is no room for personal pride. On the contrary it makes one very humble, and we can only say in the words of John Newton's hymn, "Amazing grace! how sweet the sound, that saved a wretch like me!" Moreover the doctrine of election imparts a sense of urgency to our desire to see others saved since, although we do not know whom God has elected, we **do** know that there are those whom He **has** appointed for eternal life (Acts 13:48), and therefore we preach Christ to all.

Loss of the birthright

As the brothers grew to manhood the differences in character and temperament became increasingly evident. "The boys grew up, and Esau became a skilful hunter, a man of the open country, while Jacob was a quiet man, staying among the tents. Isaac, who had a taste for wild game, loved Esau, but Rebekah loved Jacob" (Genesis 25:27–28). The divided favouritism of Isaac and Rebekah for their sons carries its own lesson for all parents since nothing is more calculated to cause dissension and unhappiness in the home. All children are a gift from God, and we should cherish them equally. But having said that we must notice that the only reason given for Isaac's preference for Esau is that he "had a taste for wild game", such as Esau the hunter could provide him with. This was hardly the best reason for Isaac's favouritism, and carries with it more than a hint of self-indulgence and fleshly appetite. Rebekah on the other hand, had already received a word from the Lord that Jacob was to be the one through whom the Messianic line would be continued, and therefore her love for him and concern for his future welfare is understandable, if not excusable, in the way she expressed it.

Esau was the rugged outdoor type, in contrast to Jacob who appeared to be a 'much paler sort of creature', quiet and fond of home life. In our society today the Esau type of character is admired by many people for he represents the macho man living life to the full. In that sense he typifies the modern man-of-the-world, sensual and materialistic, intent on gratifying his appetites and desires, sexual and otherwise, and totally unspiritual and godless. Esau's sensuality comes out in the following passage: "Once when Jacob was cooking some stew, Esau came in from the open country, famished. He said to Jacob, 'Quick, let me have some of that red stew! I'm famished!' (That is why he was also called Edom). Jacob replied, 'First sell me your birthright'. 'Look, I am about to die,' Esau said. 'What good is the birthright to me?' But Jacob said, 'Swear to me first'. So he swore an oath to him, selling his birthright to Jacob. Then Jacob gave Esau some bread and some lentil stew. He ate and drank, and then got up and left. So Esau despised his birthright" (Genesis 25:29–34).

Speaking of Esau's character the writer to the Hebrews says: "See that no one is sexually immoral, or is godless like Esau, who for a single meal sold his inheritance rights as the oldest son" (Hebrews 12:16). That was Esau's trouble, he was easy going and careless and lacked discipline of any kind. There are thousands like him in our present day society. They are often decent likeable people but their life and thought is rooted in the things of this world, and they live only for the immediate material experiences of the here and now without a thought for God or the needs of their soul. Like Esau they despise their birthright as those made in the 'image and likeness of God' and sell themselves to the trivialities and 'fading dreams' of a passing world.

His lack of discernment

Another weakness in Esau was his failure to discern between the permanent and the passing. Coming in from the field ravenously hungry the privileges of the birthright seemed at that moment a long way off, and of little value in comparison with the bowl of hot appetising stew. His sensuality and appetite got the upper hand and he blurts out, 'Quick, let me have some of that red stew! I'm famished'. He must have it right now, and in a moment or two he gulps down the stew, exchanging the value of his birthright, with all its blessings for the future, for the satisfaction of the moment. What a bad bargain! 'He lost tomorrow because he snatched so greedily at today'. He lost so much and gained so little.

But folk are doing that all the time in relation to their lack of discernment concerning salvation. They fail to see the temporary nature of the earthly life, and all the pleasures the world has to offer, in comparison with the permanent blessing of becoming a child of God and inheriting a home in heaven. Not that life in this world with its enjoyments is bad, but it is brief and fragile, and if we give ourselves to it wholly we are selling ourselves short. God made man for higher things when He "breathed into him the breath of life, and man became a living being". He meant man to have fellowship with Himself in this life, and, when it comes to its close, to enter into eternal life in His holy presence. It is in this matter of discernment that we see the essential difference between Jacob and Esau. Jacob possessed what Esau lacked, a sensitivity to eternal values. Jacob had his faults and weaknesses as his life story will show, although he overcame them with God's help, but he also had a sense of spiritual destiny and the insight to see the permanent value of the birthright which Esau so easily and lightly despised. Indeed it may have been that Rebekah had told him of the special message she had received from God that the Messianic line would be continued through him.

Our birthright

The story of Esau and Jacob carries with it a warning concerning the birthright that is ours in the Lord Jesus Christ. Peter describes it in these words: "Praise be to the God and Father of our Lord Jesus Christ! In his great mercy he has given us new birth into a living hope through the resurrection of Jesus Christ from the dead, and into an inheritance that can never perish, spoil or fade – kept in heaven for you" (1 Peter 1:3–4). If we have experienced regeneration through the New Birth by the Holy Spirit, then we cannot lose our spiritual birthright in the way Esau lost his. But, and this is where the warning comes, we can lose much of the spiritual blessing that comes with it. Through the corrosive effects of worldliness, and the pull of the glitzy life-style all around us, we can so easily drift from God and lose the joy of our salvation. Moreover we lose all that the Christian life has to offer, the appreciation of God's Word in the Bible, the encouragement and thrill that comes in the act of worship, the fellowship with other believers, the awareness that the Holy Spirit is guiding and watching over us. All these blessings we can foolishly exchange for the 'pleasures of sin' and in so doing we despise our birthright and squander our spiritual inheritance in Christ. May God keep us from losing so much to gain so little.

Isaac the pacifist

READ GENESIS CHAPTER 26

We said earlier in our study that the information given about Isaac is nowhere as full and detailed as that given about his father Abraham. Indeed this present chapter is the only one that deals exclusively with his life, and so helps us to understand something of his character and the kind of man he really was. On the whole we get the feeling that he lacked the strength of personality we associate with Abraham. Moreover we said earlier that he lived for the most part a quiet and uneventful life, and that is perfectly true, but we must not conclude from that that he had no problems or difficulties to contend with.

The truth is, no one's life is without trials of one kind or another. As the book of Job reminds us, "Man is born to trouble as surely as sparks fly upward" (Job 5:7). Trouble is a part of life for there is something in human nature that disposes man to trouble, and that 'something' is sin, whether one's own or that of other people. We live in a fallen world, therefore we ought not to be surprised when the effects of the Fall, in the form of trials and afflictions, come into our lives. What is important is not so much the trials themselves, but how we react to them when they come.

The famine

One severe trial Isaac had to contend with was the famine that developed in the part of Canaan where he was then living. "Now there was a famine in the land – besides the earlier famine of Abraham's time – and Isaac went to Abimelech king of the Philistines in Gerar" (Genesis 26:1). A hundred years or more had passed since the earlier famine during Abraham's lifetime so that the Abimelech mentioned here was either the son or grandson of the Abimelech mentioned in chapter 20. Just as some commentators regard Abraham's decision to go down to Egypt during the famine as an act of sinful disobedience, so Isaac's decision to go to Gerar is also questioned. Canaan was the land of promise, it is said, and he should have trusted God to provide for him and his family during the famine.

But we are not told that God was displeased with him, and in any case Gerar was a part of Canaan although at that time it was possessed by the Philistines. Furthermore, Isaac was acting very sensibly in going down to Gerar where the famine wasn't nearly as bad and where he could provide for his family. As we said earlier, when dealing with Abraham's servant in finding a bride for Isaac (Genesis 24), God expects us in the difficult situations of life to use our own initiative and sanctified common sense. Planning and divine guidance go together. We are not meant to wait for some miraculous intervention on God's part, when there are things we ourselves can do in the face of life's difficulties and trials.

The warning

It seems from the record that Isaac may have been contemplating going down to Egypt like Abraham before him, but God intervened with a warning, "The Lord appeared to Isaac and said, 'Do not go down to Egypt; live in the land where I tell you to live. Stay in this land for a while, and I will be with you and will bless you'" (Genesis 26:2–3). God was being very gracious to Isaac in giving him definite guidance and instruction, especially in connection with Egypt. Was this because God could see that, with his particular character, Isaac would be exposing himself in Egypt to the same temptation that had earlier faced Abraham, and where he had failed so badly? Furthermore, as if to reinforce and strengthen Isaac's resolve, God very graciously re-affirms the covenant promise. "'For to you and your descendants I will give all these lands and will confirm the oath I swore to your father Abraham. I will make your descendants as numerous as the stars in the sky and will give them all these lands, and through your offspring all nations on earth will be blessed, because Abraham obeyed me and kept my requirements, my commands, my decrees and my laws.' So Isaac stayed in Gerar" (Genesis 26:3–6).

The Bible is full of such warnings against exposing ourselves deliberately to the assaults of Satan. Sometimes we can be too confident of our spiritual strength, hence Paul's warning, "so if you think you are standing firm, be careful that you don't fall!" (1 Corinthians 10:12). Again and again in the history of warfare, citadels and fortresses have fallen because the defenders have failed to guard them at their strongest point. And sometimes we underestimate the power Satan wields over the minds and wills of men, and which is especially concentrated and malevolent where believers are concerned.

The temptation

But in spite of the warning about not going down to Egypt, and in spite of God's promise that He would protect him, Isaac nevertheless succumbed to the very temptation his father Abraham had fallen into years earlier. "When the men of that place asked him about his wife, he said, 'She is my sister,' because he was afraid to say, 'She is my wife.' He thought, 'The men of this place might kill me on account of Rebekah, because she is beautiful'" (Genesis 26:7). There is every possibility that he had learned of Abraham's experience earlier but he failed to learn anything from it. For here he was, telling a deliberate lie to protect his own life at the expense of Rebekah's virtue. It was cowardly and shameful and showed a complete lack of trust in God's promise to protect him in the land of the Philistines.

What led him to do such a thing? Was it that he thought to himself that since Abraham had not suffered too badly as a result of his deception, that he might get away with it too? But what about God? All sin in the end is not simply a sin against man but a sin against God. Remember Joseph's words when tempted by Potiphar's wife to commit adultery with her? "How then could I do such a wicked thing and sin against God?" (Genesis 39:9). Recall also Peter's words in response to the lying of Ananias and Sapphira: "What made you think of doing such a thing? You have not lied to men but to God" (Acts 5:4). If only we reminded ourselves that ultimately it is God that we are cheating on and lying to, then perhaps we wouldn't fall so easily in the face of temptation. Neither should we trade on God's mercy, telling ourselves, when we deliberately give way to temptation, that God will forgive us. We put ourselves in a perilous position when we forget that God is holy as well as loving and forgiving.

Isaac also failed to learn from the experience of another – his father Abraham. The idea that we have to experience a thing personally before we can really appreciate what it is all about is not always true. There is such a thing as learning from the collective experience of mankind. I don't have to fight in a war to know that it brings misery and suffering. I don't have to be a drug addict to know the harm drugs can do to me. I can learn about these evil effects from the experience of others, and if we put this learning process into practice where temptation is concerned it could save us from a lot of unhappiness in our Christian lives.

The rebuke

Just as had happened to Abraham as a result of his deception of the earlier Abimelech, the same thing happened with Isaac. He was eventually found out and was severely rebuked by Abimelech. "When Isaac had been there a long time, Abimelech king of the Philistines looked down from a window and saw Isaac caressing his wife Rebekah. So Abimelech summoned Isaac and said, 'She is really your wife! Why did you say, 'She is my sister?' Isaac answered him, 'Because I thought I might lose my life on account of her.' Then Abimelech said, 'What is this you have done to us? One of the men might well have slept with your wife, and you would have brought guilt upon us.' So Abimelech gave orders to all the people: 'Anyone who molests this man or his wife shall surely be put to death'" (Genesis 26:8–11).

As was said earlier when dealing with Abraham's experience, this is a picture of the man of the world rightly and justly passing judgement on the man of God. A sad and shameful picture, and one seen all too often in relation to ourselves. Worldly secular people can, and do, appear at times in a far better light morally than Christian believers. And when this happens it means that the Christian has lost his testimony, and anything he might say afterwards relating to the gospel carries no weight with the worldly person. Indeed, the world has its own way of describing such a Christian: "I cannot hear what you are saying, because your actions speak so loud".

The peacemaker

In the remaining verses of this chapter we see Isaac in a very different light. He is now settled in Gerar, and whereas before he had followed the pastoral life only with flocks and herds, he now begins to practise agriculture. "Isaac planted crops in that land and the same year reaped a hundredfold, because the Lord blessed him. The man became rich, and his wealth continued to grow until he became very wealthy. He had so many flocks and herds and servants that the Philistines envied him. So all the wells that his father's servants had dug in the time of his father Abraham, the Philistines stopped up, filling them with earth. Then Abimelech said to Isaac, 'Move away from us, you have become too powerful for us.' So Isaac moved away from there and encamped in the Valley of Gerar and settled there. Isaac reopened the wells that had been dug in the time of his father Abraham, which the Philistines had stopped up after Abraham died, and he gave them the same names his father had given them" (Genesis 26:12–18).

It was inevitable that Isaac's growing prosperity, and his decision to reopen the wells of his father Abraham, should be seen by the Philistines as a threat and claim to the land, and would eventually lead to conflict. In Abimelech's words, "you have become too powerful for us". Water was a vital commodity in that part of the world and the Philistines were determined to keep possession of it for themselves, and to use Isaac's attempts to find fresh sources of supply as an excuse to drive him from the land. "Isaac's servants dug in the valley and discovered a well of fresh water there. But the herdsmen of Gerar quarrelled with Isaac's herdsmen and said, 'The water is ours!' So he named the well Esek, because they disputed with him. They dug another well, but they quarrelled over that one also; so he named it Sitnah. He moved on from there and dug another well, and no-one quarrelled over it. He named it Rehoboth, saying, 'Now the Lord has given us room and we will flourish in the land'" (Genesis 26:19–22).

In this passage we clearly see the meek, peace-loving side of Isaac's personality and this is something for which he is to be commended. After all, had he wanted to he could have resisted the Philistines in the dispute over the wells, and in all probability defeated them, since Abimelech himself had acknowledged, "you have become too powerful for us" (Genesis 26:16). But that was not Isaac's way of doing things, and in that respect at least, God found his attitude of meekness acceptable and blessed him because of it. "From there he went up to Beersheba. That night the Lord appeared to him and said, 'I am the God of your father Abraham. Do not be afraid, for I am with you; I will bless you and will increase the number of your descendants for the sake of my servant Abraham.' Isaac built an altar there and called on the name of the Lord. There he pitched his tent, and there his servants dug a well" (Genesis 26:23–25). Furthermore,

Abimelech king of the Philistines recognised that Isaac's meekness in the face of aggression was not a sign of weakness but of God's strength and protection. "They answered, 'We saw clearly that the Lord was with you; so we said, 'There ought to be a sworn agreement between us' – between us and you. Let us make a treaty with you that you will do us no harm, just as we did not molest you but always treated you well and sent you away in peace. And now you are blessed by the Lord'. Isaac then made a feast for them, and they ate and drank. Early the next morning the men swore an oath to each other. Then Isaac sent them on their way, and they left him in peace" (Genesis 26:28–31).

Meekness is not weakness, as our Lord Himself makes clear in the beatitude: "Blessed are the meek for they shall inherit the earth" (Matthew 5:5). For the secular person such a philosophy is nonsense, because this is a tough old world and if you are meek and peaceable then you are likely to go to the wall and people will trample on you, and you certainly won't inherit the success and riches of the earth. But that kind of thinking results from a misunderstanding of the true meaning of 'meekness'. It is not a grovelling servile spirit or a lack of manliness. Moses was a born leader and a man of great moral strength, yet he is described as among the meekest on the earth (Numbers 12:3). Peter and Paul were by no means men of a timid nature and both were great leaders, but when Christ controlled their lives they showed their meekness in the willingness to accept beatings and imprisonment and eventually a martyr's death. Meekness is the harnessing of our natural powers and energies by the Spirit of God, thus enabling us to get a grip on our lives and to deny the old self or pride and arrogance to gain control over us. Above all let us not forget that those who manifest the meekness of Christ will indeed one day inherit the earth. As Peter puts it: "But in keeping with his promise we are looking forward to a new heaven and a new earth, the home of righteousness" (2 Peter 3:13).

The last two verses of this chapter are best understood in the context of what we said earlier when assessing Esau's character as sensual, earthbound, and intent mainly on satisfying his own appetites and desires.

The stolen blessing

The story contained in this chapter makes uncomfortable reading, but like other incidents in the Bible its inclusion confirms the truthfulness and honesty of the Word of God. It gives us a picture of a godly home torn apart by jealousy and deceit, and all four characters – Isaac, Esau, Rebekah and Jacob – appear in a very poor light. Nevertheless there are important lessons to be learned from a story like this, beginning with the role of Isaac.

Thwarting God's purpose

Isaac is now an old man, possibly close to 140, and he feels death approaching, although in fact he lived for a further forty years or so after the events recorded in this chapter. "When Isaac was old and his eyes were so weak that he could no longer see, he called for Esau his older son and said to him, 'My son'. 'Here I am,' he answered. Isaac said, 'I am now an old man and don't know the day of my death. Now then, get your weapons – your quiver and bow – and go out to the open country to hunt some wild game for me. Prepare me the kind of tasty food I like and bring it to me to eat, so that I may give you my blessing before I die'" (Genesis 27:1–4). There are two things we learn from this.

First of all it is evident that the seeds of dissension and unhappiness had been sown in Isaac's home a long time before when we are told: "Isaac, who had a taste for wild game, loved Esau, but Rebekah loved Jacob" (Genesis 25:28). As we noted earlier nothing is more calculated to disrupt family life than favouritism on the part of the parents. Our children are God's gift to us and we should love them alike. But even more disturbing was the fact that Isaac's 'taste for wild game' was the reason for his preference for Esau. Fleshly appetite and self-indulgence seems to have been a weakness with him, since in this chapter again his love of food appears to dominate his thinking even at the moment when he is engaged in the serious business of giving Esau the patriarchal blessing. "Prepare me the kind of tasty food I like and bring it to me to eat, so that I may give you my blessing before I die" (Genesis 27:4).

Amazing isn't it, that such a spiritual man should be governed by physical appetite? But it can be a failing with any of us, if not with regard to gluttony and food, then with other things. That is why the gospel warns us against the uncontrolled life. Paul puts it like this. "So I say, live by the Spirit, and you will not gratify the desires of the sinful nature ... The acts of the sinful nature are obvious: sexual immorality, impurity and debauchery; idolatry and witchcraft; hatred, discord, jealousy, fits of rage, selfish ambition, dissensions, factions and envy; drunkenness, orgies, and the like. I warn you, as I did before, that those who live like this will not inherit the kingdom of God" (Galatians 5:16–21).

His point is that the uncontrolled life dominated by fleshly appetite, lust, and self-indulgence means that freedom has degenerated into licence and society destroys itself. "If you keep on biting and devouring each other, watch out or you will be destroyed by each other" (Galatians 5:15). That describes a society like ours where self-restraint and self-control are out of fashion and self-indulgence and self-desire are in. In every area of activity; sex, pleasure, entertainment, artistic expression, there must be no curtailment of personal freedom and we are encouraged to do what we like. The result is we are being consumed and destroyed by the excesses of uncontrolled appetites, lusts and self-desire.

Second, and more sinful, was Isaac's deliberate intention to thwart God's purpose from being fulfilled in Jacob. Back in chapter 25 we learned that Rebekah had already been told by God, when the twins were still in her womb, that the Messianic line and Abrahamic promise would be continued through Jacob rather than Esau as the older son. She must surely have shared this knowledge with her husband Isaac, but in spite of that he still held on to the idea that Esau was his rightful heir as the older son, and that the birthright and the patriarchal blessing were rightfully his. He seems to have had a blind spot concerning Esau even when he showed his contempt for the spiritual significance of the birthright by exchanging it for a bowl of lentil stew.

Isaac's intention to subvert the will of God in giving Esau the blessing was clearly done secretly without the knowledge of Rebekah and indicates that he knew in his heart that it was wrong and sinful. More than that it was a device that was both stupid and short-sighted. For although he could hide it from Rebekah he should have known he could not hide it from God. Furthermore human devices, however clever, can never thwart the fulfilment of the purposes of a sovereign God. All through history man has been slow to learn the lesson of God's omnipotence in the control of human affairs and it has been the cause of untold suffering and misery. Even a godly man like Job had to learn the hard way to let God be God in the working out of His sovereign will, and was forced to confess at the end of his trial, "I know that you can do all things; no plan of yours can be thwarted" (Job 42:2).

The big question in the end is this; are we prepared to accept that God, with His superior wisdom and power, must be allowed to govern and control events in this world according to His plan and purpose, or do we insist on running our lives according to our own rules, and are we prepared to accept the consequences?

Ends and means

"Now Rebekah was listening as Isaac spoke to his son Esau. When Esau left for the open country to hunt game and bring it back, Rebekah said to her son Jacob, 'Look, I overheard your father say to your brother Esau, 'Bring me some game and prepare me some tasty food to eat, so that I may give you my blessing in the presence of the Lord before I die.' Now, my son, listen carefully and do what I tell you: Go out to the flock and bring me two choice young goats, so that I can prepare some tasty food for your father, just the way he likes it. Then take it to your father to eat, so that he may give you his blessing before he dies'" (Genesis 27:5–10).

Rebekah's 'listening' was probably 'eavesdropping', and immediately she is aware of Isaac's intentions for Esau she develops a strategy to prevent it happening. The plan outlined in verses 11–17 was to deceive Isaac, who was almost blind, into thinking that Jacob was Esau and to give him the patriarchal blessing. It was an audacious plan but just as sinful and short-sighted as Isaac's plan. Even Jacob, who was to benefit from the deception, was hesitant at first and could foresee the possible danger of incurring his father's curse rather than his blessing. "What if my father touches me? I would appear to be tricking him and would bring down a curse on myself rather than a blessing" (Genesis 27:12).

The only thing to be said in Rebekah's favour is that her motive was worthier than Isaac's was. She knew it was God's intention that the birthright, and the blessing associated with it, should go to Jacob, and she acted on the principle that the end justifies the means. But she was wrong. We must never justify our sin and wrongdoing by claiming that it serves some greater good. That is the very argument Paul condemns in those people who were claiming that our sin gives God a chance to show His grace and mercy towards us. "Someone might argue, 'If my falsehood enhances God's truthfulness and so increases his glory, why am I still condemned as a sinner?' Why not say – as we are being slanderously reported as saying and as some claim that we say – 'Let us do evil that good may result?' Their condemnation is deserved" (Romans 3:7–8).

Rebekah's other mistake was to think that she could do God's work for Him, as if He needed her deceitful strategy to fulfil His purpose to give Jacob the patriarchal blessing. Abraham and Sarah had made the same mistake earlier when they thought they could do God's thinking for Him when they conspired together to bring about the birth of Ishmael in the hope that he would become the promised son. But the outcome was disastrous since, with the birth of Isaac later, all they succeeded in doing was to lay the foundation for that deep hatred which has characterised relations between Jews and Arabs down to the present day. We should never forget that God not only ordains the end, but He also ordains the means to that end. In short, we must let God be God.

In spite of any misgivings he may have had at the outset, Jacob went along with his mother's plan and showed himself to be even more deceitful than she was, for one lie led to another. "He went to his father and said, 'My father'. 'Yes, my son,' he answered. 'Who is it?' Jacob said to his father, 'I am Esau, your firstborn. I have done as you told me. Please sit up and eat some of my game so that you may give me your blessing'. Isaac asked his son, 'How did you find it so quickly, my son?' 'The Lord your God gave me success,' he replied" (Genesis 27:18–20). So the miserable deception unfolds down to the point at verse 27 where Jacob receives the patriarchal blessing with a Judas kiss like that which betrayed the Lord Jesus. "So he went to him and kissed him. When Isaac caught the smell of his clothes he blessed him ..." (Genesis 27:27).

Once embarked on his course of deception Jacob was forced to tell one lie after another even verging on blasphemy by implicating God Himself in his lying. "Isaac asked his son, 'How did you find it so quickly, my son?' 'The Lord God gave me success,' he replied". This was inexcusable and in no way can we condone it, however worthy the motive. I disagree emphatically with the conclusion of Henry M. Morris in his commentary (The Genesis Record, Evangelical Press page 435) that there are certain exceptions in scripture where God approves of lying and deception. God hates lying and deception as is clear from our Lord's words when speaking of the devil, "he is a liar and the father of lies" (John 8:44). Likewise when Ananias and Sapphira conspired to deceive the early church in the matter of the sale of their property Peter said, "Ananias, how is it that Satan has so filled your heart that you have lied to the Holy Spirit ... you have not lied to men but to God" (Acts 5:3–4). Jacob, by his crafty unscrupulous deception, was not only cheating on his father but he was cheating on God. For that is what lying is in the end, and we cannot defend it.

What we can say is that God in His goodness and sovereign power overruled in the situation and allowed the blessing to be given, thus achieving His own purpose but without excusing Jacob's guilt. "When Isaac caught the smell of his clothes, he blessed him and said, 'Ah, the smell of my son is like the smell of a field that the Lord had blessed. May God give you of heaven's dew and of earth's richness – an abundance of corn and new wine. May nations serve you and peoples bow down to you. ... May those who curse you be cursed and those who bless you be blessed'" (Genesis 27:27–29). Again and again in the scriptures we see the overruling power of God intervening to prevent His sovereign purpose from being frustrated by the wilfulness and disobedience of His servants. This was certainly true of Jacob, for as we shall see it took many years before he was able, by God's grace, to rid himself of the deceitful streak in his character.

Esau's tears
No sooner had Jacob left his father's presence than Esau entered bringing

the wild game Isaac had asked for. "He too prepared some tasty food and brought it to his father. Then he said to him, 'My father, sit up and eat some of my game, so that you may give me your blessing.' His father Isaac asked him, 'Who are you?' 'I am your son,' he answered, 'your firstborn Esau'. Isaac trembled violently and said, 'Who was it then that hunted game and brought it to me? I ate it just before you came and I blessed him – and indeed he will be blessed'" (Genesis 27:31–33). The phrase 'Isaac trembled violently' is very expressive of the shock to his nervous system when he realised what had happened. It was not merely anger at being outwitted, but a sense almost of holy fear that his attempt to defy the divine will was known to God, who had overruled in the situation.

Esau on the other hand was consumed with anger and self-pity. "When Esau heard his father's words, he burst out with a loud and bitter cry and said to his father, 'Bless me – me too, my father!' But he said, 'Your brother came deceitfully and took your blessing.' Esau said, 'Isn't he rightly named Jacob? He has deceived me these two times: he took my birthright, and now he's taken my blessing!' … Esau said to his father, 'Do you have only one blessing, my father? Bless me too, my father!' Then Esau wept aloud" (Genesis 27:34–38). We can't help feeling sorry for Esau, but it was his own wilfulness that brought about his miserable condition. He was lying when he said that Jacob 'took my birthright'. The truth was he had despised it and regarded it as so worthless that he traded it for a bowl of lentil stew.

Now that he is older and wiser he tries to retrieve something as the firstborn by seeking to change his father's mind regarding the blessing. But it was too late! As the writer to the Hebrews says: "See that no-one is sexually immoral, or is godless like Esau, who for a single meal sold his inheritance rights as the oldest son. Afterwards, as you know, when he wanted to inherit this blessing, he was rejected. He could bring about no change of mind though he sought the blessing with tears" (Hebrews 12:16–17). Isaac was now convinced that God's hand was in the blessing he had given Jacob and God does not change His mind. The blessing he eventually bestowed on Esau (Genesis 27:39–40) was of a purely secondary nature and nothing whatever to do with the Abrahamic promise.

Esau's tears were not a sorrowful repentance for his wickedness in rejecting his birthright, but an expression of his anger at Jacob and his frustration at losing out on the material advantages that the blessing of the firstborn would have brought him. That is clear from what we are told in verse 41: "Esau held a grudge against Jacob because of the blessing his father had given him. He said to himself, 'The days of mourning for my father are near; then I will kill my brother Jacob'". In referring to Esau's rejection, the writer to the Hebrews is warning Christians not to treat lightly the spiritual privileges that are ours in Christ in favour of the pleasures of this world since we may lose them beyond recovery. It is also a warning to unbelievers that if they persist in rejecting the blessing of salvation, when the day of God's grace is over it will be too late to repent.

Now that Jacob's life is in danger from his brother's anger he is advised by his mother Rebekah to leave home for a while until the whole affair blows over. "'Now then my son, do what I say: Flee at once to my brother Laban in Haran. Stay with him for a while until your brother's fury subsides. When your brother is no longer angry with you and forgets what you did to him, I'll send word for you to come back from there. Why should I lose both of you in one day?' Then Rebekah said to Isaac, 'I'm disgusted with living because of these Hittite women. If Jacob takes a wife from among the women of this land, from Hittite women like these, my life will not be worth living'" (Genesis 27:43–46). The expression 'Why should I lose both of you in one day?' probably refers to Jacob's murder by Esau, and Esau's own death as a result of some judicial process following that murder. Rebekah may have thought that her unscrupulous plans were working out satisfactorily, but she little realised the trouble that lay ahead. As we follow the life of Jacob through the next nine chapters we shall see that his absence from home, far from being the 'little while' Rebekah had in mind, would in fact last twenty years, and it is almost certain that he never again saw his mother in this life.

Jacob's dream

READ GENESIS CHAPTER 28

With the opening of this chapter, it is evident that Isaac had now fully accepted that Jacob was the one God had chosen to carry on the Messianic promise since he is now concerned to provide a wife for him from among his own people, rather than from one of the surrounding tribes. "So Isaac called for Jacob and blessed him and commanded him: 'Do not marry a Canaanite woman. Go at once to Paddan Aram, to the house of your mother's father Bethuel. Take a wife for yourself there, from among the daughters of Laban, your mother's brother'" (Genesis 28:1–2). In making this provision for Jacob to take a wife from among his own people Isaac was doing what his own father Abraham had done for him many years before. The difference was he should have done it a lot earlier, and his failure to do so shows how reluctant he was to accept that Jacob was to perpetuate the Abrahamic promise.

But all that was now over and Isaac sends Jacob on his way with the patriarchal blessing. "'May God Almighty bless you and make you fruitful and increase your numbers until you become a community of peoples. May he give you and your descendants the blessing of Abraham, so that you may take possession of the land where you now live as an alien, the land God gave to Abraham.' Then Isaac sent Jacob on his way, and he went to Paddan Aram, to Laban son of Bethuel the Aramean, the brother of Rebekah, who was the mother of Jacob and Esau" (Genesis 28:3–5). As Jacob travelled on his journey he must have been deeply uneasy in his conscience since, in spite of his father's blessing, there was nothing in his recent behaviour of which he could be proud, and in addition he was leaving behind a brother who was now his bitterest enemy. But unknown to him he was about to enter into one of the greatest and most enduring experiences of his life – a personal encounter with the living God.

The Bethel experience

On the first stage of his journey Jacob arrived at the wild heights around Bethel as darkness was falling, and he lay down to sleep. "Jacob left Beersheba and set out for Haran. When he reached a certain place, he stopped for the night because the sun had set. Taking one of the stones there, he put it under his head and lay down to sleep. He had a dream in which he saw a stairway resting on the earth, with its top reaching to heaven, and the angels of God were ascending and descending on it. There above it stood the Lord, and he said: 'I am the Lord, the God of your father Abraham and the God of Isaac...'" (Genesis 28:10–13).

The first thing we learn from this concerns the symbolism of the "stairway resting on the earth with its top reaching to heaven". This was surely intended to teach Jacob, and us, that there is an open communication between earth and heaven, between man and God. More significantly, the angels ascending and descending between earth and heaven indicate that this communication is initiated by God and not by man. It is God who reaches down to man and not man who reaches up to find God, as is sometimes thought. In the book of Job, Zophar asks the question: "Can you fathom the mysteries of God? Can you probe the limits of the Almighty? They are higher than the heavens – what can you do? They are deeper than the depths of the grave – what can you know? Their measure is longer than the earth and wider than the sea" (Job 11:7–9). He is saying that man by his own efforts can never hope to reach up to God and understand him by means of his religious ritual or philosophy, and if we are to know God at all it can only be if God reveals Himself to us. And this He has done supremely in coming to earth in the person of His Son the Lord Jesus Christ.

Indeed Jesus Himself refers to this stairway in Jacob's dream as a type of Himself. When Nathaniel acknowledged Him as Messiah Jesus said to him: "I tell you the truth, you shall see heaven open, and the angels of God ascending and descending on the Son of Man" (John 1:51). He is claiming there that He Himself is the 'stairway' or communicator of God's truth to men.

God's gracious word

God spoke to Jacob and renewed the covenant He had made earlier with Abraham. "I will give you and your descendants the land on which you are lying. Your descendants will be like the dust of the earth, and you will spread out to the west and to the east, to the north and to the south. All peoples on earth will be blessed through you and your offspring. I am with you and will watch over you wherever you go, and I will bring you back to this land. I will not leave you until I have done what I have promised you" (Genesis 28:13–15). What an encouraging word that must have been to Jacob, especially as he needed it at that moment because of the things he was guilty of. He did not deserve such a word of promise; it was all of God's grace. And so it is with us. We do not deserve God's word and promise of salvation in the Gospel. We are guilty sinners, far from the spiritual realities of heaven and the eternal world. But God is gracious and merciful and loves us in spite of our sin and unworthiness and all the things we are guilty of. As Paul says: "But God demonstrates his own love for us in this: While we were still sinners, Christ died for us" (Romans 5:8).

For some folk the Bethel experience when God spoke His gracious Word to them has been a stony pillow like that of Jacob. They have found themselves faced with a hard situation, or illness, or the death of a loved one and it has made them think of eternal things. In their loneliness and sense of helplessness they have seen the foolishness of becoming absorbed with the material things of life to the neglect of their souls, and they have been made to open their lives to God so that He can speak to them His Word of love and comfort. The important thing is that they do not brush the experience aside as 'nonsense' or convince themselves that it is "all in the mind". God is being very gracious to them, as He was to Jacob, giving them the opportunity to get to know Him and the power of His love.

The awakening

"When Jacob awoke from his sleep, he thought, 'Surely the Lord is in this place, and I was not aware of it'. He was afraid and said, 'How awesome is this place! This is none other than the house of God; this is the gate of heaven'" (Genesis 28:16–17). What haunting words these are and how they have echoed in the hearts of believers down through the ages – "surely the Lord is in this place and I was not aware of it". Not that Jacob was unfamiliar with the doctrine of the omnipresence of God any more than ourselves, but now its truth was reinforced in his mind by this experience of knowing God's nearness and hearing His voice in a place and at a time when he did not expect it.

The immensity of God's presence permeates everywhere and, depending on our personal relationship with Him, it can either be a comforting thought or one too dreadful to be considered. In the book of Job, Elihu speaking of God says: "His eyes are on the ways of men; he sees their every step. There is no dark place, no deep shadow, where evildoers can hide" (Job 34:21–22). There is no escaping God's presence, even for Christians when we attempt to because we are outside of His will. Adam discovered that when he attempted to hide from God among the trees in the garden. Jonah discovered it when he fled to Joppa. And Jacob was to learn the same thing on the lonely heights of Bethel, and he was afraid. For the psalmist on the other hand it was a wonderful discovery that God not only knows all about us, down to the tiniest detail of our life, but that He is with us wherever we go. "O Lord, you have searched me and you know me. You know when I sit and when I rise; you perceive my thoughts from afar. You discern my going out and my lying down, you are familiar with all my ways … Where can I go from your Spirit? Where can I flee from your presence? If I go up to the heavens, you are there; if I make my bed in the depths, you are there. If I rise on the wings of the dawn, if I settle on the far side of the sea, even there your hand will guide me, your right hand will hold me fast" (Psalm 139:1–3 and 7–10).

Like Jacob, our love for God may at times be mixed with baseness, but it is comforting to know that His presence is still with us – as it was with him – and that He longs only to bring us closer to Himself in Christ.

The awesomeness of God

Jacob "was afraid and said, 'How awesome is this place! This is none other than the house of God: this is the gate of heaven.' Early the next morning Jacob took the stone he had placed under his head and set it up as a pillar and poured oil on top of it. He called that place Bethel, though the city used to be called Luz" (Genesis 28:17–19). To have a sense of reverential fear in the presence of God is a good thing and is something all too often lacking in the easy-going laid-back kind of approach to God, which characterises certain aspects of today's evangelical worship. The classic statement of wisdom in the Old Testament to be found in Job 28:28, Psalm 111:10 and Proverbs 9:10 is, "The fear of the Lord is the beginning of wisdom". That is both a definition of the religious basis of wisdom and of how we are to possess it. We have to humble ourselves in God's presence and recognise the limitations of our humanity, that there are things in this life that we shall never fully understand in and of ourselves, and that He alone is the One who governs and controls all things by His power.

It was this sense of God's awesome presence that transformed for Jacob that bare lonely hillside into 'the house of God' and 'the gate of heaven', and led him to set up the pillar as a memorial of the experience, and to consecrate it with oil. Henceforth that hillside was sacred ground and he would never forget that it was there that the holy transcendent God met with him. He changed the name from Luz to Bethel and at the end of his life, when close to dying, that was the one experience that he remembered and which brought him greatest hope and comfort. "Some time later Joseph was told, 'Your father is ill' … Jacob said to Joseph, 'God Almighty appeared to me at Luz in the land of Canaan, and there he blessed me…'" (Genesis 48:1–3). Throughout his long and troubled life, in times of temptation and trial and when circumstances would make him doubt the goodness and reality of God, Bethel served as an anchor to his soul and he would say to himself: "I know God is real because He made Himself known to me at Bethel and spoke to me His precious forgiving word so how can I doubt Him now? If He was real then, He is real now".

We all need a Bethel in our Christian lives, some spot, some precious moment when God revealed Himself to us in a special way and which serves as an anchor to our soul when we are tempted to doubt His presence and His love towards us. It is then that we can renew our courage and spiritual stamina by looking back to that experience and saying to ourselves, 'God met with me then and His presence was real to me, therefore I can count on Him now'.

"We have an anchor that keeps the soul,
Steadfast and sure while the billows roll,
Fastened to the rock which cannot move,
Grounded firm and deep, in the Saviour's love"

The vow of commitment

Students of scripture disagree in their interpretation of Jacob's vow. "Then Jacob made a vow, saying, 'If God will be with me and will watch over me on this journey I am taking and will give me food to eat and clothes to wear, so that I return safely to my father's house, then the Lord will be my God. This stone that I have set up as a pillar will be God's house, and of all that you give me I will give you a tenth'" (Genesis 28:20–22).

Some understand this as Jacob's wily scheming brain seeking to make a bargain with God. I do not see it that way myself. In the first place I cannot imagine him adopting such an irreverent shabby attitude so soon after his sense of holy dread in God's presence. Furthermore, God had already assured him: "I am with you and will watch over you wherever you go" (Genesis 28:15). So Jacob, in making his vow, was actually anticipating the fulfilment of that promise. In using the word 'If' he was not doubting God's goodness, but was saying in effect: "since God has promised to be with me to bless me, then I in turn promise that God will always be my God and I will give Him a tenth of all I possess as an expression of my thanksgiving and service".

Understood in this way Jacob's vow was an act of faith and commitment. He still had a long way to go to remain true to his vow, as we shall see, but it was certainly an important step in his spiritual progress. And that has something to say to us about our commitment to God's service especially in the matter of our giving. The tenth or tithe of personal income set aside for God's work is clearly laid down in the Bible (Leviticus 27, Numbers 18 and Deuteronomy 14). If it is maintained that this was under the old dispensation, and therefore does not apply to Christians in the gospel age, then the answer surely must be that if those under the law gave a tenth of their income then we who are living under God's free Grace should give at least that. The tithe or tenth should be seen not as a ceiling for our giving but as a foundation; for the New Testament talks of the free-will offering as well. I remember reading somewhere; 'God demands our tithe, but deserves our offering'.

If only in this alone we were to follow Jacob, the work of God and the progress of the gospel in the world would be greatly enhanced.

Jacob and Laban

The three chapters we are now studying cover the period of twenty years that Jacob spent in the home of his uncle Laban at Haran, and during which time he became a prosperous man acquiring wives and a large family. They were years of hard work and service on Jacob's part, and his relationship with Laban involved a good deal of mistrust and deception, and is not the most instructive reading. However there shines through it all the lovely story of his deep love for Rachel, who was to become the wife he was looking for and the very centre of his devotion in the years ahead.

Arrival at Haran

The journey from Bethel to Haran is passed over in silence, but eventually Jacob arrived at his destination. "Then Jacob continued on his journey and came to the land of the eastern peoples. There he saw a well in the field, with three flocks of sheep lying near it because the flocks were watered from that well. The stone over the mouth of the well was large. When all the flocks were gathered there, the shepherds would roll the stone away from the well's mouth and water the sheep. Then they would return the stone to its place over the mouth of the well" (Genesis 29:1–3). The story continues with Jacob enquiring of the local shepherds concerning the whereabouts of his uncle Laban and, during the conversation, Rachel arrives on the scene to water her father's sheep. "Then Jacob kissed Rachel and began to weep aloud. He had told Rachel that he was a relative of her father and a son of Rebekah. So she ran and told her father" (Genesis 29:11–12).

It may seem strange to us, coming from a different cultural background, to read of Jacob a grown man exhibiting this emotional outburst in kissing and crying aloud on meeting with Rachel. His tears were an expression of deep joy both at meeting his relatives and of thankfulness to God for guiding him on his journey. But we sometimes find such extremes of emotion embarrassing, especially in a religious context, and yet we come across it again and again in the scriptures. Esau 'burst out with a loud and bitter cry' when he missed his father's blessing (Genesis 27:34). When Joseph made himself known to his brothers, he wept so loudly that the Egyptians heard about it (Genesis 45:2). In Ezra's time the people wept and shouted for joy when the foundation of the temple was laid (Ezra 3:12). David expressed his joy by dancing before the ark of the Lord (2 Samuel 6:14). For seven days Job sat in silence and then gave vent to the great emotional conflict within him in a great lament, while his friends tore their robes and sprinkled dust on their heads (Job 2:12–13). And in the New Testament we read that Jesus entered the city to great shouts of joy from the people and said that if they were to keep quiet the very stones would cry out. Furthermore, He himself wept over Jerusalem (Luke 19:40–41). In Acts we read that 'the disciples were filled with joy and with the Holy Spirit' (Acts 13:52).

I wonder sometimes if we are afraid of expressing our emotions, especially in our approach to God in the act of worship? Does it offend us I wonder? When I was a young minister in Wales it was not unusual to hear an 'Amen' or 'Hallelujah' shouted during the preaching. One never hears it these days, which is a great pity to my mind. After all, we are not machines or robots and our emotions and feelings are a part of our God-given humanity, and He has given us tears and laughter with which to praise Him. Of course we have to keep a sense of balance in all this, and we have no wish to defend the extravagances that characterise some worship services. But where the Holy Spirit is present there must surely be warmth and fervour in the soul expressing itself in joyful worship, rather than in the cold formality encouraged by many churches in the mistaken idea that anything else would be unbecoming, irreverent and dishonouring to God.

Jacob's love for Rachel

As we continue reading we get the feeling that the moment he set his eyes on Rachel it was a case of love at first sight for Jacob. For only four weeks later he suggests to Laban that he might marry his daughter. "After Jacob had stayed with him for a whole month, Laban said to him, 'Just because you are a relative of mine, should you work for me for nothing? Tell me what your wages should be.' Now Laban had two daughters; the name of the older was Leah, and the name of the younger was Rachel. Leah had weak eyes, but Rachel was lovely in form and beautiful. Jacob was in love with Rachel and said, 'I'll work for you seven years in return for your younger daughter Rachel.' Laban said, 'It's better that I give her to you than to some other man. Stay here with me'. So Jacob served seven years to get Rachel, but they seemed like only a few days to him because of his love for her" (Genesis 29:14–20).

What a tender expression of romantic love!—Without equal in the world's literature. Nor did Jacob's feelings for Rachel diminish in any way with the passing years, not even when he was deceived by Laban into serving yet another seven years in order to make her his wife. "Then Jacob said to Laban, 'Give me my wife. My time is completed, and I want to lie with her'. So Laban brought together all the people of the place and gave a feast. But when evening came, he took his daughter Leah and gave her to Jacob, and Jacob lay with her... When morning came, there was Leah! So Jacob said to Laban, 'What is this you have done to me? I served you for Rachel, didn't I? Why have you deceived me?'" (Genesis 29:21–25). We may wonder how such a deception could have taken place. But we must not forget that the darkness combined with a heavy veil could easily have concealed Leah's identity. Laban justified his deceit on the grounds that tradition demanded that the older daughter is married first, and he then entered into a further transaction with Jacob to give him Rachel as his wife in return for a further seven years work. "Jacob lay with Rachel also and he loved Rachel more than Leah. And he worked for Laban another seven years" (Genesis 29:30).

Jacob's willingness to work fourteen years to prove his love for Rachel, is surely highly commendable in spite of all his other faults, and breathes the spirit of Paul's exhortation to the Ephesian Christian: "Husbands, love your wives, just as Christ loved the church and gave Himself up for her" (Ephesians 5:25). Here is the true basis for Christian marriage, a love that is self-sacrificing and caring, like that of Christ for His church. As the 'bride' of Christ, the church is often unworthy and full of deficiencies, but Christ still loves her. A husband may see deficiencies in his wife, but he will still love her. Rachel had her shortcomings, as we shall see, but Jacob's love for her remained constant until the day of her death.

The deceiver deceived

Jacob's life and character make a rewarding study because, as we saw at the time of his birth, he was to be God's chosen instrument, but at the same time was full of inconsistencies and contradictions. He was a mixture of the noble and despicable, of strength and weakness, of good and bad. Laban's deception in the matter of Rachel must have shaken Jacob and made him reflect upon his own cruel deception of his blind father, Isaac and Esau his brother, in the matter of the patriarchal blessing. The deceiver was himself deceived and reaping what he had sown. For we cannot expect to play fast and loose in our relationship with God without having to pay a price. God is not mocked. But the real lesson to come out of all this concerns God's discipline of his servant.

Jacob was a man who needed to be changed in the depths of his being in order to become the kind of instrument God could use to fulfil His purposes. The process had already begun with the meeting at Bethel and now, in the matter of his marriage, God was taking the moulding and shaping process of his character a step further. There would be other experiences from which Jacob would learn the lessons God was teaching him until the day would come when his name would be changed from Jacob—meaning 'supplanter' or 'deceiver'—to Israel meaning 'he struggles with God' and signifying God's blessing and acceptance of him. And this disciplinary process is a feature of the lives of many of the Old Testament saints. As we study them we are sometimes perplexed that God should have used, in such a remarkable way, men who were so unworthy and sinful, like Jephthah or Samson. But the important thing is not the characters themselves but the sovereign grace that fashioned out of them instruments for God's glory and praise.

Laying the foundation

Like his grandfather Abraham before him, Jacob's willingness to take both Leah and Rachel as his wives was bound to have repercussions. Polygamy, although accepted at the time, was not God's will and, as with Sarah and Hagar in Abraham's household, it was to lead to jealousy and friction in the home of Jacob. "When the Lord saw that Leah was not loved, he opened her womb, but Rachel was barren. Leah became pregnant and gave birth to a son. She named him Reuben, for she said, 'It is because the Lord has seen my misery. Surely my husband will love me now'" (Genesis 29:31–32). Three more sons, Simeon, Levi and Judah were born to Leah, but when we come to the opening of chapter 30, jealousy is already raising its ugly head. "When Rachel saw that she was not bearing Jacob any children, she became jealous of her sister. So she said to Jacob 'Give me children, or I'll die!' Jacob became angry with her and said, 'Am I in the place of God, who has kept you from having children?' Then she said, 'Here is Bilhah, my maid-servant. Sleep with her so that she can bear children for me and that through her I can build a family'" (Genesis 30:1–3).

"'For my thoughts are not your thoughts, neither are your ways my ways' declares the Lord" (Isaiah 55:8). That is certainly true where this chapter is concerned. In it we see God's purpose unfolding in laying the foundation of the nation Israel in the birth of Jacob's sons along with that of Benjamin later on (Genesis 35), but he accomplishes that purpose in the strangest of ways. As the jealousy and friction mounts between Leah and Rachel they both resort to the most devious and ungodly expedients to gain Jacob's favour and bear him children. And Jacob goes along with it without protest of any kind, so that at the end of the record in verse 23 he ends up with eleven sons and a daughter by four different wives. That could never have been in line with God's will, so that we are bound to ask 'what are we to learn from all this?'

In the first place it reinforces the truth concerning God's overruling of human circumstances in the fulfilment of His own purposes. We see this happening frequently in the Bible. It happened in the life of Abraham when he failed so miserably in Egypt, and also in the matter of the birth of Ishmael. We saw it too in Isaac's attempt to frustrate God's purpose in his efforts to pass on the birthright and the patriarchal blessing to Esau. And here again God overrules Jacob's disobedience in his multiple marriages and in his complicity with the devious strategy of his wives Leah and Rachel. For God's plan from the outset, contained in His promise to Abraham (Genesis 12), was to make for Himself a 'great nation' (Israel), and that purpose was achieved through the foundation laid down in the twelve sons–only one daughter–born to Jacob by his four wives. What Jacob did was wrong, but the lesson is, that however much we mess things up by our own sin and wilfulness, we cannot frustrate the ultimate will of God. But more importantly Satan, for all his wiles and manipulation of God's servants, cannot do so either. He may succeed in frustrating God's purpose in the short term, but God will always succeed in the end. That is the overall message of the Bible, and it is brought most clearly into focus in the death of Christ on the Cross, when it appeared as if Satan had won, but was followed by the triumph of the resurrection. The last word is always with God.

In the second place this does not mean that we can fly in the face of God's will for us and not suffer as a result. Jacob experienced a great deal of unhappiness and conflict in his home life through his multiple marriages, and this in turn influenced the behaviour of his sons in later years. Reuben arrogantly committed incest with one of his father's wives (Genesis 35:22), and Simeon and Levi brought great trouble to Jacob by their extreme cruelty (Genesis 34:25). In addition, the brothers collectively brought great grief to their father by their harsh treatment of his much loved son Joseph (Genesis 37). But hardest of all was the bitter disappointment Jacob experienced concerning his hopes for the future. He had every expectation that the Abrahamic promise of Messiah would be carried on through a son born of his great love for Rachel, but this was not to be, for Rachel was barren for many years. But more importantly God Himself decreed that the Messiah would come from the line of Judah, the fourth son born to Leah the unloved wife (Genesis 29:35). Nor should we overlook the fact that Rachel, the great love of Jacob's life, died at the birth of her second son Benjamin (Genesis 35:19).

In the school of God's discipline Jacob, like us, was having to learn that God is in charge, and he was learning it the hard way.

The longing for home

Fourteen years have now passed since Jacob arrived in Haran and he is now beginning to get homesick. "After Rachel gave birth to Joseph, Jacob said to Laban, 'Send me on my way so that I can go back to my own homeland. Give me my wives and children, for whom I have served you, and I will be on my way. You know how much work I've done for you'" (Genesis 30:25–26). Many of us can share in Jacob's longing for home because it is something fundamental to the human spirit. How lonely and inhospitable this world would be without the warmth and security of home and loved ones. That was God's intention for humanity when He instituted marriage and family life at the dawn of creation (Genesis 2:24 and 4:1–2). And the psalms confirm it. "God sets the lonely in families" (Psalm 68:6). And "Unless the Lord builds the house, its builders labour in vain" (Psalm 127:1). In our society, at the present time, there are forces at work with the deliberate intention of destroying marriage, home, and family life, with the result that we are witnessing, all too clearly, the loosening of those very ties that hold society together, and must lead eventually to its inevitable breakdown. Christian believers must repudiate this trend and do everything in their power to strengthen their home and family life.

Laban was loath to lose Jacob's services and readily acknowledged that he had prospered and been blessed because of him. "But Laban said to him, 'If I have found favour in your eyes, please stay. I have learned by divination that the Lord has blessed me because of you.' He added, 'Name your wages, and I will pay them'. Jacob said to him, 'You know how I have worked for you and how your livestock has fared under my care. The little you had before I came has increased greatly, and the Lord has blessed you wherever I have been. But now, when may I do something for my own household?'" (Genesis 30:27–30). Whether Laban had actually learned anything by the process of divination we cannot say, the important thing is that he himself recognised that his growing prosperity and blessing was ultimately due to God's blessing upon Jacob. That principle holds true still. The Christian believer blessed of God becomes a blessing to others, whether the worldly man recognises it or not. In our own nation, law, education, medicine and social reform have all been shaped and moulded by the Christian faith and millions have benefited as a result.

Jacob prospers

In the discussion with Laban about the wages he was to be paid for further work, Jacob puts forward his own solution: "'Don't give me anything' Jacob replied. 'But if you will do this one thing for me, I will go on tending your flocks and watching over them. Let me go through all your flocks today and remove from them every speckled or spotted sheep, every dark-coloured lamb and every spotted or speckled goat. They will be my wages. And my honesty will testify for me in the future, whenever you check on the wages that you have paid me. Any goat in my possession that is not speckled or spotted, or any lamb that is not dark-coloured, will be considered stolen'. 'Agreed' said Laban. 'Let it be as you have said'" (Genesis 30:31–34). The story continues into chapter 31 and ends at verse 21.

In the meantime Jacob carries out a strategy he had in mind to increase his flocks. Some commentators regard it as a further deception on his part, but I disagree with that. The plan he adopted arose out of his own knowledge of animal husbandry and their reproductive habits. His plan was to peel the bark in stripes from the branches of poplar, almond and plane trees and to place them at the watering troughs when the animals were in heat and came to drink. In this way he believed the animals could be influenced to give birth to striped and coloured offspring (Genesis 30:37–43). Was this just superstition? We cannot be certain but it is certainly true that in scientific circles today more attention is being given to the possibility of prenatal influence. Furthermore, it worked in Jacob's case for we are told in verse 43: "In this way the man grew exceedingly prosperous and came to own large flocks, and maidservants and menservants and camels and donkeys".

With the opening of chapter 31 the atmosphere in Laban's household had changed and there was a growing hostility towards Jacob because of his increased prosperity. "Jacob heard that Laban's sons were saying, 'Jacob has taken everything our father owned and has gained all this wealth from what belonged to our father'. And Jacob noticed that Laban's attitude towards him was not what it had been" (Genesis 31:1–2). The signs were all there that the time had come for him to return to Canaan and this was confirmed for him by a direct word from the Lord. "Then the Lord said to Jacob, 'Go back to the land of your fathers and to your relatives, and I will be with you'" (Genesis 31:3). In the verses following we read that Jacob discusses the matter with Rachel and Leah and they agreed this was the right thing to do. Before leaving this passage there are three points of interest we need to comment on.

First, Jacob is made aware that it was not his own ingenuity or knowledge of animal husbandry that brought about the increase in his prosperity, but the power of God. "'In the breeding season I once had a dream in which I looked up and saw that the male goats mating with the flocks were streaked, speckled or spotted. The angel of God said to me in the dream, 'Jacob'. I answered, 'Here I am'. And he said, 'Look up and see that all the male goats mating with the flock are streaked, speckled, or spotted, for I have seen all that Laban has been doing to you. I am the God of Bethel, where you anointed a pillar and where you made a vow to me. Now leave this land at once and go back to your native land'" (Genesis 31:10–13). At Bethel God had promised to watch over him and bring him back to the land of Canaan. And God was now keeping that promise, as He always does.

Second, we have seen that Laban was involved in the pagan practice of divination, and something of that pagan influence had rubbed off on Rachel. "When Laban had gone to shear his sheep, Rachel stole her father's household gods" (Genesis 31:19). Clearly she was under the impression that these images could give them some kind of protection on the journey they were about to undertake whilst at the same time she believed in Jacob's God. In that respect she typifies those Christians who try to serve God whilst allowing the secular world to shape and mould their thinking and outlook on life.

Third, Jacob was still not free of the deceptive streak in his make-up. "Moreover Jacob deceived Laban the Aramean by not telling him he was running away. So he fled with all he had, and crossing the River, he headed for the hill country of Gilead" (Genesis 31:20–21). Poor Jacob, his greatest battle was not with Laban, or his home environment, but with himself. And that is true of all of us in the Christian life. The down-drag of our sinful nature is always with us, but so is the inner sanctifying power of the Holy Spirit, which enables us to grow in holiness and into the likeness of the Lord Jesus Christ.

Laban pursues Jacob

READ GENESIS CHAPTER 31:22–55

Three days after Jacob's departure, Laban was informed of what had happened, and he was absolutely furious. "On the third day Laban was told that Jacob had fled. Taking his relatives with him, he pursued Jacob for seven days and caught up with him in the hill country of Gilead" (Genesis 31:22–23). The distance from Paddan Aram to Gilead was three hundred miles, and Laban must have pushed his party really hard to have completed the journey in seven days. It shows his state of mind; he was in no mood to be trifled with. It is clear he was determined, either to get back the livestock which he believed Jacob had stolen from him by trickery, or else to persuade him by some means to change his plans and return to Paddan Aram and continue in his service. After all, he had prospered greatly during the time Jacob had been with him and he had no wish to lose his services.

Reckoning without God

But Laban was a worldly thinking man and, in spite of his outward profession of religious faith — like thousands of people today — he reckoned without God. "Then God came to Laban the Aramean in a dream at night and said to him, 'Be careful not to say anything to Jacob, either good or bad'" (Genesis 31:24). This warning must have frightened Laban. Jacob, as we have seen, had his imperfections, but he was still God's man, and the instrument of God's purpose, and in no way was God going to allow an even greater sinner like Laban to frustrate that purpose from being accomplished.

Furthermore, God had already promised Jacob in the revelation given him at Bethel, that He would protect and care for him and bring him back to Canaan. "I am with you and will watch over you wherever you go, and I will bring you back to this land. I will not leave you until I have done what I have promised you" (Genesis 28:15). God never breaks his word, and this helps to explain the warning given to Laban – 'Be careful not to say anything to Jacob, neither good or bad'. We can understand why he was forbidden to say anything bad by way of threats of vengeance, but why was he forbidden to say anything good? It can only mean that he was not to try, with fine words and promises, to entice or persuade Jacob back to Paddan Aram, for this would hinder God's purpose for his servant from being fulfilled.

The confrontation

The meeting with Jacob when it came about was a heated one, but Laban was no fool and he took God's warning seriously. "Jacob had pitched his tent in the hill country of Gilead when Laban overtook him, and Laban and his relatives camped there too. Then Laban said to Jacob: 'What have you done? You've deceived me, and you've carried off my daughters like captives in war. Why did you run off secretly and deceive me? Why didn't you tell me, so that I could send you away with joy and singing to the music of tambourines and harps? You didn't even let me kiss my grandchildren and my daughters good-bye. You have done a foolish thing. I have the power to harm you; but last night the God of your father said to me, 'Be careful not to say anything to Jacob, either good or bad'. Now you have gone off because you longed to return to your father's house. But why did you steal my gods?'" (Genesis 31:25–30).

Laban's tone was one of injured innocence, but in fact his protest was a mixture of gross exaggeration and hypocrisy. His accusation that Jacob had treated his daughters like 'captives of war' was nonsense, since they were Jacob's wives and had gone with him quite willingly. Also his complaint about not having had an opportunity to express his fatherly love for his daughters and grandchildren by kissing them good-bye sounds a little hollow when we recall what those same daughters told Jacob earlier. "Then Rachel and Leah replied, 'Do we still have any share in the inheritance of our father's estate? Does he not regard us as foreigners? Not only has he sold us, but he has used up what was paid for us'" (Genesis 31:14–15). Finally, with a touch of arrogance Laban reminds Jacob that he could have done him great harm, but for the dream of the previous night. "I have the power to harm you; but last night the God of your father said to me, 'Be careful not to say anything to Jacob either good or bad.'"

There are two things worth noting here. First, Laban's threat, "I have power to harm you", reminds us of similar words used by Pilate, the representative of the greatest political power on earth at that time, when he faced the Lord Jesus. "Don't you realise I have power either to free you or to crucify you?" And then the reply of Jesus. "You would have no power over me if it were not given to you from above" (John 19:10–11). Both Laban and Pilate were ignorant of the fact that all power belongs to God. From the moment our first parents fell for Satan's big lie, when he said the them "For God knows that when you eat of it your eyes will be opened, and you will be like God, knowing good and evil" (Genesis 3:5), man has had a power complex. He likes to think he is his own god, with the power to control his own destiny and that of the world, and that he can live independently of his Creator. But such thinking has had disastrous consequences for mankind. All our human systems of thought and philosophy intended to explain the meaning of life and existence, and to establish a world of peace and harmony, of justice and brotherhood, have met only with failure. Governments and politicians, confident of their own power, have attempted — through their laws and institutions, through education and the advances in science and technology — to create this better world, but have met only with failure. What we have in reality is a world of increasing confusion and unhappiness. Of course, it would be foolish to deny the tremendous advances made in medicine, communications, transportation, and the general standard of living. But at the spiritual and moral level we seem hardly to have advanced at all. Millions still experience the brutalities of war, the threat of starvation, and the misery that stems from human violence and greed. Man continues to be, as he always has been, the victim of his own deceits and delusions and still fails to recognise that all power belongs to God.

Second, and this was more positive on Laban's part, he heeded God's warning not to harm Jacob in any way. In this respect he was a lot wiser than those people today who ignore the countless warnings given in God's word in the Bible against sin and godlessness and the rejection of the gospel of Christ. The Bible also teaches a ministry of warnings illustrated by the preaching of Daniel to Belshazzar. The preachers of God's word today are under a similar constraint to exercise a ministry of warnings as well as of comfort. We must not soft-pedal on sin and judgement, but must be careful to remind people of their final accountability to God.

The earthy and the heavenly

In listing his grievances against Jacob, the one that really upset and perplexed Laban was the theft of his household idols. "But why did you steal my gods?" Do we sense a note of perplexity in his question? Was he saying in effect, "why should you want to steal my gods when you worship the true God Jehovah?" It would not have occurred to him for one moment that his own daughter might have stolen them, therefore it must be Jacob. But why, if he was God's servant and God's hand was upon him, as Laban himself had witnessed only too clearly? I wonder if the worldly man or woman is similarly perplexed when they see Christians behaving in a way that is closer to their own outlook on life than that taught by Jesus? Are they confused and baffled because, as Paul puts it, "… the trumpet does not sound a clear call" (1 Corinthians 14:8)?

Jacob was unaware that Rachel had stolen the household gods and he invites Laban to search through the camp. "'But if you find anyone who has your gods, he shall not live. In the presence of our relatives, see for yourself whether there is anything of yours here with me; and if so, take it'. Now Jacob did not know that Rachel had stolen the gods" (Genesis 31:32). Laban searched but found nothing because Rachel had hidden the images in her camel's saddle and was sitting on them (Genesis 31:33–34). From the spiritual standpoint we can't help but notice the strange blending of the earthy and the heavenly, of paganism and spirituality, in the characters of both Laban and Rachel. They have a knowledge of God and are aware of His activity in their lives. That is clear in Rachel's case from her thankfulness to God after the birth of Joseph (Genesis 30:22–23). As for Laban, he acknowledged that God was active in Jacob's life and that he himself had been blessed because of that. He had also had the privilege of God speaking personally to him in his dream. But, at the same time, both of them were tainted with the remnants of paganism and superstition in their worship of idols. Laban also leaned heavily on divination for guidance (Genesis 30:27).

In the light of that we need to remind ourselves of John's affectionate warning: "Dear children, keep yourselves from idols" (1 John 5:21). He does not necessarily have in mind physical images, although these would be included, since the believers at that time would have been surrounded by idols. But his main concern was to warn them against the pagan influences which some of those early Christians had dragged with them into the Christian Church. And that is still a problem today. There is a lot of world-liness in the Church because Christians allow themselves to be influenced by the spirit and thinking of the age, which is a form of idolatry, a blending of the earthy with the heavenly, of paganism with true spirituality. For the essence of idolatry is anything which we allow to usurp the central place which God in Christ should have in the believer's life. And we all need to be warned against that.

The covenant

The final section in this chapter deals with Jacob's emotional and impas-sioned response to the charges Laban had levelled against him, and the covenant they finally entered into to bring the whole unsavoury episode to a peaceful end (Genesis 31:36–55). In no uncertain terms Jacob reminded Laban of the faithful service he had given him over twenty years, and the miserable treatment he had received in return. "If the God of my father, the God of Abraham and the Fear of Isaac, had not been with me, you would surely have sent me away empty-handed. But God has seen my hardship and the toil of my hands, and last night he rebuked you" (Genesis 31:42). The significant thing here is the description of God as the Fear of Isaac, which Jacob repeats in verse 53. This takes us back to chapter 28 and the Bethel experience in which God revealed himself to Jacob as the God of Isaac, and we are then told that Jacob "… was afraid and said, 'How awesome is this place! This is none other than the house of God; this is the gate of heaven.'"

Isaac had served and worshipped God with reverential fear, and that memory, coupled with his own experience at Bethel, led Jacob to do the same. This fear of God is not a slavish fear, or a cringing fear, but rather it is a profound sense of God's holiness which leads us to worship Him with reverence and awe in our souls. Such a holy fear creates within our own hearts a desire for holiness in living in a manner that is pleasing to God. In the seven-fold gift of the Spirit attributed to the coming Messiah, Isaiah says that "he will delight in the fear of the Lord" (Isaiah 11:3). Like the Lord Jesus, our fear of God does not fill us with any sense of dread, but with joy and delight in serving Him.

As a symbol and witness of the covenant both men had entered into, a pillar was set up called Mizpah (watch tower), which indicated that God would keep watch to see that they honoured the agreement. At one point in Job's pain and suffering his view of God became very distorted describing Him as the "watcher of men" (Job 7:20), keeping him under close surveillance and scrutinising his every action. God is indeed the 'watcher of men', but not in this bad sense that He wants to harm us or punish us, but because He is our creator and is concerned about us. His chief desire is to come close to us and to enter into all our human experiences. This He has done supremely in entering our world for the forgiveness of our sins.

The meeting with Esau

READ GENESIS CHAPTERS 32 AND 33

Following the encounter with Laban, Jacob continued his journey through the hill country of Gilead towards Canaan. One wonders what thoughts were going through his mind the nearer he got to the border of the old country he had left twenty years before. The struggle with the old enemy Laban was a thing of the past, but a new crisis was now looming ahead of him – the meeting with his brother Esau whom he had left in a murderous frame of mind all those years before. What kind of reception would he get? Would his brother still hold a grudge against him? Would Esau harm his wives and children even? These, possibly, were the thoughts and feelings troubling Jacob as he drew nearer to home, and the opening verses seem to indicate this.

The angels of God

"Jacob also went on his way, and the angels of God met him. When Jacob saw them, he said, 'This is the camp of God!' So he named that place Mahanaim" (Genesis 32:1–2). God was aware of Jacob's fears and gave him this special revelation to comfort him and calm his spirit. His exclamation, 'This is the camp of God!' and his naming the place 'two camps' (Mahanaim) shows how encouraged he really was. He looked at his own little camp in all its vulnerability and compared it with the mighty strength of God's camp, and his spirit was lifted up.

And isn't that how it is with us? Does it not encourage us, and calm our fears, when confronted by life's crises to have the assurance of God's presence with us? Has He not said: "Never will I leave you; never will I forsake you?" (Hebrews 13:5). For Jacob, this was his third experience of an angelic visit. First at Bethel, then at Haran (Genesis 31:11), and now at Mahanaim. We are not told in what form the angels appeared to him, whether in a dream or vision, or a physical appearance as happened with Abraham and the three visitors (Genesis 18). But the doctrine of angels in the old and new testaments is very prominent and extensive and, among their many activities, they have a special interest in caring for God's people. "Are not all angels ministering spirits sent to serve those who will inherit salvation?" (Hebrews 1:14).

Jacob's preparations

The next 18 verses in this chapter deal with the extensive preparations and precautions undertaken by Jacob in readiness for his meeting with Esau. "Jacob sent messengers ahead of him to his brother Esau in the land of Seir, the country of Edom. He instructed them: 'This is what you are to say to my master Esau: 'Your servant Jacob says, …I have cattle and donkeys, sheep and goats, menservants and maidservants. Now I am sending this message to my lord, that I may find favour in your eyes'. When the messengers returned to Jacob, they said, 'We went to your brother Esau, and now he is coming to meet you, and four hundred men are with him'. In great fear and distress Jacob divided the people who were with him into two groups, and the flocks and herds and camels as well. He thought, 'If Esau comes and attacks one group, the group that is left may escape'" (Genesis 32:3–8).

We read further that Jacob sent a generous gift of more than five hundred animals to Esau, divided into separate herds, and with the instruction to his servants, "'When my brother Esau meets you and asks, 'To whom do you belong, and where are you going, and who owns all these animals in front of you? Then you are to say, 'they belong to your servant Jacob. They are a gift sent to my lord Esau, and he is coming behind us' …For he thought, 'I will pacify him with these gifts I am sending on ahead; later, when I see him, perhaps he will receive me'" (Genesis 32:17–20).

Some Bible commentators have a strange way of interpreting these verses. They seem to think that Jacob's attitude towards Esau, and his extensive preparations, were unworthy of a man who had met with the angels of God. This is Jacob relying on his own crafty scheming brain again, instead of trusting God. One commentator describes Jacob's use of the words, 'my lord Esau' and 'your servant Jacob' as indicating "servile fear", and his attitude as "grovelling humiliation" (*Genesis*, W H Griffith Thomas page 293).

I think this analysis is to misunderstand what Jacob was about. His planning was not any kind of 'crafty scheming' but a wise precaution, and it was certainly not incompatible with his experience of the angelic presence. We saw earlier, in the story of the search for a bride for Isaac, that the servant made elaborate plans as well as depending on prayer and God's guidance. It is right and proper that we should use foresight and planning in directing our affairs, as long as we take God into our plans. And that is precisely what Jacob did, for part of his planning was prayer.

"Then Jacob prayed, 'O God of my father Abraham, God of my father Isaac, O Lord, who said to me, 'Go back to your country and your relatives, and I will make you prosper', I am unworthy of all the kindness and faithfulness you have shown your servant. I had only my staff when I crossed this Jordan, but now I have become two groups. Save me, I pray, from the hand of my brother Esau, for I am afraid he will come and attack me, and also the mothers with their children. But you have said, 'I will surely make you prosper and will make your descendants like the sand of the sea, which cannot be counted'" (Genesis 32:9–12).

I find this a very noble and beautiful prayer. He humbly acknowledges his unworthiness for the blessings God had given him, and he earnestly spells out how afraid he is, and how much he needs God's help. Furthermore, he claims the promise God had given him at Bethel (Genesis 28:14) concerning his descendants, since at this point he was unsure that his family might not be massacred by Esau. God is pleased when we claim His promises in our praying because it shows that we take His Word seriously. C H Spurgeon in his devotional work '*Faith's Cheque-book*' says that the Christian "must believingly present the promise to the Lord as a man presents a cheque at the counter of the bank. He must plead it by prayer, expecting to have it fulfilled".

Struggling with God

"That night Jacob got up and took his two wives, his two maidservants and his eleven sons and crossed the ford of the Jabbok. After he had sent them across the stream, he sent over all his possessions. So Jacob was left alone, and a man wrestled with him till daybreak. When the man saw that he could not overpower him, he touched the socket of Jacob's hip so that his hip was wrenched as he wrestled with the man. Then the man said, 'Let me go, for it is daybreak'. But Jacob replied, 'I will not let you go unless you bless me'" (Genesis 32:22–26).

I find this one of the most difficult passages in the Bible to fully understand. It is a wonderful and mysterious passage which has had a powerful influence, not only on Christians, but on the imagination of secular writers, poets and artists. Redon, Delacroix, Moreau all painted religious works based on Jacob wrestling with the Angel, and Paul Gauguin's interpretation in his famous painting '*Vision after the sermon*' introduced the Symbolist school of art in France. For our purposes we can consider the event under three headings.

When it happened

The first thing we notice is that it was night when the wrestling occurred, and Jacob was alone. These two features in themselves are significant. The hours of darkness, and Jacob's withdrawal from the rest of the family, suggest that he wanted to be alone in the quietness and to meditate and pray, without the distractions of the daytime, before meeting with Esau. We live in a busy, frenetic world, and Satan will exploit all the activities going on around us to keep us from waiting upon God. In the experience of the men and women of the Bible it was often when they were alone in the quietness that God made Himself known. Abraham was alone in the 'thick and dreadful darkness' when God spoke to him (Genesis 15:12). Jacob's first experience of meeting with God was on the lonely hillside of Bethel. Moses was alone in the wilderness when God spoke to him out of the burning bush (Exodus 3). And the Psalmist says, "…when you are on your beds, search your hearts and be silent" (Psalm 4:4), and again: "On my bed I remember you; I think of you through the watches of the night" (Psalm 63:6).

When speaking of our Lord's devotional life Luke says, "But Jesus often withdrew to lonely places and prayed" (Luke 5:16). If Jesus required these times of solitude and quietness in order to replenish his spiritual energies through prayer, then how much more do we. In an increasingly activist society like ours it is essential to build into our daily agenda times when we can be alone with our own thoughts and meditations in order that God might get through to us more clearly.

How it happened

What really did happen to Jacob during those long hours in the darkness? Did he have a dream, or vision, or was it an actual physical contest he engaged in? And was it a man he struggled with, or God, or an angel? The text is clear – "So Jacob was left alone, and a man wrestled with him till daybreak" (Genesis 32:24). But we also read, "So Jacob called the place Peniel, saying, 'It is because I saw God face to face'" (Genesis 32:30). Later, when he was near to dying, he identified God with, "… the Angel who has delivered me from all harm" (Genesis 48:16).

It seems that all three manifestations were involved and that it was an actual physical struggle with the Angel of Jehovah in human form, similar to the appearance to Abraham of the three visitors (Genesis 18). Also, the painful dislocation of Jacob's hip was certainly physical. But underlying the physical wrestling there was a spiritual struggle being carried on in prayer. This is reinforced by Hosea's remark that Jacob, "struggled with the angel and overcame him; he wept and begged for his favour" (Hosea 12:4). This surely teaches us that there are times when prayer is hard work, it becomes a tearful struggle to obtain the blessing we are seeking. God does not always give His gifts easily, but makes us struggle with Him in order to overcome in obtaining that blessing, and to show Him our earnestness.

Why it happened

This contest with the Angel of God was a watershed in the life of Jacob. From the time he had first left home with a guilty conscience, God had been dealing with him, shaping and moulding his character in conformity to His own will and purpose for him as the father of future Israel. First, in the dream at Bethel, and later in the disappointments and hardships of Paddan Aram, God was gradually teaching Jacob to learn to rely more on His grace and power and less on his own cleverness and strategies. That learning process was now coming to its climax as Jacob faced the biggest crisis in his life in the forthcoming meeting with Esau. He had come to the end of his own resources, and was now having to rely entirely on God. That explains his tenacity in hanging on in the struggle and crying with tears (Hosea 12), "I will not let you go unless you bless me" (Genesis 32:26).

The change in his name reinforces that truth. When God asked, "What is your name?" it was not because He did not know it, but to remind Jacob of the kind of man he had been in the past, and the kind of man he will now be in the future. "Then the man said, 'Your name will no longer be Jacob (deceiver), but Israel, because you have struggled with God and with men and have overcome'" (Genesis 32:28). From all this we learn the important lesson that if we are to be 'overcomers' in gaining the spiritual victory over the world, the flesh and the devil, then we must allow God to touch us deep in our souls as He touched Jacob on his thigh. He must humble us, as He humbled Jacob, so that we begin to lean more upon Him and less on ourselves.

The meeting

After all the preparations he had made so carefully, and the precautions he had taken, Jacob's meeting with Esau, when it came about, seemed to be an anti-climax. Instead of hostility, as he expected, he met only with friendship and kindness. "Jacob looked up and there was Esau, coming with his four hundred men; so he divided the children among Leah, Rachel and the two maidservants. He put the maidservants and their children in front, Leah and her children next, and Rachel and Joseph in the rear. He himself went on ahead and bowed down to the ground seven times as he approached his brother. But Esau ran to meet Jacob and embraced him; he threw his arms around his neck and kissed him. And they wept" (Genesis 33:1–4).

It must have been a touching scene, and one that filled Jacob not only with a profound sense of relief but also with real joy. The night before, he had seen God face to face and his life had been spared, and now he was seeing Esau face to face, and instead of destruction his life was again being spared. That can be the only interpretation of his words when he insists that his brother accepts the gift he has prepared for him as a mark of his favour. "'No, please!' said Jacob. 'If I have found favour in your eyes, accept this gift from me. For to see your face is like seeing the face of God, now that you have received me favourably. Please accept the present that was brought to you, for God has been gracious to me and I have all I need.' And because Jacob insisted, Esau accepted it" (Genesis 33:10–11).

Esau was a changed man, he was no longer the vengeful, bitter brother

Jacob had left twenty years before. He was kind and considerate and satisfied with what he had. "But Esau said, 'I already have plenty, my brother. Keep what you have for yourself'" (Genesis 33:9). He even suggests that he should accompany Jacob for the rest of the journey, but Jacob courteously refuses, claiming that his flocks and herds would have to travel at a much slower pace. (Genesis 33:12–15). It seems God had been working in Esau's life as well as Jacob's. We ought never to feel that anyone's life is beyond the power of God to change it for the better. "You can't make a silk purse out of a sow's ear" says the old proverb, but it seems God is doing just that all the time. The Bible is full of instances where God takes a life that is ugly and distorted by sin and greed, and changes it into something that reflects His glory. Take Rahab, her background was one of idolatry and paganism in Jericho, and there was nothing in her life of prostitution that pointed her to God. But she changed by God's grace. Jephthah was another, an outcast and gang-leader, but God changed him to become a judge in Israel. Or Zacchaeus, a hated misfit in Jewish society, but gloriously saved when Christ entered his life. Not only should we believe that God has the power to change lives, but we must make it clear to others that no one needs to stay the way they are.

We said earlier that the meeting of the brothers must have been a touching scene, especially since we are told that they embraced and wept. It is always a beautiful and joyful experience when people who have been separated by their hostility and bitterness of spirit are reconciled in love and forgiveness. Such human coming-together, however, is but a pale shadow of the reconciliation of man with God. The great difference lies in the fact that all the love and forgiveness is on God's side, and none on ours. God had no need to be reconciled to man, since He had never been estranged from him. It was man who became estranged from God through his own sin and disobedience. Whenever reconciliation takes place at the human level, someone has to take the first step, and that is what makes it so hard at times. The amazing thing is that, in the matter of our salvation, it was God who took the first step. As Paul puts it: "…God was reconciling the world to himself in Christ, not counting men's sins against them. And he has committed to us the message of reconciliation" (2 Corinthians 5:19).

In the concluding verses of this chapter (Genesis 33:16–20) Jacob continues his journey, staying at Succoth for a time, but finally arriving at Shechem in Canaan where he purchased some land from the local chieftain, and set up camp. "There he set up an altar and called it El Elohe Israel (the God of Israel)". In doing this he was acknowledging that God had kept the promise made at Bethel twenty years before to bring him back to Canaan (Genesis 28:15). His one mistake was to remain at Shechem too long, instead of making straight for Bethel, and this, as we shall see from the next chapter, was to spell big trouble.

The rape of Dinah

READ GENESIS CHAPTER 34

This is a miserable and ugly chapter full of lust, violence and cruelty of the worst kind, and it brought great shame and disgrace to Jacob's family. But, as we have seen so often in the unfolding of the history of man's redemption, the Bible's honesty and openness in revealing the more disreputable aspects of God's people is itself a testimony to its authenticity and truthfulness as the Word of God.

The rape of Dinah

"Now Dinah, the daughter Leah had borne to Jacob went out to visit the women of the land. When Shechem, son of Hamor the Hivite, the ruler of that area, saw her, he took her and raped her" (Genesis 34:1–2). If only Jacob had remained a short time in Shechem, and then continued his journey to Bethel where God had first met with him and where he had taken his vow, then things would not have turned out in the tragic way they did. But, as so often happens in this life, it is only with hindsight that we see our mistakes, and that impresses upon us our need to be sensitive to the leading of God's spirit in the decisions we make. What happened at Shechem suggests that Jacob must have stayed there for several years, for during that time his children were growing up, and Dinah — the only daughter — was now a young woman. The crime of rape with its fateful consequences is all too common in today's society, and if only for that reason alone this story has certain lessons to teach us.

It was perfectly natural as the only girl in a family of boys that Dinah should have wanted on occasions to have the company of girls of her own age, and so from time to time she "went out to visit the women of the land". The trouble was, these new-found friends were from a pagan background, and the moral standards of the Shechemites were far lower than those she had been brought up with in her father's house. It seems clear from the language used that Dinah did not encourage Shechem in any way but that he forced himself upon her. "Shechem ... saw her, he took her and raped her".

We may feel that she should have been more careful in the matter of the company she chose to mix with, but that would be a little hard on a young girl craving company. However, her experience points clearly to the need for young Christian people to be guarded in their choice of friends and the circles they move in. This is especially true when the time comes for them to leave the restraints of home, and the support and friendship of other young Christians in their local church, and go off to college or university. There they find themselves subjected to new pressures among their peers, and the temptation then is to lower their standards of morality and holiness for fear of ridicule, or of being thought weird.

The responsibility of parents

But Jacob himself was not without blame in all this. His mistake was the decision he made to settle so close to Shechem, with its pagan life-style, and to settle there for several years. This was bound to create spiritual problems, and to put his young family in moral danger. In a godless age like ours family life carries with it enormous responsibilities for Christian parents. On the one hand we do not want to be heavy-handed and deny our children their legitimate pleasures and enjoyments, but on the other hand we must not be blind to their faults and the possibility of their falling into sin.

We must realise that our children have to contend, not only with the increase in evil in today's world, but also with the down-drag of their own sinful nature. In addition there are forces at work in our society which have the deliberate aim of destroying our children's innocence and corrupting their souls. Obviously we cannot monitor every aspect of our children's lives, especially when they are outside the home, but we can and must be concerned to pray that God will protect and guard them against all that is evil.

A right view of sex

Another aspect to all this was the careless attitude of the young man Shechem to sex. What he did in seducing and raping the young Dinah was inexcusable, although we must bear in mind that he came from a godless background where such an act would not have been considered all that terrible. Moreover he loved the girl. "His heart was drawn to Dinah daughter of Jacob, and he loved the girl and spoke tenderly to her. And Shechem said to his father Hamor, 'Get me this girl as my wife'" (Genesis 34:3–4). When Shechem's father later spoke to Jacob we get the feeling that he and his son had no sense of the wrongfulness of what had happened, and thought that the offer of marriage would clear up the whole matter. Jacob and his sons, on the other hand, looking at it from the standpoint of God's people, saw it as a defilement of Dinah and a heinous sin, and they were terribly angry.

"Then Shechem's father Hamor went out to talk with Jacob. Now Jacob's sons had come in from the fields as soon as they heard what had happened. They were filled with grief and fury, because Shechem had done a disgraceful thing in Israel by lying with Jacob's daughter – a thing that should not be done. But Hamor said to them, 'My son Shechem has his heart set on your daughter. Please give her to him as his wife. Intermarry with us: give us your daughters and take our daughters for yourselves. You can settle among us; the land is open to you. Live in it, trade in it, and acquire property in it'" (Genesis 34:6–10). This illustrates in a vivid way the difference in attitude between the Christian and the world towards the whole question of sex. There are those who think that the Bible comes down heavily on sex as if God is against it. That is not so. The Bible is only against illicit sex, and that is a very different thing.

A story like this is a grave warning to Christians not to treat sex outside marriage as a private and personal indulgence, which does not harm anyone else, and therefore something one is perfectly free to engage in whenever one pleases. That is the kind of dangerous philosophy being peddled today in so many TV programmes, magazines and newspapers, and which encourages the kind of sexual activity this story is about. Such an irresponsible approach to sex can spark hatred, bitterness, violence and heart-break as a consequence. That is precisely what happened when the news broke about Dinah, and Jacob's sons took it into their own hands to do something about it.

The angry brothers

Anger is a very powerful emotion when it is uncontrolled, and can make a person act in the most vicious and appalling manner. That is what this last section in our chapter is about, and it carries with it a powerful lesson for Christian people. There is no doubt that Dinah's brothers were terribly angry, and thirsting for revenge. We read earlier, "They were filled with grief and fury, because Shechem had done a disgraceful thing in Israel by lying with Jacob's daughter – a thing that should not be done" (Genesis 34:7). Later, it was Simeon and Levi, the blood brothers of Dinah by Leah, who exacted a terrible revenge on the Shechemites, but all the brothers, it would seem, shared in the plot that made that revenge possible.

"Because their sister Dinah had been defiled, Jacob's sons replied deceitfully as they spoke to Shechem and his father Hamor. They said to them, 'We can't do such a thing; we can't give our sister to a man who is not circumcised. That would be a disgrace to us. We will give our consent to you on one condition only: that you become like us by circumcising all your males. Then we will give you our daughters and take your daughters for ourselves. We'll settle among you and become one people with you. But if you will not agree to being circumcised, we'll take our sister and go'" (Genesis 34:13–17). Motivated by anger and desire for revenge the brothers were engaging in the worst kind of deception. They were using religion and the sacred covenant rite of circumcision as a cloak for treachery and murder. For worse was to come.

"Three days later, while all of them (Shechemites) were still in pain, two of Jacob's sons, Simeon and Levi, Dinah's brothers, took their swords and attacked the unsuspecting city, killing every male. They put Hamor and his son Shechem to the sword and took Dinah from Shechem's house and left. The sons of Jacob came upon the dead bodies and looted the city where their sister had been defiled. They seized their flocks and herds and donkeys and everything else of theirs in the city and out in the fields. They carried off all their wealth and all their women and children, taking as plunder everything in the houses" (Genesis 34:25–29). It might be said in defence of Simeon and Levi that they were also motivated by a holy zeal to keep their faith in God from being polluted by amalgamation with the godless Shechemites. But zeal for God is only commendable when it is in the right spirit, and that was not true of the vengeful spirit of Jacob's sons. Indeed, we recall our Lord's reaction to James and John when they wanted to bring fire down from heaven to destroy the Samaritans. He rebuked them because they were in the wrong spirit (Luke 9:55).

Anger and the Christian

Because it is a human emotion we all experience anger at some time or other. But is it right for the Christian to express this anger? Paul has something to say on this. "In your anger do not sin: Do not let the sun go down while you are still angry" (Ephesians 4:26). So there is a place for the right kind of anger in the Christian life. There were occasions when Jesus was terribly angry. One such time was when He was about to heal a man with a withered hand on the Sabbath day, and the Pharisees resented it. We read: "He looked around at them in anger" (Mark 3:5). He was majestically angry when he whipped the moneychangers and traders out of the temple (John 2:13–17). But in both instances He was expressing a righteous indignation against the Pharisees' willingness to allow needless suffering, and against the desecration of God's house. This was a right kind of anger, and believers would do well to show it more than they do, against all sin and wickedness and injustice in the world.

The wrong kind of anger, on the other hand, is what Paul warns us against; it is uncontrolled, selfish, full of bitterness and the desire for revenge and therefore sinful. That is what made the action of Simeon and Levi so terrible; it was cruel and vindictive and did great harm to the cause of God among the surrounding nations, as is clear from the closing words of Jacob (Genesis 34:30). It is for this reason that Paul's exhortation should be heeded. "Do not take revenge, my friends, but leave room for God's wrath, for it is written: 'It is mine to avenge; I will repay' says the Lord" (Romans 12:19).

Back to Bethel

READ GENESIS CHAPTER 35

After the massacre at Shechem, Jacob's greatest fear was that the surrounding tribes would form a coalition and attack his family. "Then Jacob said to Simeon and Levi, 'You have brought trouble on me by making me a stench to the Canaanites and Perizzites, the people living in this land. We are few in number, and if they join forces against me and attack me, I and my household will be destroyed'" (Genesis 34:30). The truth was that in the affair of Dinah, Jacob had abdicated his authority as head of the household by leaving the matter in the hands of Simeon and Levi, and now he was having to suffer the consequences.

He was left with no alternative but to move on and find a new place to settle with his family. But God was very gracious to his servant and made the decision for him in a fresh revelation. "Then God said to Jacob, 'Go up to Bethel and settle there, and build an altar there to God, who appeared to you when you were fleeing from your brother Esau'" (Genesis 35:1). Some thirty years had passed since Jacob had made his vow to return to Bethel if God would watch over him. It had been a vow of faith and commitment, and although Jacob had not always been true to it, he had not entirely forgotten it either. Throughout his troubled life, with its trials and temptations, the Bethel experience kept before him the vision of the God of Bethel whose goodness and mercy had never failed him. And now God was bringing him back to that sacred spot, so that he might "build an altar there", and re-commit himself to the life of faith and obedience.

"O God of Bethel by whose hand
Thy people still are fed;
Who through this earthly pilgrimage
Hast all our fathers led".

True and false religion

Because of Bethel's sacred associations with the true and living God, Jacob made careful preparations for the return there. "So Jacob said to his household and to all who were with him, 'Get rid of the foreign gods you have with you, and purify yourselves and change your clothes. Then come, let us go up to Bethel, where I will build an altar to God, who answered me in the day of my distress and who has been with me wherever I have gone'" (Genesis 35:2–3). We have seen that Jacob found it a struggle at times to keep hold of his own faith in God, but – added to that – he had not succeeded to any great extent in getting his faith over to the members of his family either. The remnants of the old paganism still clung to them in their images and charms, and Jacob does not seem to have done anything about it. He might even have known about Rachel's household gods by this time. However, we must also keep in mind that the captured Shechemites, who were now part of his household, would have brought their images and false gods with them, and Jacob's instruction might well have been chiefly directed at them.

But the point is that Jacob was clear in his own mind that you cannot mix the true and the false in religion. And in our multi-faith society today that is a lesson the Church has often forgotten. There are church leaders who are perfectly willing to widen the ecumenical debate to include other religions, in which icons and images are objects of veneration and worship. The chief distinctive of the Gospel, on the other hand, is that Christianity is not simply one among other religions, but is totally different from them, because it is a direct revelation of God in Christ and He alone is to be revered and worshipped.

The main feature of false religion in every age is always the same – it is the product of man's own mind and imagination. Millions today worship at the shrines of the gods of man's own making in the form of pleasure, sport, sex, money, science, politics etc. And because they are the products of man's own thinking, they can be of no spiritual use to him since they share his own weakness and failings. Furthermore, these modern gods always let man down, because however much he seeks to manipulate them, they do not deliver on the sense of fulfilment and happiness they promise. But the God of Bethel cannot be manipulated to suit our own requirements, for He does only what pleases Him and is holy and just in all His ways.

Burying the past

"So they gave Jacob all the foreign gods they had and the rings in their ears, and Jacob buried them under the oak at Shechem. Then they set out, and the terror of God fell upon the towns all around them so that no one pursued them" (Genesis 35:4–5). It was not enough for Jacob that the members of his household stop worshipping their false gods, but that the idols themselves should be totally disposed of. He knew that the physical image itself was an object of veneration and thus he buries them, symbolising the burying of their past sins and idolatry, and their readiness to worship only the God of Bethel.

This is not unlike the experience of the man or woman who comes to faith in the Lord Jesus Christ. They are about to enter into a new and different life and they show it outwardly by burying the things that belong to the old past life before they came to Christ. As they set out on the Christian journey, in the way Jacob and his household set out on the journey to Bethel, they will leave behind the old sins, the old habits, the old values, the old places they went to and even, perhaps, the old circle of friends and acquaintances they moved in.

This may not happen all at once, the remnants of the old worldly life may cling to them for a while, just as the remnants of the old paganism clung to the members of Jacob's household. But if they have been truly born again of God's Spirit then they themselves will come to see that these things of the old life are now incompatible with their new life in Christ, and they will want to bury them once and for all. This will not be easy for some, and may involve an inward struggle lasting a considerable time. Their prayer then will be that of William Cowper:

"The dearest idol I have known,
What'er that idol be,
Help me to tear it from Thy throne,
And worship only Thee".

It is also important that more mature Christians should realise what an acute struggle this can be, and should not expect too much from new believers in the early stages of their Christian faith.

Rededication

On his arrival at Bethel, Jacob did exactly what God had commanded him. "Jacob and all the people with him came to Luz (that is, Bethel) in the land of Canaan. There he built an altar, and he called the place El Bethel, because it was there that God revealed Himself to him when he was fleeing from his brother" (Genesis 35:6–7). This must have been a deeply moving experience for Jacob. Here he was back in the place where he had first encountered God at a personal level thirty years before and where he had made his vow of commitment. A lot had happened during those years that had affected his spiritual life in both a negative and a positive way. At times he had been unfaithful to his vow, he had been guilty of deceit and manipulating events and circumstances to suit his own purposes. But it was not all weakness and backsliding. There was also progress and growth in his spiritual life, and at times he was overpowered by the sense of the reality of God's presence, as at Peniel.

But God was now giving him an opportunity to rededicate his life afresh. He confirmed the change of name from Jacob to Israel and reiterated the covenant promises made to Abraham (Genesis 35:9–13). Jacob responded with his own act of consecration and commemoration. "Jacob set up a stone pillar at the place where God had talked with him, and he poured out a drink offering on it; he also poured oil on it. Jacob named the place where God had talked with him Bethel" (Genesis 35:14–15).

Jacob's need to consecrate himself afresh in God's service is not unlike what happens in our own Christian experience. The spiritual journey for the believer is rarely one of continual progress in holiness. We all have our back-slidings and lose our way at times. Sanctification, or growing in holiness, is a progressive work of the Holy Spirit bringing us more and more into the likeness of Christ. Through faith in Christ's death on the Cross we are already sanctified in God's sight, and we call this Positional Sanctification. But as long as we live in a sinful world we have to struggle after holiness with the help of the Holy Spirit, and this we call Practical Sanctification. Like Jacob we fall and fail time after time, and there is always the need for renewed consecration and recommitment to God's service.

Home at last

The closing verses of this chapter deal with the final lap of Jacob's journey home to Mamre, and the double sorrow he experienced in the death of his beloved wife Rachel, and the wicked act of his eldest son Reuben. "Then they moved on from Bethel. While they were still some distance from Ephrath, Rachel began to give birth and had great difficulty. And as she was having great difficulty in childbirth, the midwife said to her, 'Don't be afraid, for you have another son.' As she breathed her last – for she was dying – she named her son Ben-Oni. But his father named him Benjamin" (Genesis 35:16–18).

Rachel's death must have caused Jacob great sorrow, since he had loved her deeply, and such devotion and constancy is to be commended today when marriage – in so many instances – seems to have little of either. But Jacob's sorrow was also mingled with happiness in the birth of his twelfth son, thus completing the foundation for the future of Israel. It might have been this thought that led Jacob to change the baby's name from Ben-Oni (son of my trouble), to Benjamin (son of my right hand), signifying his faith in the future.

Not long afterwards Jacob suffered another blow. "While Israel was living in that region, Reuben went in and slept with his father's concubine Bilhah, and Israel heard of it" (Genesis 35:22). Not only did Jacob hear of it, but he never forgot it, as is clear from what he had to say about Reuben when he was dying (Genesis 49:3–4). This was a wicked and arrogant thing for Reuben to have done, and as a result he lost his birthright as the firstborn, and his standing among his brothers. We read in Chronicles: "The sons of Reuben the firstborn of Israel (he was the firstborn, but when he defiled his father's marriage bed, his rights as firstborn were given to the sons of Joseph son of Israel; so he could not be listed in the genealogical record in accordance with his birthright)" (1 Chronicles 5:1).

Finally, Jacob arrives at his journey's end and is home at last. "Jacob came home to his father Isaac in Mamre, near Kiriath Arba (that is, Hebron), where Abraham and Isaac had stayed. Isaac lived a hundred and eighty years. Then he breathed his last and died and was gathered to his people, old and full of years. And his sons Esau and Jacob buried him" (Genesis 35:27–29). Although Isaac's death is mentioned, he did in fact live for a number of years afterwards. It is probably mentioned at this point in order to round off the record of his life, before entering on the last section of Genesis and the life of Joseph. The reconciliation between Jacob and Esau was still holding at the burial of Isaac, just as Isaac himself was reconciled to Ishmael at the death of their father Abraham. Death can be a great healer, and many lives have been reconciled over the grave of a loved one.

Joseph the dreamer

READ GENESIS CHAPTERS 36 AND 37

Although, as we saw earlier, the brothers Jacob and Esau had long since been reconciled, nevertheless following the death of their father Isaac, Esau decided to go his own way. "This is the account of Esau (that is, Edom). Esau took his wives from the women of Canaan: Adah daughter of Elon the Hittite, and Oholibamah daughter of Anah and granddaughter of Zibeon the Hivite – also Basemath daughter of Ishmael and sister of Nebaioth … Esau took his wives and sons and daughters and all the members of his household, as well as his livestock and all his other animals and all the goods he had acquired in Canaan and moved to the land some distance from his brother Jacob … So Esau (that is, Edom) settled in the hill country of Seir" (Genesis 36:1–8).

The remainder of chapter 36 then deals exclusively with the genealogical record of the descendants of Esau, and does not give much scope for the expositor since it seems to be no more than a dull catalogue of names. But we must remember that the purpose of these family records in Genesis is to show how God preserved the promised seed from generation to generation. In this instance the line was carried on through Jacob, and not Esau who separated himself from his brother both geographically and spiritually by becoming the father of the mixed race of Edomites. Chapter 36 ends with the words: "This was Esau, the father of the Edomites", and chapter 37 opens with the words: "Jacob lived in the land where his father had stayed, the land of Canaan". In this way the writer shows how the distinction was kept between the descendants of Esau and the descendants of Jacob, with Jacob remaining in the land of promise.

The favourite son

With verse 2 of chapter 37 we begin the final section in the book of Genesis. "This is the account of Jacob. Joseph, a young man of seventeen, was tending the flocks with his brothers, the sons of Bilhah and the sons of

Zilpah, his father's wives, and he brought their father a bad report about them. Now Israel loved Joseph more than any of his other sons, because he had been born to him in his old age; and he made a richly ornamented robe for him. When his brothers saw that their father loved him more than any of them, they hated him and could not speak a kind word to him" (Genesis 37:2–4).

At this opening stage of the story we do not find Joseph to be a particularly likeable individual. He is his father's darling and thoroughly spoiled. We can understand why the brothers felt as they did towards him. The sight of him strutting about in his richly ornamented robe infuriated them, especially since Joseph seems to have had the nasty habit of carrying tales about them to their father. Added to all this, as we shall see later, was the superior manner in which he recounted his dreams of future greatness to his brothers.

It seems incredible that Jacob should have shown his favouritism for Joseph in such a blatant way in view of his own upbringing. The favouritism shown to himself and Esau respectively by their parents had caused an enormous amount of damage. Jacob himself therefore was partly to blame for the hostility between Joseph and his brothers. They were as much their father's sons as Joseph was, and they wanted the same affection and consideration as he had. But the sight of that richly ornamented robe was a constant reminder that they came lower down in the order of things.

Being a parent in today's world calls for even greater wisdom, even in the Christian family, and there is no place for favouritism. The same must be true of the family of God in the local church. All members must be treated alike by the pastor and there should be no preference shown to particular individuals or encouragement given to the forming of a 'clique'. Our Lord showed no favouritism, and He loved the publicans and sinners as much as his own disciples. James has some strong words to say about favouritism. "My brothers, as believers in our glorious Lord Jesus Christ, do not show favouritism. Suppose a man comes into your meeting wearing a gold ring and fine clothes, and a poor man in shabby clothes also comes in. If you show special attention to the man wearing fine clothes and say, 'Here's a good seat for you,' but say to the poor man, 'You stand there,' or, 'Sit on the floor by my feet,' have you not discriminated among yourselves and become judges with evil thoughts?" (James 2:1–4). From that it is clear that there is no place in the Christian life for favouritism, partiality, or discrimination based on prejudice, and to adopt such an attitude is to be guilty of sin.

Human vanity and conceit

At this stage in his life Joseph appears to be very vain and conceited, and enjoyed wearing the ornamental robe that symbolised his special status in the family. But the saying: "Pride goes before a fall" was certainly true of Joseph, for we shall see that God is going to bring him very low through all kinds of harsh experiences before raising him to a position of eminence and authority in Egypt. He did undoubtedly have exceptional talent and ability, but as we shall see shortly, his air of superiority in recounting his dreams to his brothers, who were grown men, reveals him in a poor light. Of course we might be charitable and put it all down to youthful arrogance and conceit, since he is only a boy of seventeen, inexperienced in the ways of the world. If he had known what lay ahead of him, then his pride and talkativeness would have evaporated over night. But God knew him to be a young man open to His leading, and He had to teach him, through the experiences of life, that no gift or talent we possess is the product of our own making, but is given to us. Therefore the gifted, talented person ought to be the most humble of all.

A proud conceited spirit is a dreadful thing in a Christian, and the Word of God warns us against it. "Humble yourselves, therefore, under God's mighty hand, that he may lift you up in due time" (1 Peter 5:6). And when Paul advises Timothy on the kind of men he might choose to be pastors he says this: "He must not be a recent convert, or he may become conceited and fall under the same judgement as the devil" (1 Timothy 3:6). Conceit or pride was the darling sin nearest to Satan's heart when he sought to dethrone God.

On the wider front we can look at our world and see all too clearly that pride and intellectual conceit and arrogance are the mark of modern mankind. Man's attitude today says in effect: "What do we need God for, our forefathers in their ignorance may have needed that kind of naive belief, but we have progressed beyond that kind of simplistic thinking. We must believe in ourselves, in our own capacities and intellectual powers to unravel the mysteries of life and of the universe." It sounds plausible enough until, that is, you take a good hard look at the kind of world this arrogant, self-assertive attitude has produced. When we see the misery and wretchedness and violence in our world it is certainly no great testimony to man's ability to direct things on his own without the help and direction of God.

Joseph's dreams

"Joseph had a dream, and when he told it to his brothers, they hated him all the more. He said to them, 'Listen to this dream I had: We were binding sheaves of corn out in the field when suddenly my sheaf rose and stood upright, while your sheaves gathered round mine and bowed down to it.' His brothers said to him, 'Do you intend to reign over us? Will you actually rule us?' And they hated him all the more because of his dream and what he had said. Then he had another dream, and he told it to his brothers. 'Listen', he said, 'I had another dream and this time the sun and moon and eleven stars were bowing down to me'. When he told his father as well as his brothers, his father rebuked him and said, 'What is this dream you had? Will your mother and I and your brothers actually come and bow down to the ground before you?' His brothers were jealous of him, but his father kept the matter in mind" (Genesis 37:5–11).

In the Christian life there is a right time to speak to others of our deepest experiences of God, and there is a time to be quiet. Peter, James and John must have strongly desired to tell the other disciples of the profound experience they had had on the mountain of transfiguration, but we read: "Jesus gave them orders not to tell anyone what they had seen until the Son of Man had risen from the dead" (Mark 9:9). Joseph, in his youthful arrogance and pride, was very unwise therefore to tell his brothers and father of his dreams. The brothers were bound to feel even more resentful. The dreams were given by God for Joseph's own encouragement, and not to be paraded openly to the mortification of his brothers. Even his father Jacob rebuked him.

As to the dreams themselves, the manner in which Joseph interpreted them reflect his immature thinking at the time. He is the centre round which all things turn on earth (the sheaves) and in heaven (the sun, moon and stars). It suggests he had an unhealthy pre-occupation with the self, and other people were there to gratify his desires. That at least was how the brothers saw it. But God would change his thinking as he brought him to spiritual maturity.

Some of us may need to have our thinking changed in the same way. We too can become too absorbed with the self, too subjective and inward-looking, and there may be more than one self that God has to slay in us as He leads us on to spiritual maturity. The lustful self, assertive self, ambitious self, over-sensitive self; any one of these can hold us back in making spiritual progress, and with God's help must be dealt with.

But however unwise Joseph may have been in telling his brothers about his dreams, he clearly had some definite awareness that God's hand was on him for some great work in the future. It is a wonderful feeling when one has some intuitive stirring that God is calling us to some special work, perhaps to the ministry of the word, or to evangelism, or the mission field, or some other kind of Christian service. We can thank God for all those in history who had their dreams and inspiration of doing a work for God, people like Wilberforce and the slave trade, Elizabeth Fry and the prisons, Shaftesbury and the poor, William Booth and the Salvation Army.

But if we want to realise our dreams and aspirations to do a work for God we need to keep in mind two things. First, we must expect people to respond differently. Joseph's brothers hated him, and his father gave him no encouragement. Some may pour cold water on our enthusiasm or try to discourage us. But if we know God is speaking to us, then we must hold on to our dream. Joseph never forgot his dreams, in spite of all that happened to him, and eventually God helped him to fulfil them. Second, there may be a cost involved. In his youthful conceit Joseph dreamed of the day when God would exalt him, but the pit in which he nearly died and the years in prison did not figure in his dreams at all. But that was the price he had to pay. Any worthwhile work for God carries a cost in terms of time, or material loss, or disappointment and sacrifice. But it is all part of God's discipline. It happened with the Lord Jesus. "... he humbled himself and became obedient to death – even death on a cross. Therefore God exalted him to the highest place and gave him the name that is above every name"

(Philippians 2:8–9). Our salvation in Christ was a great work, but only at a great cost.

A murderous intent

In the second half of chapter 37, Joseph's troubles really begin. "Now his brothers had gone to graze their father's flocks near Shechem, and Israel said to Joseph, 'As you know, your brothers are grazing the flocks near Shechem. Come, I am going to send you to them.' … So Joseph went after his brothers and found them near Dothan. But they saw him in the distance, and before he reached them, they plotted to kill him. 'Here comes that dreamer!' they said to each other. 'Come now, let's kill him and throw him into one of these cisterns and say that a ferocious animal devoured him. Then we'll see what comes of his dreams'" (Genesis 37:12–20).

It seems that the brothers had nursed their grievance towards Joseph day after day until it had become an obsession with them, and when the opportunity came, nothing less than murder would satisfy it. Resentment is like that. If we brood upon it, it will become a fixation and distort our personality, twist our thinking and destroy our relationship with God and other people. The only wise thing to do with a spirit of resentment is to strangle it at birth.

Reuben's failure

It was Reuben's intention to try and save Joseph from his brothers. "When Reuben heard this, he tried to rescue him from their hands. 'Let's not take his life', he said. 'Don't shed any blood. Throw him into this cistern here in the desert, but don't lay a hand on him'. Reuben said this to rescue him from them and take him back to his father. So when Joseph came to his brothers, they stripped him of his robe – the richly ornamented robe he was wearing – and they took him and threw him into the cistern. Now the cistern was empty, there was no water in it" (Genesis 37:21–24).

Reuben's intention was good enough, but he lacked the strength of character to carry it out. Later on in the story his father Jacob described him as "Turbulent as the waters" (Genesis 49:4); meaning that he was weak and indecisive. As the eldest son he should have stood up to his brothers and warned them of the sinfulness of their actions. But ever since his act of incest with his father's wife (Genesis 35:22) he had lost the respect of his brothers and with it his status as the firstborn and leader of the family. The result was that when he returned to rescue Joseph it was too late, his brothers had already sold him as a slave to some passing Midianites.

"So when the Midianite merchants came by, his brothers pulled Joseph up out of the cistern and sold him for twenty shekels of silver to the Ishmaelites, who took him to Egypt. When Reuben returned to the cistern and saw that Joseph was not there, he tore his clothes. He went back to his brothers and said, 'The boy isn't there! Where can I turn now?'" (Genesis 37:28–30). Reuben serves as a warning to all those who would aspire to leadership in the work of God. It calls for the spiritual and moral strength that wins the respect of others, and a spirit of decisiveness in decision making. In addition there must be no failure of nerve when it comes to standing up for what is right before God, even when it makes one unpopular.

Evil promotes evil

The brothers were guilty of committing a crime against Joseph, but it did not end there. They now had to commit the further sins of lying and hypocrisy in order to hide the first. "Then they got Joseph's robe, slaughtered a goat and dipped the robe in the blood. They took the orna-mented robe back to their father and said, 'We found this. Examine it to see whether it is your son's robe.' He recognised it and said, 'It is my son's robe! Some ferocious animal has devoured him. Joseph has surely been torn to pieces'. Then Jacob tore his clothes, put on sackcloth and mourned for his son many days. All his sons and daughters came to comfort him, but he refused to be comforted" (Genesis 37:31–35).

We saw earlier in the life of Jacob how deliberate sin has a multiplying effect, especially that of lying. One lie leads to another, like an inverted pyramid with each lie making it more top heavy until the whole edifice comes crashing down. This happened with the brothers, as we shall see in the following chapters. In the years ahead their initial crime against Joseph, and the lying and hypocrisy in the face of their father, was to lead them deeper into a situation which they could not control, until it all came crashing down around their ears. Truth, on the other hand, is like a pyramid properly built, broad at the base and cannot be overturned, that is why the gospel of Christ can never ultimately be defeated by the forces of sin and darkness in the world. Falsity and hypocrisy will pass away but God's truth will stand. That is His promise. "Heaven and earth will pass away, but my words will never pass away" (Mark 13:31).

What of Joseph in all this? "Meanwhile, the Midianites sold Joseph in Egypt to Potiphar, one of Pharaoh's officials, the captain of the guard" (Genesis 37:36). Disillusionment had come early, and he was already learning that life is not such an easy business after all. He was going to discover that if he was to reach the heights he had dreamed of, he would have to rely much more upon God, and less upon himself.

Judah's sin

A t first glance this chapter appears to be a misplacement, since it breaks the continuity of the story of Joseph. Chapter 37 ended with Joseph being taken down to Egypt by the Midianites, and chapter 39 begins with his being sold as a slave to Potiphar, the captain of Pharaoh's guard. But in between we have this glimpse into the family life of Judah and his sin with Tamar his daughter-in-law. It is not a very edifying story and, on the face of it, totally irrelevant to the continuing history of Joseph.

Why then is it here? One answer sometimes given is that it is meant to show the contrast between the sinful conduct of Judah in relation to Tamar, and the purity of Joseph's conduct in relation to the wife of Potiphar in the following chapter. But there is a more important reason than that.

A separated people

The answer lies in the opening verses: "At that time, Judah left his brothers and went down to stay with a man of Adullam named Hirah. There Judah met the daughter of a Canaanite man named Shua. He married her and lay with her; she became pregnant and gave birth to a son, who was named Er. She conceived again and gave birth to a son and named him Onan. She gave birth to still another son and named him Shelah. It was at Kezib that she gave birth to him" (Genesis 38:1–5).

Following the rough treatment of Joseph, Judah – for whatever reason – decided to leave his brothers and went to live among the Canaanites in Adullam, where he eventually married a Canaanite woman and had three children. Altogether this must have covered a period of something like twenty-two years, during which time Judah was strongly influenced by the customs of the pagan Canaanites, including religious prostitution. This mixing with the Canaanites was contrary to God's purpose, since the Israelites were meant to be God's special and separated people. And it is here that we see the explanation for the inclusion of this chapter at this point. God has already, through the sale of Joseph, put into operation his plan to remove his people to Egypt at a later date to prevent them from being absorbed by the pagan Canaanites. The story of Judah's transgression is meant to reinforce the need for this removal by showing how likely it was that the Israelites would intermarry with the Canaanites, and lose their distinctiveness as God's people.

As the people of God we are meant to be different from the people of the world simply because we **are** different from them. The idea, in circulation in some quarters today, that Christians should make every attempt to convince non-Christians that they are not really any different from them, is wrong and dangerous. The reason given is that we then become accepted by those outside the Church, and are better placed to evangelise them. Jesus, they say, was "the friend of publicans and sinners". That is perfectly true, but the same publicans and sinners had no doubt what He stood for and where He was coming from. By all means let us befriend the people around us, but let us make it perfectly clear at the same time that we are in fact different, simply because we belong to Jesus Christ. Otherwise, like Judah, we shall become infected by the pagan values of the world and become seduced from our love of Christ.

Paul puts it very clearly: "Do not be yoked together with unbelievers. For what do righteousness and wickedness have in common? Or what fellowship can light have with darkness? What harmony is there between Christ and Belial? What does a believer have in common with an unbeliever? … 'Therefore come out from among them and be separate' says the Lord" (2 Corinthians 6:14–17).

Judah's hypocrisy

The remaining verses form a long and complicated story, which we can summarise before bringing out the main lesson. "Judah got a wife for Er, his firstborn, and her name was Tamar. But Er, Judah's firstborn, was wicked in the Lord's sight; so the Lord put him to death" (Genesis 38:6–7). We do not know why Er was put to death, or what his wickedness was, so it is useless speculating. "Then Judah said to Onan, 'Lie with your brother's wife and fulfil your duty to her as a brother-in-law to produce offspring for your brother.' But Onan knew that the offspring would not be his; so whenever he lay with his brother's wife, he spilled his semen on the ground to keep from producing offspring for his brother. What he did was wicked in the Lord's sight; so he put him to death also" (Genesis 38:8–10).

Onan married Tamar in accordance with the custom known as 'levirate marriage' (Deuteronomy 25:5–6). He had no wish to raise children to his brother's memory and practised a form of birth control (coitus interruptus, sometimes called Onanism), and was put to death for his refusal to carry out the levirate law. That left Shelah, the youngest son, and Judah promised Tamar (Genesis 38:11) that when he was old enough he would be allowed to marry her. But as time passed Tamar could see that Judah had no intention of keeping his promise and devised a strategy to force his hand. She disguised herself as a shrine prostitute and enticed Judah to have sexual relations with her and she became pregnant.

"About three months later Judah was told, 'Your daughter-in-law Tamar is guilty of prostitution, and as a result she is now pregnant'. Judah said, 'Bring her out and have her burned to death!'" (Genesis 38:24). What an appalling act of hypocrisy this was on the part of Judah, a senior member of the patriarchal family and one destined to carry on the messianic line. He had himself used the services of a prostitute, although unaware who she was, and at the same time he condemns her to death. Outwardly he was righteously indignant at the sin of Tamar, but inwardly he was full of self-righteousness since he was guilty of the same sin.

On several occasions our Lord was deeply scathing of the hypocrisy of the Pharisees. "Woe to you, teachers of the law and Pharisees, you hypocrites! You are like whitewashed tombs which look beautiful on the outside but on the inside are full of dead men's bones and everything unclean" (Matthew 23:27). The picture he painted is clear. They were outwardly intensely religious, but in their hearts they were foul and putrid with sin. What they did, they did to obtain the praises of men, not of God. Hypocrisy is a form of play-acting, when one pretends to be righteous but in reality is self-righteous.

There is nothing the worldly man despises more than a religious hypocrite. He wants the Christian to be what he claims to be, even if he does not agree with him. Hiding behind the mask of a hollow false religion is the one thing he will not tolerate. If we have a faith at all it must be real and not a façade. God is not concerned with any outward show of religion but with the state of our heart.

God's grace

The one thing to be said in mitigation of Judah's offence is that he admitted his guilt and was fully repentant. "As she was being brought out, she sent a message to her father-in-law. 'I am pregnant by the man who owns these' she said. And she added, 'See if you recognise whose seal and cord and staff these are.' Judah recognised them and said, 'She is more righteous than I, since I wouldn't give her to my son Shelah.' And he did not sleep with her again" (Genesis 38:25–26).

God is very gracious and forgiving when we fall into sin, and does not cast us off, but continues to use us, and even – by his grace – brings something positive and purposeful out of the evil we have done. Judah himself became a transformed man in the years ahead, and incredible though it seems, it was through him and Perez, the son born of his sin with Tamar, that the Messianic line would be continued. We gather this from Matthew's genealogy of Jesus:

"A record of the genealogy of Jesus Christ
the son of David, the son of Abraham:

Abraham was the father of Isaac,
Isaac the father of Jacob,
Jacob the father of Judah and his brothers,
Judah the father of Perez and Zerah whose mother was Tamar" (Matthew 1:1–3).

Joseph's temptation

READ GENESIS CHAPTER 39

In this chapter we come to a turning point in Joseph's life. Back in Canaan he was a rather vain and proud young man, but at the same time we saw too that he was sensitive to the moving of the Spirit of God in his life. But now he is in a strange country and only a slave. How will he react?

God was with him

"Now Joseph had been taken down to Egypt. Potiphar, an Egyptian who was one of Pharaoh's officials, the captain of the guard, bought him from the Ishmaelites who had taken him there. The Lord was with Joseph and he prospered, and he lived in the house of his Egyptian master" (Genesis 39:1–2). The key phrase here is: "The Lord was with Joseph". It occurs again in verse 23 and it tells us that God had great things in store for young Joseph, and was going to keep a close watch on him. We also read that "he prospered". That is, not only materially in the house of Potiphar, but spiritually. Because of his circumstances he was going to grow in his relationship with God pretty fast. He would depend more on God and less on himself.

"Man's extremity is God's opportunity". We have often heard that saying, which means that when we find ourselves in a situation where, like Joseph, we realise our inadequacy, then God has the opportunity to come in and do what He has to do. And it follows that others begin to see us in the way Potiphar saw Joseph.

"When his master saw that the Lord was with him and that the Lord gave him success in everything he did, Joseph found favour in his eyes and became his attendant. Potiphar put him in charge of his household, and he entrusted to his care everything he owned" (Genesis 39:3–4). Potiphar was a pagan, but he could see that there was an honesty and integrity about Joseph that related in some way to his faith in the eternal God. That tells us that it is not enough to be a child of God, but it must be seen that we are. The truly Christ-like life cannot be concealed, it is bound to break through in some way, in our conversation, attitude, quality of work and relationships.

So Joseph at this point, although he is a slave, is on top of things and life is purposeful and worthwhile. But it was not to last.

Satan's activity

Satan watches God's people very closely, every move we make, assessing our strengths and weaknesses as he devises ways and means to bring us crashing down. And he is never more interested in us than when we are being blessed of God. It happened with Joseph. Everything was going fine with him in Potiphar's house when Satan suddenly struck, and Joseph found himself in a very dangerous situation. "Now Joseph was well-built and handsome, and after a while his master's wife took notice of Joseph and said, 'Come to bed with me!'" (Genesis 39:6–7).

Here was a woman of wealth and position who spent her days in idleness, and because of the emptiness and boredom such a life brings, she set herself deliberately to seduce Joseph. We learn later (Genesis 41:46) that he was thirty years old when he entered the service of Pharoah, so he was possibly in his mid-twenties at this time, and being handsome and well-built he was a real catch for an older designing woman. Even so he would only be her 'toy boy' to bring a little sexual spice into her otherwise boring life.

In our society today there are thousands like her, young and old, often with time on their hands, money to spare, and so utterly bored with life that they are constantly looking for something to spice things up a bit. It may be promiscuous sex, drink, drugs, crime, wild living, anything to bring some colour into life and make it worth living. And in the light of the spirit of the age they would have no difficulty in rationalising Joseph's reaction to the temptation to commit adultery. They would argue something like this: "He's young and healthy and it's only natural he should want to express his sexuality. Anyway, he's not to blame really since she invited him to it. In any case he won't be found out because she isn't going to say anything, is she? Get your fun while you can, I say". So goes the philosophy by which thousands live their lives today, and the misery it brings is all around us.

Joseph's resistance

But how did Joseph manage to resist such a powerful temptation – for resist he did. "But he refused. 'With me in charge' he told her, 'my master does not concern himself with anything in the house; everything he owns he has entrusted to my care. No one is greater in this house than I am. My master has withheld nothing from me except you, because you are his wife. How then could I do such a wicked thing and sin against God?' And though she spoke to Joseph day after day, he refused to go to bed with her or even to be with her" (Genesis 39:8–10).

Here was one very persistent woman. She kept up the pressure on Joseph day after day, telling herself perhaps, "he's only human and will give way eventually". But he did not. And we can learn from that. Temptation comes to everyone, even the Lord Jesus (Luke 4). Writing to the Corinthians Paul says: "No temptation has seized you except what is common to man" (1 Corinthians 10:13). God will not allow us to avoid temptation because, from His standpoint, it is a test and challenge for the strengthening of our faith. But there are things we can keep in mind when faced with temptation, which will help us to overcome.

Joseph reminded himself that he would lose his spiritual testimony as God's man in a pagan household. "But he refused. 'With me in charge' he told her, 'my master does not concern himself with anything in the house; everything he owns he has entrusted to my care". Potiphar had seen the effect of this young slave's religion upon his life and work and trusted him completely as a result. His religion and testimony would count for nothing if he were to give way. And the same can happen to us when we give way to temptation. We can lose our Christian testimony in the eyes of the world.

Joseph reminded himself that giving way would hurt not only his own character but also Potiphar who had treated him so generously. "My master has withheld nothing from me except you, because you are his wife". Our sin always involves others. Some one may say, "it's my life, I can do what I like with it". What they don't realise is that others get hurt through the things we do, for we do not live to ourselves alone. We can all be affected by the moral atmosphere of the community to which we belong. John Donne the seventeenth century poet put it like this in a sermon he preached at St. Paul's Cathedral:

"No man is an island, entire of itself; every man is a piece of the continent, a part of the main; any man's death diminishes me, because I am involved in mankind".

Most important of all Joseph reminded himself that to give way to temptation was a violation of God's holiness. "How then could I do such a wicked thing and sin against God?" In the last analysis all sin is sin against God. We may hurt ourselves and others in the process of sinning, and that is bad enough, but above all we hurt God. We "grieve the Holy Spirit of God" (Ephesians 4:30). This consideration overshadowed all others with Joseph, and enabled him to withstand the temptation.

Fleeing temptation

Sometimes the best way to overcome temptation is to put as great a distance as you can between yourself and the object of temptation. That is what Joseph did finally. "One day he went into the house to attend to his duties, and none of the household servants was inside. She caught him by his cloak and said, 'Come to bed with me!' But he left his cloak in her hand and ran out of the house" (Genesis 39:11–12). There are some temptations we cannot avoid and we have to meet them head on in the strength God gives to us. But there are others we bring on ourselves by getting into situations where we are exposed to Satan's attack. We know our own weakness in certain areas of our life, it may be in relation to the opposite sex, or in the matter of drink. Whatever it may be, the important thing is to keep it at a safe distance by avoiding those situations whenever we can.

Faith under trial

"Hell hath no fury like a woman scorned". That was certainly true of Potiphar's wife. "When she saw that he had left his cloak in her hand and had run out of the house, she called her household servants. 'Look', she said to them, 'this Hebrew has been brought to us to make sport of us! He came in here to sleep with me, but I screamed. When he heard me scream for help, he left his cloak beside me and ran out of the house'. … When his master heard the story his wife told him, saying, 'This is how your slave treated me', he burned with anger. Joseph's master took him and put him in prison, the place where the king's prisoners were confined" (Genesis 39:13–20).

"There's no justice in this life". Have we been tempted to say that at times? I wonder if Joseph felt like that? After all, he had honoured God by resisting temptation and doing what was right, and all he got out of it was a spell in prison. It seems on the face of it that there is something radically wrong with the way God organises things in this life. We know of people who cheat and steal and care nothing for God and morality, and yet seem to live full and satisfying lives. On the other hand, those who seek to please God can sometimes suffer the real hardships and injustices of life. Like many of us the Psalmist was perplexed by this state of affairs. "But as for me, my feet had almost slipped; I had nearly lost my foothold. For I envied the arrogant when I saw the prosperity of the wicked" (Psalm 73:2–3).

But the history of Joseph teaches us that, whilst we may be perplexed by the twists and turns of life, God is not. He knows exactly what He is doing. "But while Joseph was there in the prison, the Lord was with him; he showed him kindness and granted him favour in the eyes of the prison warder. So the warder put Joseph in charge of all those held in the prison, and he was made responsible for all that was done there. The warder paid no attention to anything under Joseph's care, because the Lord was with Joseph and gave him success in whatever he did" (Genesis 39:20–23).

Notice the repetition of the phrase we referred to earlier: "the Lord was with him" (Genesis 39:21 and 23). God had not deserted him, and He will not desert us when our faith is under trial. We have to remember that God's mind is not like our mind, and He has His own way of doing things. God says through Isaiah "As the heavens are higher than the earth, so are my ways higher than your ways and my thoughts than your thoughts" (Isaiah 55:9). All God asks is that we learn to trust Him where we do not understand.

In the prison

W e are dealing with these two chapters together because they cover the same material – Joseph's experiences in the prison.

The cupbearer and baker

"Some time later, the cupbearer and the baker of the king of Egypt offended their master, the king of Egypt. Pharaoh was angry with his two officials, the chief cupbearer and the chief baker, and put them in custody in the house of the captain of the guard, in the same prison where Joseph was confined. The captain of the guard assigned them to Joseph, and he attended them" (Genesis 40:1–4). We may get the impression at first that Joseph's imprisonment was not that bad, since he is given the job of caring for these two high officers of State.

This was a trusted position and was given him because once again, as in Potiphar's house, his godliness and spiritual integrity asserted itself and he gained the confidence of the prison warder. But prior to that his time in prison was no picnic. Speaking of Israel's migration to Egypt the psalmist says: "… he sent a man before them – Joseph, sold as a slave. They bruised his feet with shackles, his neck was put in irons, till what he foretold came to pass, till the word of the Lord proved him true" (Psalm 105:17–19). But he came through the hard time, and the experience was not wasted because God was using it to prepare him for the great task of leadership that lay ahead. Looking back on some heavy trial many a Christian has said, "I never thought I would be able to carry on, but it's amazing how the strength comes". And it is true! With the trial comes the strength.

Joseph the interpreter

"After they had been in custody for some time, each of the two men – the cupbearer and the baker of the king of Egypt, who were being held in prison – had a dream the same night, and each dream had a meaning of its own" (Genesis 40:4–5). We have already touched upon the importance of dreams in the Bible when dealing with Abraham's encounter with Abimelech in Gerar (Genesis 20:3f). What interests us now is not so much the dreams of these men as the part they themselves had in the overall plan of God's providence to bring Joseph to the attention of Pharaoh, and finally out of prison.

"When Joseph came to them the next morning, he saw that they were dejected. So he asked Pharaoh's officials, … 'Why are your faces so sad today?' 'We both had dreams', they answered, 'but there is no-one to interpret them'. Then Joseph said to them, 'Do not interpretations belong to God? Tell me your dreams'" (Genesis 40:6–8). Here is Joseph beginning to see himself as the prophetic agent of God's truth. He hears the dreams, and rightly interprets them with God's help. The cupbearer is restored to his former position, and the baker is hanged (Genesis 40:9–23). We are meant to see in this the working out of God's plan to transform Joseph into the leader and saviour of his people. Back in Horeb his character was in danger of being warped and emasculated by the unwise petting of his father Jacob. But God took him out of that situation and made him a slave and a prisoner, but all with the purpose of putting a finer edge on his character. With a pretty robe Jacob would have made him an ornament, but God wanted to make him an instrument.

When Joseph said: "Do not interpretations belong to God?" he was showing his sensitivity to God's Spirit, and had no doubt that the dreams were divinely sent. At the same time he knew that he was the one to give the interpretation or to be the channel through whom the interpretation would be made known. God is the source of revelation, but he uses the human messenger, an Isaiah or Jeremiah, a Peter or Paul, to convey the revelation to others. And that is still the function of the preacher. He is not there to give people his own ideas and opinions but to give God's message from the Bible. Nor does he rely on his own abilities and insights alone to do this, but he is empowered by the Holy Spirit so that the Word preached becomes "the power of God for the salvation of everyone who believes" (Romans 1:16).

Forgetfulness

It was a happy day for the chief cupbearer when he walked free from the prison, just as Joseph said he would when interpreting his dream. But before he left, Joseph made a request, "But when all goes well with you, remember me and show me kindness; mention me to Pharaoh and get me out of this prison. For I was forcibly carried off from the land of the Hebrews, and even here I have done nothing to deserve being put in a dungeon" (Genesis 40:14–15). Because both had been unfairly treated, Joseph might well have expected the cupbearer to help him by using his influence to get him his freedom. It is disappointing therefore to read in the last verse "The chief cupbearer, however, did not remember Joseph; he forgot him" (Genesis 40:23).

The sin of forgetfulness is common enough and touches a good many of us at some point or other. We so easily forget the vows and promises we make, the kindnesses we receive, and the debt we owe others. We do not forget intentionally, but – like the cupbearer – we make no real effort to keep the matter in the forefront of our minds. He probably intended to help Joseph, but in the bustle of palace life Joseph was forgotten. The psalmist said "Praise the Lord O my soul … and forget not all his benefits" (Psalm 103:1–2). But forget is exactly what we do. We forget God's benefits and mercies because we become so absorbed in the rush of daily life that a myriad other lesser things dominate our thoughts and feelings. The truth is we can always remember the things that are really important to us. We forget God's mercies because firstly, we do not take them seriously enough and secondly, because we do not make the effort of will, and exercise the discipline of mind, to keep them in the forefront of our thinking.

The waiting time

We learn, from the opening verses of Genesis chapter 41, that two more years passed before a circumstance arose that caused the cupbearer to remember Joseph in prison. "When two full years had passed, Pharaoh had a dream … Then the chief cupbearer said to Pharaoh, 'Today I am reminded of my shortcomings. Pharaoh was once angry with his servants, and he imprisoned me and the chief baker in the house of the captain of the guard. Each of us had a dream the same night, and each dream had a meaning of its own. Now a young Hebrew was there with us, a servant of the captain of the guard. We told him our dreams, and he interpreted them for us, giving each man the interpretation of his dream. And things turned out exactly as he interpreted them to us: I was restored to my position, and the other man was hanged'. So Pharaoh sent for Joseph, and he was quickly brought from the dungeon. When he had shaved and changed his clothes, he came before Pharaoh" (Genesis 41:1 and 9–14).

For the first few weeks after the cupbearer had left the prison Joseph would have been in a hopeful frame of mind, expecting to hear some news of his release. But as time passed he had to accept that the cupbearer had forgotten him, and there was nothing for it but to settle down to the routine of prison life and continue to wait – wait to see what God would do next. Sometimes that can be the most difficult thing in the world for the believer to have to do, simply wait upon God. We want to be active, up and doing, getting things done.

Waiting can be difficult for the person who feels God is calling them to some special work. We know God had a great purpose in store for Joseph, and that he himself had been given a glimpse of that in the dreams God gave him at the age of seventeen. But here he was, thirteen years later (Genesis 41:46), still waiting, and everything seemed to have turned out the wrong way. Moses was forty years shepherding in the wilderness before he became the leader of God's people. David was only a shepherd boy when Samuel anointed him, but he was thirty years old before he became king. John the Baptist spent years in the wilderness waiting on God before he became the forerunner of the Messiah. We may feel God is calling us to some special work and we are eager to get started, but the way is not opening up. We must not get frustrated but get on with the business in hand, building up our prayer life, growing in our understanding of the gospel, and waiting upon God. What we must not do is give way to the temptation to take some short cut to achieve our goal. God will honour our patient waiting as he did with Joseph.

Before Pharaoh

"Pharaoh said to Joseph, … 'I had a dream and no one can interpret it. But I have heard it said of you that when you hear a dream you can interpret it'. 'I cannot do it', Joseph replied to Pharaoh, 'but God will give Pharaoh the answer he desires'" (Genesis 41:15–16). Back in verse 8 we are told that Pharaoh was troubled by his dreams; he had a vague feeling of uneasiness that both he and his kingdom were threatened by something beyond his control. "In the morning his mind was troubled so he sent for all the magicians and wise men of Egypt. Pharaoh told them his dreams, but no-one could interpret them for him". Joseph too admits that he cannot explain the mystery of the dreams, but says: "God will give Pharaoh the answer he desires".

What we have here is the impotence of man, represented by the magicians and astrologers of Egypt on the one hand, and the power of God, represented by Joseph on the other. There is a Will that governs and guides the destinies of men, but it is not to be known by consulting one's horoscope in the daily newspaper, or by trying to learn the astrological significance of the stars and planets as thousands still do today. For this power is not something vague and undefined, but it is real, positive, personable and knowable. It is the eternal God of whom Joseph speaks with such confidence to Pharaoh, and who has revealed the meaning of life's mystery in the gospel of His Son the Lord Jesus Christ.

The dreams

As Pharaoh recounts his dreams to Joseph it is clear that they are both essentially Egyptian in character. "Then Pharaoh said to Joseph, 'In my dream I was standing on the bank of the Nile, when out of the river there came up seven cows, fat and sleek, and they grazed among the reeds. After them, seven other cows came up – scrawny and very ugly and lean. I had never seen such ugly cows in all the land of Egypt. The lean, ugly cows ate up the seven fat cows that came up first. But even after they ate them, no-one could tell that they had done so; they looked just as ugly as before. Then I woke up. In my dreams I also saw seven heads of corn, full and good, growing on a single stalk. After them, seven other heads sprouted – withered and thin and scorched by the east wind. The thin heads of corn swallowed up the seven good heads. I told this to the magicians, but none could explain it to me'" (Genesis 41:17–24).

For centuries the fertility and prosperity of Egypt depended upon the annual flooding of the river Nile. Joseph explains that the seven fat cattle and the seven full ears of grain represent seven years of prosperity coming upon Egypt, and the seven lean cattle and seven withered ears of grain represent seven years of famine. He explains further that "The reason the dream was given to Pharaoh in two forms is that the matter has been firmly decided by God, and God will do it soon" (Genesis 41:32).

The two things that strike us in all this are Joseph's confidence on the one hand, and his humility on the other. But his confidence is in God alone – "God will do it soon". He insists on making it clear to Pharaoh that his ability to interpret the dreams is not the result of his own cleverness but came from the illumination God gave him. A man must humble himself and acknowledge that he has come to the end of all his questioning and reasoning concerning the mystery of human life and existence. He must confess that his own endowment and ability can take him so far and no further, and then God will open the eyes of his understanding. "Trust in the Lord with all your heart and lean not on your own understanding; in all your ways acknowledge him, and he will make your paths straight" (Proverbs 3:5–6).

Joseph the statesman

Joseph did more than interpret the king's dreams, he outlined an agrarian policy that would help to meet the national crisis during the years of famine. "And now let Pharaoh look for a discerning and wise man and put him in charge of the land of Egypt. Let Pharaoh appoint commissioners over the land to take a fifth of the harvest of Egypt during the seven years of abundance. They should collect all the food of these good years that are coming and store up the corn under the authority of Pharaoh, to be kept in the cities for food. This food should be held in reserve for the country, to be used during the seven years of famine that will come upon Egypt, so that the country may not be ruined by the famine" (Genesis 41:33–36).

Pharaoh's response was to select Joseph himself as the man to put the new policy into operation. Although a pagan he recognised that Joseph had the political insight and the spiritual integrity arising out of his belief in God to carry the policy through. "Then Pharaoh said to Joseph, 'Since God has made all this known to you, there is no-one so discerning and wise as you. You shall be in charge of my palace, and all my people are to submit to your orders. Only with respect to the throne will I be greater than you'" (Genesis 41:39–40). In the verses that follow (41–45) Joseph, along with the trappings of high political office, is given an Egyptian name and an Egyptian wife. This was intended possibly to make him more acceptable to the Egyptian people.

But does this investiture of Joseph to high political office teach us anything? Well, it says something about the influential role God-fearing men and women can play in public and political life, and of which there are several examples in the Bible. Isaiah was active in the court of King Uzziah; Nehemiah was the civil governor during the rebuilding of Jerusalem after the exile; and Daniel held the highest political office in the Babylonian Empire. Political office and strong faith in God are not mutually exclusive, and it shows all too clearly how we are lacking such people in public life today when we keep hearing of so much corruption and immorality among those in positions of leadership in our nation.

When the Lord Jesus was asked about paying taxes to Caesar he replied: "Give to Caesar what is Caesar's and to God what is God's." (Mark 12:17). Whilst distinguishing between God and the state, Jesus was saying that Caesar does have certain claims upon the Christian. And Paul says the same thing. "Everyone must submit himself to the governing authorities, for there is no authority except that which God has established" (Romans 13:1). He also urges all Christians to pray for those in positions of authority in the life of the nation (1 Timothy 2:1–2). What is needed today, I believe, is for more godly men and women to play an active role in public and political life.

Manasseh and Ephraim

"Before the years of famine came, two sons were born to Joseph by Asenath daughter of Potiphera, priest of On. Joseph named his firstborn Manasseh and said, 'It is because God has made me forget all my trouble and all my father's household'" (Genesis 41:50–51). Joseph needed to forget all the bitterness of his past experiences – the hatred of his brothers and their attempt to kill him by putting him in a pit, the years spent in slavery, and his unjust imprisonment. By naming his son Manasseh he was saying that God helped him to do that.

We all need God's help to forget the bitterness associated with past hurts and disappointments, and even when the memory persists in rising to the surface on occasions, let us ask His help to take the sting out of it.

"The second son he named Ephraim and said, 'It is because God has made me fruitful in the land of my suffering'" (Genesis 41:52). Past bitterness was forgotten but the blessings Joseph enjoyed in the present were remembered. His life was indeed fruitful with his elevation over the kingdom of Egypt and the joy of home and family life. And we have equal cause to remember all the blessings we enjoy and give thanks and praise to Almighty God.

In the closing verses of this chapter (53–57) the seven years of famine have started, and thanks to Joseph's agrarian policy there was food in Egypt, whereas the neighbouring countries were suffering badly.

Corn in Egypt

READ GENESIS CHAPTERS 42, 43 AND 44

In the first of these three chapters we have a flash back to life in Jacob's household in Canaan, and the beginning of the final phase in the unfolding of God's plan of redemption for His people.

The famine

"When Jacob learned that there was grain in Egypt, he said to his sons, 'Why do you just keep looking at each other?' He continued, 'I have heard that there is corn in Egypt. Go down there and buy some for us, so that we may live and not die'" (Genesis 42:1–2). Because of Joseph's wise foresight and planning there was plenty of bread in Egypt but hunger and need everywhere else. In that sense Joseph was indeed a saviour and giver of life, and through him God was opening up the way to preserve his own people during the time of famine. It is for this reason chiefly that many have seen in Joseph a type of the Lord Jesus Christ as our Saviour.

Why then were the brothers so slow and seemingly reluctant to go down to Egypt for corn? Their father had to say to them: "Why do you just keep looking at each other?" Was it that, in spite of their need, they were incapable of translating it into action? Or did the mention of Egypt, and its connection with the Joseph of long ago, make them uneasy about going down there? Whatever the explanation only one thing mattered to Jacob: they were experiencing famine and their need was desperate, whereas Egypt had plenty of food to spare.

From the spiritual standpoint this is a picture of our nation today. We are suffering from a spiritual famine, or what Amos calls "a famine of hearing the words of the Lord" (Amos 8:11). God has provided food for our souls, just as He provided corn in Egypt. We have God's Word in the Bible and in the ongoing preaching of the gospel, but there is no appetite for it in our nation. Like Joseph's brothers people are reluctant to turn to the one place where their spiritual needs can be met – in the Lord Jesus Christ. And yet, again like the brothers, who on reflection did go to Egypt, if people do not turn to Christ for salvation they will die in their sins as surely as the brothers would have died of starvation. As Jacob urged his sons to go down to Egypt, so we must continue to urge men and women to accept the truth of the gospel.

Meeting with Joseph

Urged on by their father the brothers set out for Egypt and eventually met with Joseph. "Then ten of Joseph's brothers went down to buy corn from Egypt. But Jacob did not send Benjamin, Joseph's brother, with the others, because he was afraid that harm might come to him. So Israel's sons were among those who went to buy corn, for the famine was in the land of Canaan also. Now Joseph was the governor of the land, the one who sold corn to all its people. So when Joseph's brothers arrived, they bowed down to him with their faces to the ground" (Genesis 42:3–6). Here was Joseph's dream of twenty years before, when his brother's sheaves bowed down to his, coming true. Twenty years may seem a long time for the divine promise in the dream to come true, but God is in no hurry and works according to His own time-scale. In the book of Revelation we have a graphic picture of God's timetable relating to His judgement. "And the four angels who had been kept ready for this very hour and day and month and year were released" (Revelation 9:15). For every one of us, Christian and non-Christian alike, there is an hour or day or month or year when God acts in salvation or in judgement. That is a solemn thought.

"As soon as Joseph saw his brothers, he recognised them, but he pretended to be a stranger and spoke harshly to them. 'Where do you come from?' he asked. 'From the land of Canaan' they replied, 'to buy food'. Although Joseph recognised his brothers, they did not recognise him. Then he remembered his dreams about them and said to them, 'You are spies! You have come to see where our land is unprotected'" (Genesis 42:7–9). So the dialogue continues down to verse 17 when he puts them in custody for three days. But why does he treat them so harshly? Is it a desire for revenge? Hardly that, since as the story unfolds it is clear that his one purpose is forgiveness and reconciliation. But before that can happen he wants to bring them to repentance. Their eyes needed to be opened to the sinfulness of their behaviour years before, and he would accomplish that through a process of discipline. It is a hard lesson we ourselves have to learn in relation to God, as the letter to the Hebrews reminds us. "My son, do not make light of the Lord's discipline, and do not lose heart when he rebukes you, because the Lord disciplines those whom he loves, and he punishes everyone he accepts as a son" (Hebrews 12:5–6). In spite of his harshness Joseph loved his brothers; and likewise God's discipline of us, though seemingly harsh at times, is intended as a corrective for our spiritual development as His children.

The fear of God

"On the third day, Joseph said to them, 'Do this and you will live, for I fear God: If you are honest men, let one of your brothers stay here in prison, while the rest of you go and take corn back for your starving households. But you must bring your youngest brother to me, so that your words may be verified and that you may not die.' This they proceeded to do" (Genesis 42:18–20).

We may wonder why Joseph was able to recognise his brothers but they did not recognise him. But we must remember that they were grown men twenty years before whereas he was only a boy of seventeen. Also he was in Egyptian dress and spoke through an interpreter (Genesis 42:23). It was even more surprising therefore when this Egyptian governor told them that he was treating them in this way because, "I fear God". We recall how Jacob had earlier described God as the Fear of Isaac (Genesis 31:42), and we said then that this does not imply a craven fear or an abject fear, but a sense of awe and reverence in our soul before the holiness of God. It was said at the death of John Knox, the fiery Scots reformer: "here lies one who feared God so much that he never feared the face of man". That was also true of Joseph. He did not trifle with God, he feared Him, and so must we.

The stirring of conscience

"They said one to another, 'Surely we are being punished because of our brother. We saw how distressed he was when he pleaded with us for his life, but we would not listen; that is why this distress has come upon us'" (Genesis 42:21). Their minds and emotions were in turmoil at the strange turn events were taking, and their consciences were awakened concerning their former treatment of Joseph. As we read down to the end of the chapter we learn that their consciences were stirred still further when each of them discovered that the money he had paid for the grain was in his sack. Joseph may have intended this as a kindness, but their consciences turned it into a nemesis of guilt.

When God created us He gave us a conscience as part of the moral equipment of the soul, and it is one of the things that distinguishes us from the animals. Animals do not have feelings of guilt such as we experience. And – because it is a part of our moral frame-work – the Bible says that those who have never heard the gospel will be judged according to how they have obeyed the dictates of conscience (Romans 2:14–15). But the conscience can lose its sensitivity to wrongdoing. That is what happened to the brothers of Joseph. For twenty years their conscience had not disturbed them. Like any piece of equipment, the conscience – if it is to function properly – has to be serviced and cared for. We do that by exposing it to God's word through the reading of scripture, prayer, and the regular worship of God.

The second journey

Chapter 43 opens with a family conference in which Jacob and his sons are forced to accept that a second journey to Egypt can be delayed no longer. The food situation was desperate. "Now the famine was still severe in the land. So when they had eaten all the corn they had brought from Egypt, their father said to them, 'Go back and buy us a little more food' (Genesis 43:1–2). But Judah said to him, 'The man warned us solemnly, 'You will not see my face again unless your brother is with you'. If you will send our brother along with us, we will go down and buy food for you. But if you will not send him, we will not go down, because the man said to us, 'You will not see my face again unless your brother is with you'" (Genesis 43:3–5). As we continue reading down to verse 14 we find Jacob finally giving way to the insistence of his sons that Benjamin should accompany them. He advised them to take a gift for the Egyptian governor, and after committing them to 'God Almighty' sends them on their second journey.

We have seen already that it was God's intention to bring His people down to Egypt, and through Joseph to draw the brothers closer to Himself through repentance. To do that, God used the pressure brought on the family by famine. They were desperate for food, and had to make another journey to Egypt. That is how God works in our lives at times. He uses the pressure of the ordinary circumstances of life to drive us closer to Himself. It may be the pressure of sickness, or bereavement, or unemployment or the break-up of a marriage. We find ourselves in a desperate situation, and are made aware of our vulnerability, which in turn drives us to seek refuge in God.

Unexpected treasure

On arrival in Egypt the brothers, to their surprise and apprehension, are told by Joseph's steward that they are to dine with the governor. "The man did as Joseph told him and took the men to Joseph's house. Now the men were frightened when they were taken to his house. They thought, 'We were brought here because of the silver that was put back into our sacks the first time. He wants to attack us and overpower us and seize us as slaves and take our donkeys'" (Genesis 43:17–18). But what is of special interest is the reply of the steward.

"'It's all right' he said, 'Don't be afraid. Your God, the God of your father has given you treasure in your sacks; I received your silver'" (Genesis 43:23). His words could mean that he himself had come to faith in the eternal God through the witness of Joseph. Be that as it may, a preacher's thought will linger on the suggestiveness of the words, "the God of your father, has given you treasure in your sacks". He did not mean that the silver appeared miraculously, but Joseph's God had moved his heart to restore the money. But what a marvellous text for the preacher to expound the theme – "treasure in unexpected places". The gifts and treasures of God are all around us in the ordinary places of life if we have the eye of faith to see and to appreciate them – in our homes and families, in the love of friends and in the beauties of nature. And we ourselves have sometimes described a person as a 'real treasure' when they have come to our help or stood by us in a desperate situation. Then there are the hidden treasures of gifts and abilities, often unexpected, in the lives of church members, which are suddenly quickened by the Spirit. And God Himself describes His people as "my treasured possession" (Malachi 3:17), and there was a time when some of us certainly did not expect that!

Joseph was deeply moved when he saw Benjamin, and the special relationship he had with him as "his own mother's son" (Genesis 43:29) became evident when they all sat down to the meal. "When portions were served to them from Joseph's table, Benjamin's portion was five times as much as anyone else's. So they feasted and drank freely with him" (Genesis 43:34). The fears of the brothers had now disappeared and they must have been in high spirits as they set out on the journey home. But as we pass into chapter 44 we see that it did not last, but was simply part of the mounting drama whereby Joseph would test them even more severely.

The silver cup

"Now Joseph gave these instructions to the steward of his house: 'Fill the men's sacks with as much food as they can carry, and put each man's silver in the mouth of his sack. Then put my cup, the silver one, in the mouth of the youngest one's sack, along with the silver for his corn'. And he did as Joseph said. As morning dawned, the men were sent on their way with their donkeys. They had not gone far from the city when Joseph said to his steward, 'Go after those men at once, and when you catch up with them, say to them, 'Why have you repaid good with evil? Isn't this the cup my master drinks from and also uses for divination? This is a wicked thing you have done'" (Genesis 44:1–5).

Reference to Joseph's divining cup may seem strange, but we do not know that he actually used it for that purpose, and mention of it was probably part of his strategy to convince the brothers of his Egyptian identity. The tension continued to mount as the steward searched their sacks. "Each of them quickly lowered his sack to the ground and opened it. Then the steward proceeded to search, beginning with the oldest and ending with the youngest. And the cup was found in Benjamin's sack. At this, they tore their clothes. Then they all loaded their donkeys and returned to the city" (Genesis 44:11–13). The expression "they tore their clothes" shows how distraught the brothers were as they felt the nemesis of their old guilt once more catching up with them. For again it was the youngest beloved son of their father who was involved.

Repentance and transformation

But why did Joseph feel it necessary to put them through this further test? The answer to that comes out in the remaining verse of this chapter. As they appear before Joseph, Judah becomes the chief spokesman. "What can we say to my lord?' Judah replied. 'What can we say? How can we prove our innocence? God has uncovered your servants' guilt'" (Genesis 44:16). What a significant remark! Judah knew they were innocent of stealing the cup, so what was the guilt he was referring to? He could only have meant the sin that had festered in their hearts for the past twenty years, and of which they were now truly repentant.

This is what Joseph had been looking for. Had they changed over the years? And would they show that change in their attitude towards Benjamin? Would they be willing to sacrifice Benjamin as the supposed guilty party to save themselves, just as they had once sacrificed him? Judah, in a speech (verses 18–34) that is deeply moving and poignant, and one of the finest passages in the Old Testament, shows clearly that they really are transformed men. He ends by asking to become Joseph's slave in the place of Benjamin. "Now then, please let your servant remain here as my lord's slave in place of the boy, and let the boy return with his brothers. How can I go back to my father if the boy is not with me? No! Do not let me see the misery that would come upon my father" (Genesis 44:33–34).

Here was the man who twenty years before led the brothers into selling Joseph into slavery, and with them deceived their father into thinking he had been killed by wild animals (Genesis 37:26–33). But he was now a transformed character, willing even to give his life as a substitute for young Benjamin. True repentance is like that. The French cynic Voltaire said: "God pardon? Of course He will, it's His job". But that is to presume on God's forgiveness, and it will not be forthcoming if our repentance is not genuine and does not show itself in a change of heart and mind and behaviour.

Reconciliation

In this chapter we come to the climax of our story. The willingness of the brothers to stand by Benjamin, and the moving appeal made by Judah, convinced Joseph that they really were changed men, and truly repentant. He was overcome with emotion and wanted to be alone with his brothers to make himself known to them. "Then Joseph could no longer control himself before all his attendants, and he cried out, 'Make everyone leave my presence!' So there was no one with Joseph when he made himself known to his brothers. And he wept so loudly that the Egyptians heard him, and Pharaoh's household heard about it" (Genesis 45:1–2).

Joseph not only wanted privacy to speak with his brothers, but he was being considerate in wanting to spare them the shame and embarrassment of having their past wickedness exposed to strangers. The announcement he was about to make would come to them as a great shock.

Reconciliation begins with God

"Joseph said to his brothers, 'I am Joseph! Is my father still living?' But his brothers were not able to answer him, because they were terrified at his presence. Then Joseph said to his brothers, 'Come close to me'. … I am your brother Joseph, the one you sold into Egypt! And now, do not be distressed and do not be angry with yourselves for selling me here, because it was to save lives that God sent me ahead of you. For two years now there has been famine in the land, and for the next five years there will not be ploughing and reaping. But God sent me ahead of you to preserve for you a remnant on earth and to save your lives by a great deliverance. So then, it was not you who sent me here, but God'" (Genesis 45:3–8).

We can only imagine the scene when Joseph revealed himself to his brothers. Every kind of emotion was present; joy, shock, tenderness and amazing forgiving love. There is not a word of recrimination on Joseph's part, and the memory of all the years of suffering his brothers had caused him is wiped out in the moment of reconciliation. Little wonder that, in this too, Joseph is seen as a type of that greater reconciliation which we have experienced in the Lord Jesus Christ. For it was Joseph who acted to bring about the reconciliation. He need not have done so, since he owed his brothers nothing.

And so it is with God and us, as we pointed out earlier when considering the reconciliation between Jacob and Esau (Genesis 33). It is not God who needs to be reconciled to man, but man who must be reconciled to God. It is man who became estranged from God through his sin and disobedience, but it was God who took the initiative in healing the relationship by giving His Son as a sacrifice for sin. As Paul puts it: "All this is from God, who reconciled us to Himself through Christ" (2 Corinthians 5:18).

Another thing is this. Joseph regarded his own reconciliation with his brothers, not simply as patching up an old family quarrel, but as part of the wider purpose of God for His people. "But God sent me ahead of you to preserve for you a remnant on earth and to save your lives by a great deliverance" (Genesis 45:7). God would save the family from extinction by the famine because He would one day fulfil the promise given to Abraham to make them into a great nation through whom He would accomplish his purpose in the world. That purpose is nothing less than the reconciliation of the world. "God was reconciling the world to Himself in Christ, not counting men's sins against them" (2 Corinthians 5:19). And we, through our own reconciliation are now instruments in furthering that work through our preaching and witness. For God "has committed to us the message of reconciliation. We are therefore Christ's ambassadors, as though God were making his appeal through us. We implore you on Christ's behalf: Be reconciled to God" (2 Corinthians 5:19–20).

Doctrine of the remnant

In making himself known to his brothers Joseph mentions the prophetic concept of the remnant. "God sent me ahead of you to preserve for you a remnant on earth and to save your lives by a great deliverance" (Genesis 45:7). A remnant is a part of the whole, and the Bible teaches that out of the mass of humanity God always has those who, by His grace, remain faithful to His truth no matter what the circumstances at any stage in history.

Joseph was part of the remnant and so too was the family of Jacob whom God would bring down to Egypt. Elijah, in his depressed state of mind, thought that he was the only one faithful to God's truth, but God pointed out that—scattered throughout the villages of Israel—there was a remnant of seven thousand who had not bowed the knee to Baal (1 Kings 19:18). Paul refers to this example of the remnant in Elijah's day to support his claim that God had not cast off His people but has "a remnant chosen by grace" (Romans 11:5).

This doctrine has a twofold application. It speaks to us as individual Christians. Do we stand apart from the mass of humanity today as one of God's faithful remnant? Like Elijah we may feel at times that we are alone in our stand for evangelical truth, perhaps where we work, or in the home, or on the university campus, or even in the church where we worship. But we must encourage ourselves with the knowledge that God has many others who belong to His remnant in shops and offices, in factories, schools and colleges who have not bowed the knee to our modern Baals.

This doctrine also speaks to the Church today. Isaiah pictures Zion in her spiritually weak state as 'a hut in a field of melons' – a tottering broken down shed isolated in an open field. He says further that if God had not left them a remnant all would have been lost, they would have become like Sodom and Gomorrah (Isaiah 1:8–9). The Church today is weak and spiritually impoverished, a mere wreck of what God wants it to be. But the spiritual life of our nation would be infinitely worse were it not that God still has His godly remnant in churches where the gospel is faithfully preached, where the authority of God's word is accepted and where evangelisation and the missionary work is zealously supported. And whatever spiritual blessing or revival God may again bring to our nation, it will come through that faithful remnant.

The doctrine of the remnant also teaches us that at any point in history the true Church will always be a minority. Jesus confirmed this when He said; "But small is the gate and narrow the road that leads to life, and only a few find it" (Matthew 7:14). Also: "For many are invited but few are chosen" (Matthew 22:14). This cancels out the idea taught by some that salvation is universal, and that ultimately all will be saved because God is merciful and will allow none to be lost. That is not the view of the Bible, and people must be shown that, if they want to be part of God's remnant, then the responsibility rests with themselves to respond in faith to the message of the gospel.

The invitation

Following the reconciliation, Joseph instructs the brothers to return to Canaan and invite his father and his whole family to come and live with him in Egypt. "Now hurry back to my father and say to him, 'This is what your son Joseph says: God has made me lord of all Egypt. Come down to me; don't delay. You shall live in the region of Goshen and be near me—you, your children and grandchildren, your flocks and herds, and all you have. I will provide for you there, because five years of famine are still to come. Otherwise you and your household and all who belong to you will become destitute'" (Genesis 45:9–11).

There are several things here. To begin with it is a very generous invitation Joseph gives since it extends to the brothers as well as to his father Jacob. He was under no obligation to do this, considering the years of suffering they had caused him, and we can only interpret it as the action of a true man of God. He was not intoxicated with a spirit of revenge, as many are at the pleasurable prospect of 'getting their own back'. Instead, the trials he had undergone, rather than twisting and distorting his outlook, had made him a bigger and more generous personality. And it was his faith in the goodness and reliability of God that enabled him to achieve that. That is something we can all learn from, since there is always the tendency to allow the adverse experiences of life to corrode our finer feelings.

Another point to notice is that Joseph gave all the glory to God for the success he now enjoyed. "God has made me lord of all Egypt" (Genesis 45:9). As a young man he had been conceited and self-centered. But all that had changed as God kindled in him a deeper sense of His loving purposes. Clearly he was a man of considerable ability and gifts, which also helped him to reach such heights, and we may not be able to emulate him in that. But whatever level of success we achieve in the work of the gospel, we should always have an eye to the glory of God. It will keep us from feelings of resentment at the greater success of others and, more importantly, when all the successes and praises of this life are past there is nothing else left to us but the glory of God. Jeremiah put it so well: "This is what the Lord says: 'Let not the wise man boast of his wisdom or the strong man boast of his strength or the rich man boast of his riches, but let him who boasts boast about this: that he understands and knows me, that I am the Lord, who exercises kindness, justice and righteousness on earth, for in these I delight' declares the Lord" (Jeremiah 9:23–24).

Seeing is believing

Pharaoh himself confirmed Joseph's invitation to his father and brothers. "Pharaoh said to Joseph, 'Tell your brothers, "Do this: Load your animals and return to the land of Canaan, and bring your father and your families back to me. I will give you the best of the land of Egypt and you can enjoy the fat of the land." You are also directed to tell them, "Do this: Take some carts from Egypt for your children and your wives, and get your father and come. Never mind about your belongings, because the best of all Egypt will be yours"'" (Genesis 45:17–20).

As they set out for home, loaded with gifts and provisions (Genesis 45:21–23), the brothers' feelings must have been in a whirl. Never in their wildest moments had they ever anticipated life turning out like this. As they left, Joseph gave them a final word of advice: "Then he sent his brothers away, and as they were leaving he said to them, 'Don't quarrel on the way!'" (Genesis 45:24). He was afraid they would begin blaming one another for the way they had acted towards him years before, whereas he wanted them to forget the whole unsavoury business and start afresh. They had received his forgiveness and he wanted them now to forgive each other. Paul reminds us of the same thing. "Be kind and compassionate to one another, forgiving each other, just as in Christ God forgave you" (Ephesians 4:32).

On arriving home they told their father the good news but Jacob could not take it in at first. "Jacob was stunned; he did not believe them" (Genesis 45:26). But then we read: "… and when he saw the carts Joseph had sent to carry him back, the spirit of their father Jacob revived. And Israel said, 'I'm convinced! My son Joseph is still alive. I will go and see him before I die'" (Genesis 45:27–28). Seeing the carts was the solid evidence Jacob needed to convince him of the good news that Joseph was alive. And so it is in the Christian life. We have good news to give people that God in Christ changes lives, and we do it by our preaching, our personal witness, our prayers, and acts of worship. But the secular man and woman also want to see the solid evidence of that truth, and we have to give it to them in practical ways. Our society today is conditioned by performance. It underlies everything, sport, politics and commercial life. The psychology behind many of the commercials on television is based on the idea that performance proves the value of the product. And people often judge the gospel in the same way. They watch us as believers to see if our performance verifies the gospel we preach, and like Jacob they are more likely to be convinced of its truth when they see the evidence that it does.

Jacob's fears

Jacob was delighted at the prospect of seeing his son Joseph again, but at the same time he was nervous and apprehensive about leaving Canaan, the land God had promised to Abraham and his descendants. Hence he did what God's people should always do when confronted by a situation we are not sure about and which calls for a decision. He sought God's guidance. "So Israel set out with all that was his, and when he reached Beersheba, he offered sacrifices to the God of his father Isaac" (Genesis 46:1).

Beersheba was a sacred spot to Jacob for both his grandfather Abraham, and his father Isaac, had worshipped God there (Genesis 21:33; 26:23–24). And now Jacob does the same, believing that God would calm his fears. "And God spoke to Israel in a vision at night and said, 'Jacob! Jacob!' 'Here I am' he replied. 'I am God, the God of your father' he said. 'Do not be afraid to go down to Egypt for I will make you into a great nation there. I will go down to Egypt with you, and I will surely bring you back again. And Joseph's own hand will close your eyes'" (Genesis 46:2–4). This was the word of guidance Jacob needed as he set out for Egypt. God calmed his fears and assured him that the covenant promise made to Abraham concerning the Promised Land would still be fulfilled, even in Egypt.

We have already said something about guidance when considering the story of the search for a bride for Isaac, and Jacob's preparations for his meeting with Esau. In both we saw that it is right and proper to use foresight and planning in directing our affairs as long as we take God into our plans. But there is more here. God calmed Jacob's fears, and that is a comforting thought. For we all have our fears, sometimes hidden from others but very real nevertheless. Fear of sickness, fear of old age when we have no one to look after us, fear of possible redundancy in our place or work, fear of death and the unknown and so on. And if we allow these fears to haunt us they can make us depressed and unhappy, and life becomes unbearable. The best antidote for our fears is to know that God loves us and cares about us. John says: "There is no fear in love. But perfect love drives out fear ..." (1 John 4:18). God's love to us in Christ drives out not only the fear of judgement, but all our other fears as well. In the gospels Jesus uses the phrase, 'do not be afraid' some fourteen times, and among his last words to the disciples were these: "Do not let your hearts be troubled, and do not be afraid" (John 14:27).

How sweet the name of Jesus sounds
In a believer's ear!
It soothes his sorrows, heals his wounds,
And drives away his fear.

A separated people

The middle section of chapter 46 is simply a list of those who accompanied Jacob down to Egypt, but from verse 28 we have an account of his meeting with Joseph. "Now Jacob sent Judah ahead of him to Joseph to get directions to Goshen. When they arrived in the region of Goshen, Joseph had his chariot made ready and went to Goshen to meet his father Israel. As soon as Joseph appeared before him, he threw his arms around his father and wept for a long time. Israel said to Joseph, 'Now I am ready to die, since I have seen for myself that you are still alive'" (Genesis 46:28–30). This was clearly an emotionally charged meeting, but when it was all over Joseph got down to the real business of settling his family in their new home.

"Then Joseph said to his brothers and to his father's household, 'I will go up and speak to Pharaoh and will say to him, My brothers and my father's household, who were living in the land of Canaan, have come to me. The men are shepherds; they tend livestock, and they have brought along their flocks and herds and everything they own. When Pharaoh calls you in and asks, 'What is your occupation?' you should answer, 'Your servants have tended livestock from our boyhood on, just as our fathers did.' Then you will be allowed to settle in the region of Goshen, for all shepherds are detestable to the Egyptians" (Genesis 46:31–34).

On the face of it, it seems strange advice Joseph gave his brothers, that they should tell Pharaoh they were shepherds, knowing as he did that the Egyptians detested shepherds. Unlike the Hebrews the Egyptians were not nomads but urban dwellers, who despised the wandering desert tribes. In this way Joseph was ensuring that his family would be settled in Goshen as far as possible from the Egyptians themselves. The reason was that God had covenanted to make them a great nation, and this was possible only if they lived a separated life, worshipping God and following His ways, rather than being assimilated into Egyptian society with its materialism and idolatry.

The question of God's people living a life separate from the world was considered earlier when dealing with the search for a wife for Isaac (Genesis 24). And the fact that it comes up again shows what an important matter it is. God has called us in Christ out of the world, to be a people for Himself, and that involves separation from prevailing attitudes and the current of popular opinion in today's society. This will not always be easy, and we must be prepared to incur people's hostility, and the unpopularity that goes with it. But the gospel insists that we are to be different from the world around us, and not crave to be like it. The world's culture and values are alien to the teaching of Christ, and no amount of mental gymnastics can make it otherwise. We either love God or Mammon.

Joseph's administration

READ GENESIS CHAPTERS 47 AND 48

In the first six verses of chapter 47, Joseph presents his brothers to Pharaoh, and following Joseph's advice they inform the king that they are shepherds. As Joseph had anticipated, Pharaoh was agreeable to the suggestion that they should settle in Goshen, and in addition put them in charge of his own livestock. Joseph then presented his father Jacob to Pharaoh.

Life's pilgrimage

"Then Joseph brought his father Jacob in and presented him before Pharaoh. After Jacob blessed Pharaoh, Pharaoh asked him, 'How old are you?' And Jacob said to Pharaoh, 'The years of my pilgrimage are a hundred and thirty. My years have been few and difficult, and they do not equal the years of the pilgrimage of my fathers'. Then Jacob blessed Pharaoh and went out from his presence" (Genesis 47:7–10). Jacob's age of a hundred and thirty gave him great dignity in the eyes of Pharaoh, who seems to have treated the elderly patriarch with enormous respect even to the point where he willingly received his blessing. In view of the 'generation gap' we hear so much of in our churches today it ought to be remembered that those well on in years have something which only time can give — experience! Those who have lived so much longer must have learned something about life which is of value to younger people, and they would do well to listen to them.

But it is Jacob's description of life as a pilgrimage that is of greatest interest. All through the Bible we get this idea that life is a journey, and the world is a temporary residence for God's people who dwell in it as strangers and aliens. The writer to the Hebrews speaks of the patriarchs in this way. "All these people were still living by faith when they died. They did not receive the things promised; they only saw them and welcomed them from a distance. And they admitted that they were aliens and strangers on earth" (Hebrews 11:13). Peter uses the same language. "Dear friends, I urge you as aliens and strangers in the world…" (1 Peter 2:11). Christians belong to two worlds. We live in this world of time, but we belong to eternity. We come from God and spend a little time in this lodging place called earth, and then we return to God who is our home. The worldly secular man does not have this pilgrimage view of life, for in his thinking he has no final destination. He lives for this life and this world alone.

Does it make any difference to have this pilgrimage view of life? It certainly does to my mind. It helps us keep life in perspective. The danger for all of us is to make material security the dominant factor in our lives, whereas the pilgrim view helps us see the impermanence of this world, and that it is passing away. We are meant to enjoy the material blessings of life, but we do not depend upon them, they are only a means and not an end, for the true end and destination for the believer is heaven towards which we are journeying.

A brief pilgrimage

Jacob described his life as a brief pilgrimage: "My years have been few and difficult and they do not equal the years of the pilgrimage of my fathers". His 130 years were indeed few in comparison with the 175 years of Abraham and the 180 years of Isaac. But more significant is the fact that the life of the oldest person on earth is brief compared with the vastness of eternity. That is why the Bible uses many figures to describe the brevity and transitoriness of life on this earth. Life is "like a watch in the night", "like the new grass of morning, … by evening it is dry and withered" (Psalm 90:4–6). For Job, life is a "flower that withers away", and "a fleeting shadow" (Job 14:2). For Isaiah it is "a shepherd's tent removed", and "a weaver's thread cut off from the loom" (Isaiah 38:12). In the New Testament James asks and answers the question: "What is your life? You are a mist that appears for a little while and then vanishes" (James 4:14).

Since life is so brief people ought not to waste it, or think there is plenty of time to start thinking about the serious issues like religion, God and the soul. The only time we have is now, tomorrow may be too late. Christians too should realise that, since life is so brief, we should treat the work of the gospel with urgency. The Lord Jesus said: "As long as it is day, I must do the work of Him who sent me. Night is coming, when no-one can work" (John

9:4). The time is short and the work of evangelisation is urgent, so let us get on with it.

Joseph's administration

In the second half of this chapter we see Joseph as the great statesman and public administrator during the years of famine. "There was no food however in the whole region because the famine was severe; both Egypt and Canaan wasted away because of the famine. Joseph collected all the money that was to be found in Egypt and Canaan in payment for the corn they were buying...When the money of the people of Egypt and Canaan was gone, all Egypt came to Joseph and said, 'Give us food. Why should we die before your eyes? Our money is used up'. 'Then bring your livestock' said Joseph...And he brought them through that year with food in exchange for all their livestock. When that year was over they came to him the following year and said, 'We cannot hide from our lord the fact that since our money is gone and our livestock belongs to you, there is nothing left for our lord except our bodies and our land'...Joseph said to the people, 'Now that I have bought you and your land today for Pharaoh, here is seed for you, so you can plant the ground'...'You have saved our lives' they said. 'May we find favour in the eyes of our lord; we will be in bondage to Pharaoh'" (Genesis 47:13–25).

By today's standards Joseph's policy may be regarded as hard and despotic, since he reduced the people to servitude. But he was a man of his time, and there is no doubt that by his wise planning and political insight he probably saved half the population of Egypt from being wiped out by the famine, as the people themselves recognised. "'You have saved our lives' they said". He insisted on the people paying for their food rather than receiving it free of charge, probably because he knew the danger of any policy whereby people get something for nothing on a regular basis. It seems that under our own welfare system in our country we are learning that lesson, hence the tightening up of social policy at the present time.

But another aspect of all this is the role God's people should play in political and public life. Apart from Joseph we have other instances in the Bible of men that God used in a powerful way in guiding the affairs of the nation. Isaiah was not only a prophet but also an adviser in the courts of

King Uzziah and Hezekiah. Daniel for most of his life served the Babylonian empire with great distinction. Nehemiah was the governor of Jerusalem under the Persian king Artaxerxes. Jesus showed the contribution Christians must make to the nation's political life in the matter of payment of taxes—"Give to Caesar what is Caesar's and to God what is God's" (Mark 12:17). He is showing there the dual responsibility of the Christian. Caesar and the state do have claims upon the Christian, because the civil authority is part of God's economy for the government of mankind. Paul makes the same point: "Everyone must submit himself to the governing authorities, for there is no authority except that which God has established" (Romans 13:1).

The moral failure of so many in the leadership of our nation today, and the frequent allegations of bribery and corruption in public life, are an indication of how far we have fallen as a nation from the biblical view of government and political life. Christians need to take an interest in political life, either by being actively engaged at the local or national level, or by the responsible use of their vote. Furthermore, the scriptures teach that we should pray for those in positions of leadership in public and political life. "I urge, then, first of all, that requests, prayers, intercession and thanksgiving be made for everyone—for kings and all those in authority that we may live peaceful and quiet lives in all godliness and holiness" (1 Timothy 2:1–2). But we should especially pray for those Christians in responsible positions in political and public life who come under particular pressure when conscience clashes with policy, and spiritual conviction is challenged by compromise.

The approaching end

In the closing verses of chapter 47 Jacob is aware that his life is coming to its close. "Jacob lived in Egypt seventeen years, and the years of his life were a hundred and forty-seven. When the time drew near for Israel to die, he called for his son Joseph and said to him, 'If I have found favour in your eyes, put your hand under my thigh and promise that you will show me kindness and faithfulness. Do not bury me in Egypt, but when I rest with my fathers, carry me out of Egypt and bury me where they are buried,' 'I will do as you say' he said. 'Swear to me' he said. Then Joseph swore to him, and Israel worshipped as he leaned on the top of his staff" (Genesis 47:28–31). The alternative reading here is "Israel bowed down at the head of his bed". Indeed, both the staff and the headboard might have supported him since he was a very old man.

Hebrews 11:21 refers to this incident as an example of Jacob's faith. It does so because Jacob's insistence that he be buried in Canaan was an expression of his faith in the covenant promise that the land would be the possession of his descendants.

Jacob remembers

With the opening of chapter 48 Jacob is dying and it takes a tremendous physical effort for him to speak his final words to Joseph and his other sons. "Some time later Joseph was told, 'Your father is ill'. So he took his two sons Manasseh and Ephraim along with him. When Jacob was told, 'Your son Joseph has come to you,' Israel rallied his strength and sat up on the bed. Jacob said to Joseph, 'God Almighty appeared to me at Luz (Bethel) in the land of Canaan, and there he blessed me and said to me, 'I am going to make you fruitful and will increase your numbers. I will make you a community of peoples, and I will give this land as an everlasting possession to your descendants after you'" (Genesis 48:1–4).

Of all the many and varied experiences in Jacob's long life, the one that stands out at the last was his meeting with God at Bethel. Why was that? Well, it was at Bethel that the reality of God first broke in on his life. Up to that point he had given little thought to God; his life had been somewhat selfish and self-centred. But in that never-to-be-forgotten dream God had disturbed him, and made him think about the reality of the things of the spirit, and faith was born in his heart. That is an experience every man and woman needs—to meet with God in the awakening of faith in the heart. And it can come to us in different ways. For one person their Bethel can be a gospel service where Christ is preached, for another the witness of a Christian friend, for yet another a passage in the Bible or in a devotional book when the eyes of the understanding are opened to spiritual truth. However it comes, the important thing is that it should be a heart-felt experience that nothing can erase from our memory, and which brings us—in our dying moments—the comfort and hope that Jacob had at the last.

"O happy day that fixed my choice
On Thee, my Saviour and my God!
Well may this glowing heart rejoice,
And tell its raptures all abroad.

High heaven, that heard the solemn vow,
That vow renewed shall daily hear,
Till in life's latest hour I bow,
And bless in death a bond so dear"

Phillip Doddridge

Great expectations

Joseph had brought his sons Manasseh and Ephraim to his father so that they might receive his blessing. "When Israel saw the sons of Joseph, he asked, 'Who are these?' 'They are the sons God has given me here,' Joseph said to his father. Then Israel said, 'Bring them to me so that I may bless them'. Now Israel's eyes were failing because of old age and he could hardly see. So Joseph brought his sons close to him, and his father kissed them and embraced them. Israel said to Joseph, 'I never expected to see your face again, and now God has allowed me to see your children too'" (Genesis 48:8–11).

I find this a very moving scene; the old patriarch blessing his grandsons whom he could hardly see properly because of encroaching blindness. And of special significance are his words, "I never expected to see your face again, and now God has allowed me to see your children too." Earlier he had given up all hope of ever seeing Joseph again, and now he has the enjoyment of seeing his grandsons as well. God had exceeded all his expectations, as he does ours so often. Many of us would say that we never had any expectation that we would ever have come to know Christ as our Saviour. We did not even think about it. Or if we did, it was to criticise the gospel. But God went beyond our thinking, and by His grace brought us into the joy of salvation.

Others would say that when they became believers they never thought or really expected their experience to go beyond that. But God thought otherwise, and later they found themselves preparing for the ministry, or missionary work, or some other full-time Christian service. This was way beyond all their expectations. Paul puts it so well in his doxology: "Now to Him who is able to do immeasurably more than all we ask or imagine, according to his power that is at work within us, to him be glory in the church and in Christ Jesus throughout all generations, for ever and ever! Amen" (Ephesians 3:20–21).

The blessing
"Then Joseph removed them from Israel's knees and bowed down with his face to the ground. And Joseph took both of them, Ephraim on his right towards Israel's left hand and Manasseh on his left towards Israel's right hand, and brought them close to him. But Israel reached out his right hand and put it on Ephraim's head, though he was the younger, and crossing his arms, he put his left hand on Manasseh's head, even though Manasseh was the firstborn" (Genesis 48:12–14).

Why did Jacob do that, because it certainly displeased Joseph. "When Joseph saw his father placing his right hand on Ephraim's head he was displeased; so he took hold of his father's hand to move it from Ephraim's head to Manasseh's head. Joseph said to him, 'No, my father this one is the firstborn; put your right hand on his head'" (Genesis 48:17–18). "But his father refused and said, 'I know, my son, I know. He too will become a people, and he too will become great. Nevertheless, his younger brother will be greater than he, and his descendants will become a group of nations … ' So he put Ephraim ahead of Manasseh" (Genesis 48:19–20).

Joseph may have thought that his father's mistake was because of his blindness but Jacob knew exactly what he was doing. He was acting with prophetic insight concerning the future of the tribes that would descend from Ephraim and Manasseh. Ephraim did indeed become the most powerful of the tribes, and a synonym for the nation Israel. We see the same thing occurring elsewhere in Genesis. God blessed Abel the younger over Cain, Isaac over Ishmael, Jacob over Esau, and now Ephraim over Manasseh. What this tells us is that God is sovereign in his choices, and is not controlled by men's customs and traditions. And sometimes His choices surprise and even displease us, as happened with Joseph, but God knows exactly what He is doing, as history has proved again and again.

As to the blessing itself which Jacob invoked on both Joseph and his sons, three things stand out.

"May the God before whom my fathers Abraham and Isaac walked" (Genesis 48:15). He is the God of history who makes known His power in the witness of His people from generation to generation.

"… the God who has been my Shepherd all my life to this day" (Genesis 48:15). Here is a truth that shines out all through the Bible. God protects and watches over his people. "He tends his flock like a shepherd: He gathers the lambs in his arms and carries them close to his heart; he gently leads those that have young" (Isaiah 40:11). He is mindful of our needs and is able to meet all of them in Christ Jesus.

"… the Angel who has delivered me from all harm—may he bless these boys" (Genesis 48:16). God alone is able to deliver us from all the harm that Satan, and the powers of darkness and evil in the world, would inflict upon our souls. He does this in Christ. "She will give birth to a son, and you are to give him the name Jesus, because he will save (deliver) his people from their sins" (Matthew 1:21).

Jacob blesses his sons

READ GENESIS CHAPTERS 49 AND 50

In this section the dying words of Jacob are described as his 'blessing' on his sons, but that is not strictly accurate since some of his predictions are anything but pleasant and happy. "Then Jacob called his sons and said: 'Gather round so that I can tell you what will happen to you in days to come. Assemble and listen, sons of Jacob; listen to your father Israel'" (Genesis 49:1–2).

The scene is a dramatic one with the sons gathered round the bed of the old patriarch, anxious to hear what he has to say about each of them personally, and about the future developments of their respective tribes. Jacob's words, spoken under the influence of the Spirit of God, are prophetic and full of poetic imagery containing both encouragement and warnings.

Reuben

"Reuben, you are my firstborn, my might, the first sign of my strength, excelling in honour, excelling in power. Turbulent as the waters, you will no longer excel, for you went up onto your father's bed, onto my couch and defiled it" (Genesis 49:2–4). Reuben had enjoyed all the advantages of the firstborn, and in him were centred all his father's hopes and aspirations. But he proved a great disappointment. The expression 'turbulent as the waters' suggests instability, indecisiveness and weakness, making him unfit for leadership. He showed this by committing incest with one of his father's wives (Genesis 35:22). In later history no great leader ever emerged from the tribe of Reuben.

That is a warning to us, to guard against instability and self-indulgence in our Christian life which could cause us to forfeit our spiritual birthright in Christ. Today, especially, Christians need to be firm and strong where their convictions are concerned.

Simeon and Levi

"Simeon and Levi are brothers—their swords are weapons of violence. Let me not enter their council, let me not join their assembly, for they have killed men in their anger and hamstrung oxen as they pleased. Cursed be their anger, so fierce, and their fury, so cruel! I will scatter them in Jacob and disperse them in Israel" (Genesis 49:5–7). Linked together as brothers, not only physically, but also in outlook and spirit, and they had shown their violence and cruelty in the massacre of the Shechemites in Genesis 34:25f.

As foretold, their tribes were 'dispersed' throughout Israel, Simeon being swallowed up in Judah, and Levi—as a priestly tribe—had no inheritance of its own but lived in various cities scattered among the other tribes. Ours is a violent world full of hatred and continual warfare, which is symptomatic of that malignancy of the human heart the Bible calls sin. And only God can deal with that, as the Lord Jesus made clear. "For from within, out of men's hearts come evil thoughts, sexual immorality, theft, murder, adultery, greed, malice, deceit, lewdness, envy, slander, arrogance and folly. All these evils come from inside and make a man unclean" (Mark 7:21–23).

Judah

"You are a lion's cub, O Judah; you return from the prey, my son. Like a lion he crouches and lies down, like a lioness—who dares to rouse him? The sceptre will not depart from Judah, nor the ruler's staff from between his feet, until he comes to whom it belongs and the obedience of the nations is his. He will tether his donkey to a vine, his colt to the choicest branch; he will wash his garments in wine, his robes in the blood of grapes. His eyes will be darker than wine, his teeth whiter than milk" (Genesis 49:9–12).

The name Judah means 'praise'. His brothers and their tribes would praise him and bow down to him, for he would be as strong and powerful as a lion in the nation. The sceptre and ruler's staff symbolised kingship, and David—Israel's greatest king—came from the tribe of Judah. The prophetic statement that the sceptre would not depart from Judah "until he comes to whom it belongs and the obedience of the nations is his", is Messianic in content. In Revelation 5:5 the Lord Jesus is described as 'the lion of the tribe of Judah'. Symbolising His kingship over the nations, and His triumph over the forces of sin and darkness.

Jacob's blessing on each of the remaining sons, except Joseph, is much shorter and of less significance.

"Zebulun will live by the seashore and become a haven for ships, his border will extend towards Sidon" (Genesis 49:13). With access to the sea Zebulun had the opportunity for maritime and commercial prosperity but never realised it—an opportunity lost that is the lesson.

"Issachar is a scrawny donkey lying down between two saddlebags. When he sees how good is his resting place and how pleasant is his land, he will bend his shoulder to the burden and submit to forced labour" (Genesis 49:14–15). Issachar enjoyed rich pasturelands and opted for the easy life paying tribute to the other tribes rather than sharing actively in the affairs of the nation. Spiritually we can all too easily give way to a flabby kind of faith and a laid-back Christianity, without ever getting involved in the work of God's Kingdom.

"Dan will provide justice for his people as one of the tribes of Israel. Dan will be a serpent by the roadside, a viper along the path, that bites the horse's heels so that its rider tumbles backwards" (Genesis 49:16–17). Samson came from the tribe of Dan and was a judge in Israel, thus fulfilling the first part of this prophecy. The allusion to the serpent and viper causing the horse to fall backwards may refer to the fact that it was the tribe of Dan who first introduced idolatry in Israel (Judges 18) which ultimately brought about its downfall. Dan is a mixture of justice and treachery. And we have these opposing forces in ourselves—our new nature in Christ and the old nature which seeks to drag us along the way of the old serpent Satan. And only the grace of God can help us gain the victory.

Suddenly in the middle of his blessing Jacob exclaims, "I look for your deliverance O Lord" (Genesis 49:18). Is this simply a prayer for God's help? Or is Jacob expressing the hope that God will bring his prophecies to pass? Or, as some commentators suggest, is the prayer for deliverance (salvation) connected with the biting of the serpent (Satan) in the previous verse, which takes our minds back to the prophecy in Genesis 3:15? "And I will put enmity between you and the woman, and between your offspring and hers; he will crush your head, and you will strike his heel."

"Gad will be attacked by a band of raiders, but he will attack them at their heels" (Genesis 49:19). This can only mean that Gad would be successful in overcoming his enemies, and from the spiritual standpoint it points to the promise of the victory which is ours in Christ over sin and the powers of this world.

"Asher's food will be rich, he will provide delicacies fit for a king" (Genesis 49:20). A love of luxury and soft living was to characterise the tribes of Asher in the rich fertile land around Mount Carmel. The prophecy carries with it a warning against self-indulgence and the uncontrolled life. Paul gives the same warning: "So I say, live by the Spirit, and you will not gratify the desires of the sinful nature" (Galatians 5:16).

"Naphtali is a doe set free that bears beautiful fawns" (Genesis 49:21). It is difficult to see what this means, except that it refers to freedom, possibly a free independent spirit. Any application to ourselves as Christians must be that we have freedom in Christ to produce the good things of life but we must never allow it to degenerate into licence.

The blessing of Joseph extends from verse 22 to 26. "Joseph is a fruitful vine, a fruitful vine near a spring, whose branches climb over a wall" (Genesis 49:22). That spells a fruitful and productive life, which was certainly true of Joseph himself, and of his descendants Ephraim and Manasseh who became strong and powerful among the other tribes. It reminds us of the words of Jesus: "I chose you to go and bear fruit—fruit that will last" (John 15:16).

"With bitterness archers attacked him; they shot at him with hostility. But his bow remained steady, his strong arms stayed flexible, because of the hand of the Mighty One of Jacob, because of the Shepherd, the Rock of Israel, because of your father's God, who helps you, because of the Almighty who blesses you" (Genesis 49:23–25). In the early part of his life Joseph was attacked on all sides by hostility and hatred from his brothers, and later from Potiphar's wife. But through it all he remained steady because God strengthened him. The believer too is attacked on all sides by "the flaming arrows of the evil one", and that is why Paul urges us to 'stand firm' and 'Put on the full armour of God' (Ephesians 6:10–18).

"Your father's blessings are greater than the blessings of the ancient mountains, than the bounty of the age-old hills. Let all these rest on the head of Joseph, on the brow of the prince among his brothers" (Genesis 49:26). Jacob is reminding Joseph that throughout his long life and experience he had never known God's love and mercy fail him. They are as certain as the age-old hills and will likewise rest on the head of Joseph and his descendants whom God had set apart from his brothers for special blessing.

The Christian too has the same comfort of knowing that, whatever the circumstances or situation, God's promises cannot fail and His blessings towards us in Christ will never cease.

"Benjamin is a ravenous wolf; in the morning he devours the prey, in the evening he divides the plunder" (Genesis 49:27). Benjamin was the smallest of the tribes, but became prominent for its power and success in warfare. Ehud the judge, Saul and Jonathan were all Benjamites. But mention of the 'ravenous wolf' may also contain a warning against allowing this martial spirit to degenerate into fierce cruelty. This indeed is what happened, according to Judges 19 and 20, when the tribe of Benjamin was virtually annihilated.

Death and Burial of Jacob

Following the blessing of Jacob's sons the closing verses of chapter 49 record his death, and the opening section of chapter 50 records his burial. With his last words he repeats the request he had made earlier to Joseph that he should be buried in Canaan. "Then he gave them these instructions: 'I am about to be gathered to my people. Bury me with my fathers in the cave in the field of Ephron the Hittite, the cave in the field of Machpelah, near Mamre in Canaan, which Abraham bought as a burial place from Ephron the Hittite, along with the field.' ... When Jacob had finished giving instructions to his sons, he drew his feet up into the bed, breathed his last and was gathered to his people" (Genesis 49:29–33).

Although the covenant promise God had made concerning possession of the Promised Land was not fulfilled during Jacob's lifetime, he was nevertheless certain it would be fulfilled. That explains his detailed knowledge of the purchase and site of the family tomb during the time of his grandfather Abraham. He kept that knowledge in readiness for his own burial, which was a testimony to his faith in God's promise.

Another point of significance is in the words: 'I am about to be gathered to my people'. This cannot simply mean that he would be buried in the same tomb as Abraham and Isaac, since we have seen that he gave special directions for that. It is a phrase that must refer to his hope of an after life when he would be reunited with his loved ones. Speaking of the faith of the patriarchs the writer to the Hebrews says: "they were longing for a better country—a heavenly one" (Hebrews 11:16). Unlike their hope, which was only dimly perceived, our hope of the heavenly city is more certain because Christ has already gone ahead to prepare it for us. "In my Father's house are many rooms; if it were not so, I would have told you. I am going there to prepare a place for you" (John 14:2).

The burial of Jacob, which takes up the first fourteen verses of chapter 50, is given in greater detail than any other burial mentioned in the Bible. It was a very impressive affair since Pharaoh, out of respect for Joseph, had made it a state funeral with many Egyptian officials and dignitaries in attendance. One interesting insight is in the words of Joseph, in his request to Pharaoh, to be allowed to bury his father in Canaan. "Now let me go up and bury my father; then I will return" (Genesis 50:5). He assures Pharaoh that he and his people will not remain in Canaan now that the years of famine were over, but will return to live in Egypt. It would be another four hundred years before God would call his people out of Egypt, but Joseph was prepared to wait on God's time.

Failure to appropriate forgiveness

"When the brothers saw that their father was dead, they said, 'What if Joseph holds a grudge against us and pays us back for all the wrongs we did to him?' So they sent word to Joseph saying, 'Your father left these instructions before he died: 'This is what you are to say to Joseph: I ask you to forgive your brothers the sins and the wrongs they committed in treating you so badly'. Now please forgive the sins of the servants of the God of your father'. When their message came to him, Joseph wept" (Genesis 50:15–17).

This is a very sad passage, and we can understand why Joseph wept when he received the message of his brothers. It meant that after all the years since he had truly forgiven them they still doubted his word, and found it necessary to make up a fictitious story about their father in order to be reassured. It was deeply hurtful to him. And it is equally hurtful to the heart of God when we do the same. For there are folk who make their lives a burden and a misery by persisting in feeling guilty about some sin committed perhaps years before. They repented of it at the time and even reminded themselves of the verse: "If we confess our sins, he is faithful and just and will forgive us our sins and purify us from all unrighteousness" (1 John 1:9). But they did not really appropriate that forgiveness, and so they still feel uneasy and guilty about it.

These people must realise that what they are doing is wrong, and the sense of fear and guilt they feel, like Joseph's brothers felt, is totally unnecessary. Just as Joseph had truly forgiven them and wiped out the memory of what they had done to him, so God assures us that His forgiveness is real and He has blotted out our sins. "Who is a God like you, who pardons sin and forgives the transgression of the remnant of his inheritance? You do not stay angry for ever, but delight to show mercy. You will again have compassion on us; you will tread our sins underfoot and hurl all our iniquities into the depths of the sea" (Micah 7:18–19). How can we doubt a promise like that? When we sin, we must truly repent, then put the matter behind us as God does. We must not go behind God's back digging up the same old sins, and feeling guilty about them all over again.

God's overruling

Joseph's reply to his brothers is truly amazing. "But Joseph said to them, 'Don't be afraid. Am I in the place of God? You intended to harm me, but God intended it for good to accomplish what is now being done, the saving of many lives. So then, don't be afraid. I will provide for you and your children.' And he reassured them and spoke kindly to them" (Genesis 50:19–21). He assures them he has no thoughts of revenge. 'Am I in the place of God?' He meant that he did not have the power to do what only belongs to God; the right of vengeance. As Paul says: "Do not take revenge, my friends, but leave room for God's wrath, for it is written: 'It is mine to avenge; I will repay' says the Lord" (Romans 12:19).

But even more remarkable are Joseph's next words, "You intended to harm me, but God intended it for good to accomplish what is now being done, the saving of many lives". The overruling sovereignty of God brings good out of evil and makes even man's sinful intentions to serve his eternal purposes. Men may plan, and scheme, and work out their own evil designs to thwart the purposes of God, and they may even succeed in the short term. But ultimately there is nothing that can prevent God's intention to bring to fruition the unity of all things in the Lord Jesus Christ.

Joseph's death

"Joseph stayed in Egypt, along with all his father's family. He lived a hundred and ten years and saw the third generation of Ephraim's children. Also the children of Makir son of Manasseh were placed at birth on Joseph's knees. Then Joseph said to his brothers, 'I am about to die. But God will surely come to your aid and take you up out of this land to the land he promised on oath to Abraham, Isaac and Jacob'. And Joseph made the sons of Israel swear on oath and said, 'God will surely come to your aid, and then you must carry my bones up from this place'. So Joseph died at the age of a hundred and ten. And after they embalmed him, he was placed in a coffin in Egypt" (Genesis 50:22–26).

So the story of Genesis comes to a close. It began in Eden and ends in Egypt, with the dying words of Joseph expressing a prophetic faith equal to any to be found in the Bible. More than three hundred years would pass before God, through Moses, would bring His people out of bondage in Egypt. During those centuries of suffering the embalmed body of Joseph in their midst would symbolise God's promise that He would visit them again, and bring them into the joy and freedom of the Promised Land.